ETHICAL PERSPECTIVE IN THE NOVELS OF THOMAS HARDY

Kennikat Press
National University Publications
Literary Criticism Series

General Editor
John E. Becker
Fairleigh Dickinson University

ETHICAL PERSPECTIVE IN THE NOVELS OF THOMAS HARDY

Virginia R. Hyman

National University Publications
KENNIKAT PRESS • 1975
Port Washington, N.Y. • London

PR
4757
.E8
H9

Copyright © 1975 by Kennikat Press Corp. All Rights Reserved.
No part of this publication may be reproduced, stored in a retrieval system, or transmitted, in any form or by any means, electronic, mechanical, photocopying, recording, or otherwise, without the prior written permission of the publisher.

Manufactured in the United States of America

Published by
Kennikat Press Corp.
Port Washington, N.Y. / London

Library of Congress Cataloging in Publication Data

Hyman, Virginia R   1929–
    Ethical perspective in the novels of Thomas Hardy.

    (National university publications)
    Bibliography: p.
    Includes index.
    1. Hardy, Thomas, 1840–1928–Religion and ethics.
I. Title.
PR4757.E8H9   823'.8   75-23334
ISBN 0-8046-9128-2

CONTENTS

	Introduction	3
One	Metaphysics and Morality	8
Two	Ethical Evolution and "The Science of Fiction"	18
Three	Character as Ethical Type	29
Four	The Early Novels	39
Five	*Far From the Madding Crowd*	46
Six	*The Hand of Ethelberta*	52
Seven	Eustacia Vye: The Romantic Egotist	56
Eight	The Evolution of Clym Yeobright	65
Nine	Historical Perspective: The Minor Characters	76
Ten	*Two on a Tower*	87
Eleven	*The Mayor of Casterbridge*	99
Twelve	The Evolution of Tess	106
Thirteen	Tess as Agent of Change	122
Fourteen	Angel Clare	127
Fifteen	*The Well-Beloved*	141
Sixteen	The Disillusionment of Jude	151
Seventeen	The Relapse of Sue Bridehead	165
	Bibliography	175
	Index	178

ETHICAL PERSPECTIVE IN THE NOVELS OF THOMAS HARDY

INTRODUCTION

> *"The very fact of my having tried to spread over art the latest illumination of the time has darkened counsel in respect of me."*
>
> Hardy, The Life *(February, 1904)*

In saying that he had "spread over [his] art the latest illumination of the time," Hardy was referring, as the first few chapters of this book will show, to the theory of ethical evolution as it came to him through Comte, Mill, Darwin, and Leslie Stephen. The phrase is significant because it conveys both the essence of Hardy's belief in ethical evolution and his concept of his role as its proponent. For the ethical evolutionist, time was the great illuminator, destroying past illusions and revealing more sober and necessary truths. Hardy saw himself as time's surrogate, not only in illuminating the past but in stimulating his readers to move into the future. His plots imitate the inexorable movement of time, and his characters reveal varying degrees of ability to adapt to it. His novels not only express his view of the past and the present but attempt to restructure the responses of his readers in such a way as to accommodate them to the only future he believed possible. By becoming time's surrogate, Hardy hoped to provide his contemporaries with time's illuminations soon enough to make them its allies rather than its victims.

One of the major difficulties for us as modern readers is that Hardy seems to have one foot in the past and one in the present. There is much in Hardy that we can identify with; and yet there is a great deal that makes him seem archaic. One way of dealing with this problem is to ignore the differences—the archaisms, the moralizing, the creaky plots, and the weak psychology and concentrate on his similarities with us—his irony, his sense of each individual's isolation, his sensitivity to natural phenomena, and his own psychological conflicts. Studies of these similarities have been made and some have proved extremely useful. But the modern nets

INTRODUCTION

we cast allow much to escape and often raise more questions than they resolve. Furthermore, by imposing our own criteria we merely reinforce our own views rather than allowing the novels to reveal other views with which we are not so familiar. In doing so, we deprive ourselves of the advantages of another perspective.

In order to free ourselves from our own perspectives, we should attempt to look at the novels from Hardy's angle of vision. By examining his attitudes and values we can begin to see how they shaped the structures and characterizations of the novels.

Most of us have some general belief in historical progress. We believe, for example (or have believed until quite recently), in social and technological "advances" and tend to contrast "underdeveloped" countries with "developed" ones. On the other hand, we see the lives of individuals as separate from that process. We believe that men's lives are determined not by history but by deep unconscious forces and by their own particular past and present environment. If we see any pattern in the life of an individual, we see that pattern as cyclic rather than linear, following universal mythic patterns established from the beginning of time.

Such a view of the disjunction between historical processes and individual lives is very different from Hardy's. Hardy saw a direct relationship between historical processes and individual lives: both, like natural processes, were evolutionary; human character evolved as history evolved.

This view of the relationship between history and the individual has a profound effect on fictional technique. If men are in some way connected with historical processes, they are impelled by its progress to move forward. If they do not move forward, as many of Hardy's tragic characters do not, their actions are seen as relapses. Many of Hardy's characters, like Joyce's, seem to move in a circular way. But Hardy's circles are not Joyce's. They are not Viconian cycles, running harmoniously and concentrically within the larger cycles of life and time. Rather, when Hardy's characters move in circles, they move *against* a larger linear pattern. Their circular movement indicates loss of direction. They have spun themselves off from the general forward direction and are forced to move in ever-narrowing circles until they sink into obscurity. Hence, the counterpoint between the linear progression of history and the cyclic pattern of individual lives, which we view as the norm, is presented by Hardy as an aberration. We feel this tension as we read such novels as *Tess of the D'Urbervilles* and *Jude the Obscure;* but unless we are aware of Hardy's value system, we cannot fully account for it.

Hardy's view of the relationship between the individual and the historical process affects not only the dynamics of his plot structures but his method of characterization as well. Rather than regarding the individual

INTRODUCTION

as a unique and separable creature with a unique personal history and indeterminate future, as we do, Hardy saw the individual as representative of a particular stage of human history. His characters are clearly distinguishable types, exhibiting clearly recognizable traits, which, in turn, lead to predictable ends. Generally, the novelist placed his characters along a historical spectrum, with each character representative of a certain stage in human history.

This much may, indeed, be obvious. We certainly recognize how he contrasts the "rustics" with the urbane, civilized types. But what we may not be so aware of is that Hardy's view of history differs considerably from our own. We view history "scientifically," that is, as ethically neutral. We define progress in terms of social or economic advance. But progress, for Hardy, as well as for the other ethical evolutionists such as Comte and Mill, was essentially *ethical.* In their view history showed men generally advancing from early egotistic stages to dawning altruistic ones. At each stage, they saw the culture's social, economic, and religious structures reflecting the ethical attitudes of the group, and they regarded an individual's success or failure as dependent upon his ability to "keep up" with history. According to the ethical evolutionists, one's survival was dependent not so much on his ability to move up the social or economic ladder as on his ability to progress along the ethical one, to move out of the egotistic stage and into the altruistic one. The more intransigent his egotistic traits were, the more likely a man was to fail; the more "advanced" his altruistic ones were, the more likely he was to succeed.

What gets in the way of a full understanding of Hardy's work is the limited connotations that we give to the terms "egotism" and "altruism." And the limited connotations we assign to these words reflect our view of the whole subject of ethics. With our modern viewpoint we discount ethics as being too rigid and confining a way of dealing with individual motivation and action. We prefer to explain motivation in psychological terms. But, like our history, our psychology is generally ethically neutral. Hence, our psychological equivalents are too narrow to catch the cluster of meanings Hardy associated with the terms "egotism" and "altruism." The Freudian concept of the id-ego conflict is a rough equivalent to Hardy's terms; yet the connotations of these terms are not large enough to embrace all that Hardy meant by altruism and egotism. The very difference in terminology indicates the contrast in value systems. The ethical neutrality of the modern terms suggests that we value both id and ego and see the need for some kind of balance between the two. In contrast, Hardy's terms are mutually exclusive and hierarchical. Altruism is clearly superior to egotism. There is no question of balance. The one must be destroyed for the other to survive.

INTRODUCTION

Perhaps what is most difficult for us to understand about Hardy's value system is that it seems to embrace our own while attempting to supersede it. Caught up by our own sense of progress, we tend to think we have advanced beyond Hardy's perspective. What is so strange is that Hardy seems to have been fully aware of many of our modern values and to have rejected them for others he thought superior. What happens, then, is that *we* identify with Hardy's major characters while the novelist does not. For example, we identify with Michael Henchard, for we share his values and his perspective. For, much as we do, Henchard sees himself as a free and separate entity, entitled to happiness and deserving of love. He strives for happiness by trying to move up the social and economic ladders. We identify with these values and assumptions and overlook his faults, seeing his wife-selling, the faulty grain-dealing, his shabby treatment of Elizabeth Jane and rivalry with Farfrae as natural, and therefore forgivable. What we do not see, or if we see prefer to ignore, is the novelist's system of values running a counter-course, moving Henchard ineluctably to the "destiny" his character had prepared him for. And unless we are aware of the contrast between the two value systems, we miss the creative tension that accounts for the novel's dramatic effects. While Henchard is treated sympathetically, his values are not endorsed. The novelist is at a greater distance from his character than we are.

Hardy's view of Henchard is that he is, indeed, acting naturally in following his impulses for freedom, happiness, and love. But Hardy does not, as we would, accept these actions as natural and therefore right. On the contrary, he indicates that survival in the complex modern world requires more than "natural" actions. To Hardy, Henchard's values are those of the egotist; his fate, the consequence of his acting upon his egotistic impulses. Hardy shows Henchard increasingly as belonging to an older order and as acting upon impulses that are essentially self-destructive. Over against Henchard's values he sketches in his own, in the characterizations of Farfrae and Elizabeth Jane. They are the new breed of altruist who survive after the old tragic hero is extinct. However much we may wish to disregard this alternative as unattractive and therefore unconvincing, we cannot assume that it was unconvincing to Hardy. Hardy believed the values of the altruist to be superior to those of the egotist, and the progress of the novel outlines the decline of the old system and the rise of the new. If we, as readers, choose the "old system," we must be aware that it is we, rather than Hardy, who have chosen to remain "behind."

As moderns, many of us have come to see all natural life as random and indeterminate and man's life as corresponding to the absurdity of the universe. Hardy is a modern in that he accepts the modern view of the

INTRODUCTION

amorality of the universe (although he finds it more orderly and determinate than we do). He is a Victorian, however, in maintaining a deep faith in the morality of the human world and in man's ability to create laws higher than the natural ones. Whether such a view is more or less advanced than our own is open to conjecture. That it is different from our own is clear. And the emphasis on the differences should prove useful by allowing us to distinguish between what is created within the novel and what we project onto it. By examining the attitudes and values that went into the novels, we should be better able to ascertain what emerges from them. By using Hardy's base rather than our own, we should be able to see both their scope and their limitations from another angle.

Since all that Hardy meant by such terms as "egotism" and "altruism" is generally forgotten, this study will begin by reconstructing the sources of Hardy's ideas and by describing them in some detail. Next it will show how these ideas and attitudes provided the basis for his fictional structures, his plots and characterizations, and his evocative techniques. Finally, it will show the gradual refinement of these techniques as Hardy moved from one novel to the next. What should become evident during the course of the study is that while the techniques become more refined the ethical base remains the same; and, hence, whatever we may finally conclude about Hardy's ethics, we must acknowledge that it provided the novelist with a useful structure for his fiction.

One

METAPHYSICS AND MORALITY

Almost from the first, the major portion of criticism that has concerned itself with Hardy's ideas has tended to place a great deal more emphasis on his metaphysics than on his ethical views. And there are good reasons that this should be so. For until recently, what has appeared unique to Hardy has been his metaphysics; furthermore, although recent critics have begun to argue that Hardy's theories of the Unconscious First Cause and the Immanent Will were not so strange to the Victorians as had been commonly thought, nor that they need be so alien to us, there is no doubt that Hardy's terminology has required a somewhat extensive explanation.[1] As for his moral philosophy, it is difficult at first to discern whether it is really there at all. Most readers and critics have recognized that Hardy argues against certain social conventions in the novels, but such attacks were common among Victorian writers and need not be considered part of a personal ethic. They certainly do not account for the particular aesthetic effect of his works. Besides, Hardy himself minimized his attacks on social conventions, asserting that in "opposing institutions to individuals" he was not "questioning their necessity or urging their nonnecessity."[2] Critics have also recognized that Hardy makes some remarks about his moral intentions in his essays and prefaces, but these remarks seem to be part of every Victorian writer's stock-in-trade. Similarly, few readers or critics can miss the value Hardy places on "loving-kindness" or altruism; but such comments seem so commonplace as to be almost embarrassing clichés. They certainly do not constitute anything like what could be considered a fully worked-out moral philosophy. Why, then, should a study be made of a moral philosophy that is seemingly nonexistent?

METAPHYSICS AND MORALITY

The first, and perhaps most important, reason is that during his lifetime Hardy constantly complained that he was being misunderstood by critical emphasis on his metaphysics. He was continually trying to escape being labeled a pessimist for his metaphysics and insisted that his emphasis was primarily meliorist and moral. For example, the "one thing he was certain of" before publishing *Jude the Obscure* was that it would "make for morality" (*The Life*, p. 274). And when this novel, like previous ones, was attacked for its amorality and fatalism Hardy complained to William Archer: "My pessimism — if pessimism it be — does not involve the assumption that the world is going to the dogs. . . . On the contrary, my practical philosophy is distinctly meliorist. What are my books but one plea against 'man's inhumanity to man,' woman, and to the lower animals? . . . Whatever may be the inherent good or evil in life, it is certain that men make it much worse than it need be. . . . "[3] He claims that he left off writing novels and went to poetry because he felt that his "ideas and feelings" had been misunderstood. In poetry he felt he could "perhaps express more fully . . . ideas and emotions which run counter to inert crystallized opinion—hard as a rock—which the vast body of men have vested interest in supporting" (Oct. 17, 1896, p. 284). Such complaints surely warrant another look in the direction toward which the author seems to be pointing.

Another reason for looking more deeply into Hardy's ethical ideas is that, unlike most other Victorian writers, he emphasizes one value so consistently. Although the one virtue he selects for special emphasis is by no means original, he seems to prize it almost to the exclusion of all others. Calling it "altruism" at times and "loving-kindness" at others, he alludes to it again and again in his novels, in his poetry, and in *The Life*. Even later in life, after he had rejected any claim to having developed or expressed a systematic philosophy, Hardy continued to "hold fast" to the view that in the future pain should be "kept down to a minimum by loving-kindness, operating through scientific knowledge. . . . "[4] This belief seems to coincide with the one emotional effect most sensitive readers of Hardy have noted as characteristic. His works seem both to express and to evoke a kind of sympathy for all living creatures. The consistency of such remarks would seem to indicate that his choice of emphasis was not arbitrary or casual but quite deliberate and well thought out. If this is so, this idea must certainly have been important enough to have affected his work in a more profound way than has previously been recognized.

Of further significance is the fact that, in the same passage, Hardy "allies himself" with "those few" who "hold fast" to the belief that altruism will eventually prevail. Later on in the essay he disassociates himself from more recent philosophers like Schopenhauer, Von Hartmann, and

Einstein who have only a "supercilious regard of hope." In other words, he seems to be placing himself within a tradition which had, by 1922, become a part of the past. What is that tradition and who are "those few" who "hold fast" to the belief that altruism will eventually prevail? Unfortunately, we do not know who, besides Hardy, was still holding to this belief in 1922. We do know, however, what that tradition had been and who had held it. Hardy himself has provided the list. And it is to these writers that we must go if we are to understand the full significance of Hardy's references.

Hardy's remarks about his ethical views are admittedly scant. He certainly never wrote out a systematic science of ethics. But interestingly enough, the "one man whose philosophy influenced him the most — indeed more than any other contemporary" did write one (*The Life*, p. 100). That man was Leslie Stephen: the work is entitled *The Science of Ethics*. Nor was Leslie Stephen the only writer to concern himself with ethics whose influence Hardy acknowledges. Although we tend to think of the writers whom Hardy mentions (that is, Darwin, Huxley, Spencer, and Mill) primarily as agnostics, they all were also concerned with ethics.[5] Not only were they concerned, to one degree or another, with establishing a scientific basis for ethics, but, even more remarkably, they also believed in cooperation or altruism as the highest ethical value. Like Hardy, they believed that, by a process of social evolution, this value would eventually prevail. They derived this belief, as well as the term, ultimately from Comte, whom Hardy also read.[6]

Biographers have established that Hardy was reading Darwin, Spencer, and Mill during the 1860s, the period of his religious disillusionment, and they have attributed a good deal of his skepticism to their influence. This is no doubt true. But we must also be aware that they offered an alternative set of values to those that they found obsolete. And if it is true, as Irving Howe has remarked, that "what Hardy was searching for was not merely, and not even so much a metaphysical system that might replace Christian theology," but "philosophical cues by means of which human solidarity might be maintained," he could have found them in the very writers he was reading.[7] For, despite the fact that most of them rejected the notion of Divine Providence, they were by no means hopeless with regard to man's position or to his future. Indeed, as Gertrude Himmelfarb has pointed out, the more skeptical the Victorian thinkers were about the supernatural world, the more they insisted upon human values in this one.[8] The social evolutionists simply transferred their faith from the supernatural world to the human one.

To put the ideas quite simply, the Positivists saw human history in terms of intellectual and moral progress. All of them believed, like Comte, that man was progressing from egotism toward cooperation or altruism, and that this moral progress was paralleled by various stages of intellectual progress. Comte had clearly defined the historic stages as theological, metaphysical, and sociological; he had also asserted that every individual could, and eventually would recapitulate the history of the race. "Every man is a theologian in his childhood, a metaphysician in his youth, a sociologist in maturity."

Such a view is clearly an anodyne for the sense of loss that accompanies religious disillusionment. The rejection of belief in the supernatural need not leave one entirely without a sense of moorings. Rather, such a rejection of belief could place the individual in a responsible position within an historic human framework. The rejection of religious belief was a step forward in terms of intellectual and moral progress. If one could no longer recognize ties with the supernatural, he could still be a part of human history; and indeed, if one were lucky enough to be more advanced than his contemporaries, he might gain a new kind of immortality by affecting the intellectual and moral future of humanity.[9]

But merely to state that a system of values was available to Hardy from among the very writers that he claims were most influential in forming his views is no proof that he adopted those values. It is certainly not being argued that Hardy adopted the views in exactly the same form in which they were presented. Certainly, for example, Comte's almost athletic optimism would have been uncongenial to Hardy's temperament. However, as the next chapter will demonstrate, with each writer the views shifted; and Stephen's reading of Comte is a good deal closer to Hardy's stated position. There is, however, one major difference between the views of the social evolutionists and Hardy's that has tended to obscure the similarities between them: none of the social evolutionists seemed to regret, as Hardy did, the loss of their religious beliefs. Hardy's expressed regrets would seem to indicate that he did not, in fact, embrace the Positivist philosophy wholeheartedly. This apparent difference between Hardy and the Positivists can be explained in several ways. First, his statements of regret over the loss of his religious beliefs — and particularly his belief in a Divine Providence — appear most often in his poetry. Such statements, like his poetic utterances after the death of his wife, can be considered as only partially autobiographical. That is, they tell only part of the story. They may be, as he insisted they were, "dramatic utterances," reflecting only certain moods and impressions. There are an equal number of poems that offer his moral substitutes. And certainly his attacks on the destructive effects of religious dogmatism in *Tess of the D'Urbervilles* and *Jude the Obscure* (which resemble similar attacks made by Mill and Stephen) indicate that Hardy did not altogether regret the loss. And there is other,

11

more objective evidence that Hardy did not regret the loss of his faith so much as he sometimes professed and that he welcomed and embraced the new views with some enthusiasm — particularly during the time when he was writing the novels.

In the biography, for example, he notes that he had been one of the "earliest acclaimers" of *The Origin of Species* (p. 153). In a later note he comments on the *beneficial* effect of Darwin's ideas; he does not see them as destroying his previous religious ideas and values but rather as reaffirming and extending his ethical ones:

Few people seem to perceive fully as yet that the most far-reaching consequence of the establishment of the common origin of all species is ethical; that it logically involves a readjustment of altruistic morals by enlarging as a *necessity of rightness* the application of what has been called "The Golden Rule" beyond the area of mere mankind to that of the whole animal kingdom. Possibly Darwin himself did not wholly perceive it, though he alluded to it. (April 10, 1910, p. 349)

In another note Hardy considered writing an article arguing against any further need for the Christian religion, basing his argument on the belief that it had evolved into an ethical system no different from other moral religions which teach the same things: that is, "emotional morality and altruism" (p. 332).

But if we accept the idea that Hardy did, indeed, accept the ideas of the English Positivists, how do we account for his preoccupation with metaphysics? If he accepted, during the period 1870-1890, the time when he was writing the novels, the social evolutionists' view that the center of interest must be man, why did he, when he turned to the poetry and *The Dynasts*, preoccupy himself with speculation regarding Unconscious First Causes and the growing consciousness of an Immanent Will? According to the Positivists, such a preoccupation with abstractions would indicate regression to an earlier "metaphysical" stage of thought. And if he accepted the Positivists' theories during the time when he was writing the novels, why are his novels not as morally deterministic as those of George Eliot, for example, who also shared the Positivist view and who had first used the term "meliorism" to describe it? Why does he insist on the persistence of coincidence or chance in the novels?[10]

Once again, Hardy supplies the answer to the apparent inconsistency. He had come, he claimed, to his theory that the Immanent Will was growing conscious by "reflecting that what has already taken place in a fraction of the whole (i.e., so much of the world as has become conscious) is likely to take place in the mass." Further, he hoped that this mass would become not only conscious but "ultimately sympathetic" (June 2,

1907). What Hardy is saying here is that since man has become conscious and is becoming increasingly sympathetic, so might the Universe. What he is doing is projecting his vision of moral history onto the metaphysical sphere. His metaphysics is therefore an extension of his ethics. The reason that he gives for having made use of this theory (i.e., that the Immanent Will is growing conscious) in *The Dynasts* is even more significant. He had used it, he asserts, primarily for its ethical effect, believing that such a theory would "strengthen the involuntary inter-social emotions which affect men's lives and actions."[11] Thus, he has projected his vision of moral history onto the metaphysical sphere in order to reinforce the social sympathies, or altruistic feelings, in his readers. If, according to the Positivists, at each stage in his intellectual and moral history man creates his gods out of his own needs, then Hardy, who considered himself in advance of his time, would create a projection of the responsive and sympathetic values he most prized in order to stir men to prize them also. In other words, he seems to have built his metaphysics on the groundwork of his moral philosophy and to have used it for his moral purposes. For Hardy, the relationship between his morality and his metaphysics was continuous, with the morality taking precedence over the metaphysics.

If his metaphysics may be regarded as heuristic, so might his poetic statements expressing regret over his loss of faith. That is, he may not only be expressing a sense of personal loss in the poems but also dramatizing a stage of consciousness which he believed his readers must also eventually sympathize with and accept. This was, as the subsequent chapters will show, his method in the novels. He portrayed his characters in various "fetishistic," "theological," and "metaphysical" stages sympathetically, but he was nevertheless conscientious about pointing out the reactionary and destructive effects of maintaining these attitudes in the face of ongoing history. There is a similar continuity between his emphasis on chance in the novels and his equally important moral comments. By emphasizing the power of chance to affect men's lives, he was also emphasizing the correspondingly increased need for moral responsibility among men. The dice game between Wildeve and Diggory Venn in *The Return of the Native* can be taken as a kind of paradigm of how Hardy handles the relationship between chance and moral responsibility. Venn eventually wins the game because he persists with a kind of dogged patience and selflessness that Wildeve, a more passive victim of chance and his own whims, lacks. Similarly, Hardy treats with detached irony those characters who rely on Divine Providence to provide them with a disproportionate amount of happiness. Thus, for example, when Eustacia Vye waits on Providence for happiness and eventually blames a "dark Prince of the World" for her destiny, the author comments: "nothing could save her

13

from censure for not answering the first knock. Yet, instead of blaming herself for the issue, she laid the fault upon the shoulders of some indistinct, colossal Prince of the World, who had framed her situation and ruled her lot."[12]

The difficulty, however, is one that every Hardy reader has experienced. Unfortunately, despite Hardy's ironic comments reminding us that we, as readers, should know better, we *do* sympathize with his characters' assumptions that they should be happy; like them, we tend to blame chance for their failures, and we fail to see how carefully Hardy has placed the major responsibility upon the characters themselves.[13] Despite their popular success, critical reaction to the novels apparently made Hardy aware of the difficulty, for he abandoned the form of the novel after *Jude the Obscure* and turned to poetry, as a more effective vehicle for his ideas.

In writing *The Dynasts,* which dramatized the victory of the Allies over Napoleon, Hardy could make use of his own moral vision of history, which, instead of running counter to "inert crystallized opinion," rather coincided with the Englishman's view of history. When Part I of *The Dynasts* received mixed criticism, Hardy responded in somewhat the same way as he had to the critical reception of the novels. He still asserted that he was expressing "philosophies and feelings as yet not well established or formally adopted into general teaching." His attitude this time, however, is less accusatory. He is willing to admit that he is in part responsible for the critical misunderstanding. He admits to having "handicapped" himself by expressing his advanced notions. "The very fact of my having tried to spread over art the latest illumination of the time has darkened counsel in respect of me" (Feb. 1904, p. 320). Unfortunately, the "philosophies and feelings" which Hardy expressed never became well established, nor were they, as he had hoped, ever "formally adopted into general teaching."[14]

Even a brief review of his theories will reveal why. They are full of logical inconsistencies and unfounded assumptions. Hardy himself seems to have recognized this, and his recognition of the weakness of those theories may account for his own later reticence in discussing them.[15] While he never abandoned the fundamental beliefs that he shared with those writers he had named after writing the novels and *The Dynasts,* he did not attempt to apply the theories systematically or to insist on their scientific validity. (He even began to describe his works as "impressions," reflecting only an "idiosyncratic mode of regard.") But if the ideas are without much value philosophically, they are crucial to an understanding of Hardy's aims and methods, particularly in the novels. Their chief value now lies in their having provided Hardy with a coherent structure for the novels. For they were able to solve, in a unique way, what Ian Watt has described as one of the central problems of the novel: "how to impose a

METAPHYSICS AND MORALITY

coherent moral structure on the narrative without detracting from its air of literal authenticity."[16] The subsequent chapters will attempt to reveal what "the latest illumination of the time" was for Hardy, and how it still casts light on his works.

NOTES

1. Of significance to this study is that two recent critics have seen J.S. Mill as having been far more influential than has previously been recognized. Kenneth Marsden sees parallels between Mill's remarks in *Utilitarianism* and Hardy's meliorism (*The Poems of Thomas Hardy* [New York: 1969], pp. 49-50). Harold Orel points out that Mill had, in the second of his *Essays on Religion*, formulated the theory that a conscious Mind may be produced by unconscious processes (*Thomas Hardy's Epic-Drama: A Study of the Dynasts* [Kansas: 1963], p. 24).

Further, both critics have argued that too literal an emphasis on the metaphysics has tended to detract from our appreciation of the poetry, and that it serves primarily as a structural device. Marsden makes a comparison between Hardy's metaphysics and Yeats's cosmology.

2. Florence Emily Hardy, *The Life of Thomas Hardy* (New York: 1962) entry dated Dec. 1895, p. 274.

3. William Archer, in *Real Conversations* (London: 1904), pp. 46-47, quoted by Harvey Webster, in *On a Darkling Plain* (Chicago: 1964), p. 199.

4. The full sentence runs as follows:

"And, looking down the future, these few hold fast to the same: that whether the human and kindred animal races survive till the exhaustion or destruction of the globe, or whether these races perish and are succeeded by others before that conclusion comes, pain to all upon it, tongued or dumb, shall be kept down to a minimum by loving-kindness, operating through scientific knowledge and actuated by the modicum of free will conjecturally possessed by organic life when the mighty necessitating forces — unconscious or other — that have 'the balancing of the clouds' happen to be in equilibrium which may or may not be often" (*Collected Poems* [New York: 1926], p. 527). This essay first appeared as the preface to *Late Lyrics* in 1922.

5. Rejecting the attribution of his philosophy to Schopenhauer, Hardy

provided the following list of "influences": "my pages show harmony of view with Darwin, Huxley, Spencer, Hume, Mill and others, all of whom I used to read more than Schopenhauer" (quoted by Carl Weber, *Hardy of Wessex* [New York: 1965], pp. 246-247), Hume is obviously excepted from the subsequent discussion.

6. This view, as John Wyon Burrow has pointed out, is not to be confused with the amoral, deterministic brand of Social Darwinism which became popular later. Burrow demonstrates that theories of social evolution developed independently of Social Darwinism, and that even Spencer, whose name is most closely associated with the theory, did not make much use of "natural selection," using it only as a garnish for theories he had already developed (*Evolution and Society* [Cambridge: 1966], p. 115).

7. Irving Howe, *Thomas Hardy* (New York: 1967), p. 13.

8. Gertrude Himmelfarb, *Darwin and the Darwinian Revolution* (New York: 1962), p. 37.

9. According to Burrow, the very fact that the theories about social evolution were so intellectually and emotionally satisfying accounted for their popularity. They "satisfied the need for reassurance, for guarantees that all was, ultimately at least, well with the human situation, and for ethical and political certainty, for ethical premises which should not be arbitrary and recommendations which should be more than piecemeal" (p. 93).

10. Critics who have recognized the moral element in his works have also recognized the apparent dichotomy between his morality and his metaphysics. Webster, for example, notes that the social protests running through the novels are "based upon a hope for the ultimate melioration" of man's condition, and "are as much a part of his reading of life as his emphasis upon the tragedy he regards as inherent in the nature of things." Webster says that this is a logical inconsistency which Hardy, as an artist, is incapable of resolving (p. 171).

Kenneth Marsden, in commenting upon the contrast Hardy makes between the moral world and the amoral universe, indicates something of the connection that the social evolutionists saw between the two by paralleling Hardy's belief that he could affect the Unconscious Will with similar comments in Mill's *Utilitarianism* (pp. 49-50).

11. Harold Orel, *Thomas Hardy's Personal Writings* (Kansas: 1966), p. 146. This passage first appeared in "The Dynasts: A Postscript," *Times Literary Supplement,* Feb. 19, 1904, p. 53.

12. *The Return of the Native* (New York: 1959), p. 298.

13. One of the first critics who recognized the emphasis Hardy places on the characters' responsibility in affecting their lives is Charles Walcutt, *Man's Changing Mask* (Minnesota: 1966), pp. 159-174. Roy Morrell's work on this subject has been largely ignored. Cf. *The Will and The Way* (Singapore: 1965).

14. G. E. Moore, in his *Principia Ethica* (1903), pointed out the "naturalistic fallacy" in the theories of social evolution, thereby giving the death blow to a movement that had, by the time of Moore's publication, lost most of its impetus.

15. In a note dated Dec. 31, 1901, Hardy made the following remark:

METAPHYSICS AND MORALITY

"After reading various philosophic systems, and being struck with their contradictions and futilities, I have come to this: *Let every man make a philosophy for himself out of his own experience.* He will not be able to escape using terms and phraseology from earlier philosophers, but let him avoid adopting their theories if he values his own mental life. Let him remember the fate of Coleridge, and save years of labour by working out his views as given him by his surroundings."

The date, as well as the tone of the entry, suggest that this may have been a kind of New Year's Resolution. In rejecting the philosophic systems of others for the future, he implies that he had accepted them in the past. The date also coincides with his turning away from fiction to poetry and to the metaphysics of the Immanent Will in *The Dynasts*.

16. *The Rise of the Novel* (Berkeley, California: 1967), p. 117.

Two

ETHICAL EVOLUTION AND "THE SCIENCE OF FICTION"

> *Altruism, or The Golden Rule, or Whatever "Love your Neighbour as Yourself" may be called, will ultimately be brought about, I think, by the pain we see in others reacting on ourselves, as if we and they were a part of one body.*
>
> The Life *(March-April 1890, p. 224)*

This statement, perhaps more than any other, characterizes Hardy's belief in moral progress and expresses his idea about the means necessary to achieve it. It is really the heart of his moral philosophy and, perhaps more important, a clue to his aims and techniques, particularly in the novels. Unfortunately, it is too brief to convey all of his assumptions about the nature of history and the function of literature. Although Hardy made other relevant comments in the biography and the essays, he never presented a coherent system which the reader could apply to his works. (His reluctance to do so may have been because he became aware of the logical inconsistencies already suggested or of the psychological and ethical inconsistencies that will become clear during the course of the discussion.)

But if Hardy did not provide a fully developed system himself, he did, by locating himself within an intellectual tradition, provide enough clues for a critic to be able to examine, to some extent at least, the presuppositions behind his somewhat cryptic statements. He had attempted, he asserted in 1904, to "spread over art the latest illumination of the time," and as late as 1922 he continued to ally himself with "those few" who "held fast" to the belief in the eventual triumph of loving-kindness. His comment that his pages "show harmony of view with Darwin, Huxley, Spencer, Hume, Mill, and others" give some indication of what that tradition was that provided him with views that were "advanced" until the 1900s and apparently forgotten by 1922. His biography provides even further elucidation, for it provides two other names which should be included among the "others" referred to in the list. The first name that is mentioned several times is that of Comte.[1] But the second name is even more important. Strangely enough, it has been almost totally ignored by critics. The name is that of Leslie Stephen. Although Frank Southerington, in *Hardy's Vision of Man* (New York, 1971) notes some general similarity between Stephen's evolutionary theories and Hardy's, he concludes that Hardy's view "was formulated on premises which were different from Stephen's. While he sees both men believing that man could shape his future, Southerington sees Hardy stressing the role of intellect, rather than feeling, in creating such a change (pp. 223-236). In the biography Hardy asserts that Leslie Stephen was "the one man whose philosophy influenced my own for many years, indeed, more than that of any other contemporary" (p. 100). Certainly such a direct statement of his indebtedness to Stephen deserves some attention. What was Stephen's "philosophy" and how was Hardy "influenced" by it?

Like the other writers whom Hardy mentions, Stephen was an agnostic. We know that Stephen wrote and Hardy praised an article entitled "Are We Christians?"[2] Even more important, however, are the reasons Stephen gives for his agnosticism. Stephen rejects religion in general and Christianity in particular because it is immoral. "By cultivating aimless contemplations of an imaginary ideal," religion "renders men insensitive to the miseries and sufferings of the world" (p. 372). By its pre-occupation with the Omnipotence of God it renders men too passive to act either on their own behalf or, more important, on the behalf of others. By its emphasis on personal salvation it encourages concern only with the self. "The figments of theology are a consecration of our delusive dreams; the teaching of the new faith should be the utilization of every emotion to the bettering of the world of the future" (p. 388).

These same criticisms of religion had been made by Mill in his essay "On Liberty," which Hardy admired so much as to have learned by heart.[3] Earlier still, Comte had used similar arguments. He had attempted to demonstrate that religion was a reflection of an earlier stage in man's intellectual and spiritual progress. According to Comte's theory, during his "theological phase" man had attempted to satisfy his need to find ultimate causes behind phenomena. What man found, however, was but a reflection of his own needs. Thus, the idea of Divine Omnipotence reflected that same intellectual pride and egotism in man which assumed that he could and should discover ultimate causes. According to Comte, however, and indeed to all the subsequent ethical evolutionists, man had passed beyond the "theological phase" of his development. Every new branch of science indicated his growing interest in more immediate concerns. His interest in the world around him had led him to a more objective understanding of natural laws. Philosophy, mathematics, and biology particularly, reflected this tendency, and were reflections of his progress out of

19

the "theological" and into the "metaphysical" stage of development. In the nineteenth century, according to Comte, man was moving beyond the "metaphysical" stage and into the "sociological" one. Having discovered, primarily from biology, what the natural laws were, man was beginning (with Comte) to apply the study of external nature to his own. Those who, like Comte, had reached this last sociological stage recognized that knowledge of ultimate causes is not only inaccessible, but even if accessible, useless. They also contended that even the study of the sciences should be limited to what is directly useful for man. "We have no concern with anything but the laws of phenomena which affect human beings."[4]

Far from seeing the disbelief in Divine Providence as regrettable, Comte, like Stephen and Mill, saw it as having positive value: "Theology's vague notion of Providence . . . prevents men from forming a true conception of Law, a conception necessary for prevision, on which all wise intervention must be based" (*GV*, p. 443). "Accepting the truths of science, [Positivism] teaches that we must look to our own unremitting activity for the only providence by which the rigour of our destiny can be alleviated" (*GV*, p. 392). The idea that man is "the arbiter, within certain limits, of his own destiny" is not to be regretted or merely accepted, but actively embraced as "far more satisfying than the old belief in Providence which implied our remaining passive" (*GV*, p. 33).

This view, which perhaps prompted Comte to term his philosophy "Positivist," was shared by all of the writers Hardy mentions. Even more important, it corresponds to Hardy's treatment of religion in the novels. Mercy Chant, for example, is his most devastating caricature of the egotism that the ethical evolutionists claimed religion fostered, but the parents of Angel Clare, although treated more sympathetically, also exhibit a degree of moral insensitivity and passivity. And, as the discussion of Eustacia Vye will demonstrate, her reliance on Providence and her subsequent denunciation of "some indistinct, colossal Prince of the World, who had framed her situation and ruled her lot," is treated ironically. Tess's rejection of the sign-painter's warnings of Divine Wrath as "too crushing" reflects the view held by all of the ethical evolutionists.

What is remarkable in Stephen's criticism of religion, and what makes it so similar to Comte's and Mill's, is that he is not really concerned with theological questions at all. He does not attempt to disprove the existence of God by scientific or rational argument. He begins by assuming that such a debate had already been won. What concerns him is the contention that religion, even if it lacks objective validity, is still necessary because of its moral value. In order to establish the validity of his own ethic, Stephen had first to attack this assumption. Once having refuted the argument that religion fostered the moral qualities he valued most, he could go on to demonstrate the "scientific" basis of his own ethic. In 1882 Stephen's *Science of Ethics* was published. In a refreshingly honest remark, he prefaces the work by confessing that none of the arguments he uses are new: "I do not believe ... that there is a single original thought in the book from beginning to end."⁵ He admitted, indeed, to owing much of his philosophy to Comte. Since, however, Hardy admits to having been most influenced by his philosophy, a brief review of Stephen's theories should prove rewarding.

The Science of Ethics, like Comte's works on Positivism, has as its two major premises the belief that altruism is the highest moral value and that it is also the highest stage of man's development. Stephen, like Comte, believed that man, unlike the other animals, was continuing to evolve. Man's progress, however, was no longer physical, according to Stephen, but intellectual and moral; his entire social and intellectual history demonstrated his evolution from the egotistic to the altruistic stage of development. In the past, man had progressed by adapting himself to increasingly complex forms of social organization, and with each adaptation he achieved a new and better kind of equilibrium. In the future, Stephen believed, man would become increasingly aware of the relationship of the parts to the whole. His increasingly complex social organizations would foster a greater sense of interdependence.⁶ Hardy's statement that man will eventually begin to see and feel itself as part of one body says the same thing.

Up to this point, Stephen's views coincide with those of Comte and Mill. He is not so sanguine, however, about man's automatic progress to the next stage of development, for he does not believe that further progress can be achieved without some losses. Mill had hoped that a morality could be established which would "neither sacrifice the individual to the aggregate nor the aggregate to the individual."⁷ "For my part," Stephen asserts, "I accept the altruist theory, and I accept what I hold to be its legitimate and inseparable conclusion – the conclusion namely, that the path of duty does not coincide with the path of happiness" (*SE,* p. 431). It is this difference which distinguishes Stephen and the later ethical evolutionists like Spencer and Huxley from Comte and Mill, and it is this latter position that Hardy adopted when he asserted his belief that altruism would "be brought about" by pain. For apparently Hardy, like the later ethical evolutionists, saw the claims of egotism as far more persistent than Comte had. The transition from egotism to altruism would not be, these later writers felt, either as natural or as conducive to happiness as Comte had assumed. On the contrary, since altruism required giving up one's selfish desires, it required the necessary sacrifice of hopes for personal happiness. Unlike Comte, the later English ethical evolutionists believed

21

that you cannot be both selfless and happy: you must choose the one or the other, and be willing to take the consequences of that choice. "To exhort a man to be virtuous," said Stephen, "is to exhort him to acquire a quality which will in many cases make him less fit than the less moral man for getting the greatest amount of happiness from a given combination of circumstances" (*SE,* p. 432). For Huxley, pain was a "necessary consequence of man's attempting to live as a member of an organized polity." It was "a baleful product of evolution" and it would increase in quantity and intensity as evolution progressed. In order to progress, man must learn altruism through self-restraint and renunciation. "This is not happiness," Huxley admits, "though," he adds characteristically, "it may be something much better."[8]

For the ethical evolutionists there was no question as to which was the proper choice: it was better to be good than happy. It was, moreover, not only better but essential if man wished to progress. Huxley's statement characterizes this position. In order to progress, he says, "man must cast aside the notion that the escape from pain and sorrow is the proper object of life" ("Prolegomena," p. 94). Obviously, this was also Hardy's position. Altruism, he believed, would come about through pain. Like Huxley and Stephen, he believed that happiness and altruism were mutually antagonistic. It was his aim, in the novels and the poetry, to dramatize this conflict. In the "Apology" he explains that what is taken for pessimism in his writing is really intended to be curative. His aim is not simply to describe man's present unhappiness but to indicate his future direction. He first quotes his own lines from "In Tenebris": "If a way to the Better there be,/It exacts a full look at the worst." He explains the lines in the following way: "that is to say, by the exploration of reality, and its frank recognition, stage by stage along the survey, with an eye to the best consummation possible: briefly, evolutionary meliorism" (pp. 526-527). Failure to recognize the fact that Hardy saw unhappiness and pain not as the final end for modern man but as a necessary condition for his future moral growth has been one of the chief stumbling blocks in critical interpretations of his works. Subsequent chapters will reveal how crucially Hardy's preference for altruism over happiness affected his works.

While all of the ethical evolutionists believed that man's progress up to this point had been automatic, all but Spencer agreed that his future progress would require conscious effort. Even Comte, who had the most optimistic attitude about the ease of the transition, recognized that "the great problem was to raise the social feelings by artificial effort to the position which, in the natural condition, is held by the selfish feelings" (*GV,* p. 102). Further, all of the ethical evolutionists agreed that one way of raising the social feelings was to make man intellectually aware of the

ETHICAL EVOLUTION

past. Comte's whole *Cours de Philosophie Positive* had been an attempt to do just this. Mill, too, felt that "the science of history affords the only means of predicting and guiding the future, of unfolding the agencies which have produced and still maintain the Present" ("Essay on Coleridge," p. 144). His own essay "Civilization" had been an attempt to prove that "there is no more accurate test of the progress of civilization than the progress of the power of cooperation." Stephen's study of eighteenth-century literature is an attempt to trace men's recent intellectual and moral history through literature. As the chapter on Hardy's literary methods will indicate, Hardy also attempted to do this by creating types representative of each successive intellectual and moral stage of man's history. *The Dynasts*, which traces the defeat of the Arch-Egotist, Napoleon, by the cooperative efforts of the Allies, was Hardy's most ambitious attempt to impose his moral values on historic fact.

But to make men intellectually aware of their history was only a part of what could be done by "artificial means" to "raise the social feelings." Even Comte was aware of the limitations of rational discourse. It soon became evident to him that no amount of moral argument, however "logical" or "scientific," would change men's moral natures.

The study of moral questions, intellectually speaking, is most valuable; but the effect it leaves is not directly moral, since the analysis will refer, not to our own actions, but to those of others.... Now to judge others without immediate reference to self, is a process which may possibly result in strong convictions, but so far from calling out right feelings, it will, if carried too far, interfere with or check their natural development. (p. 111)

Mill criticized Comte's system as being too intellectual to be effective, endorsing Spencer's statement that "ideas do not govern and overthrow the world; the world is governed and overthrown by feelings, to which ideas serve only as guides." Spencer had contended that men's moral nature could be changed only by experience, by the "continuous discipline of social life." Spencer admitted that the process was long, arduous, and wasteful. The other ethical evolutionists were more impatient, and were willing to interfere with the "natural" process in order to hasten it.

But if feelings, rather than ideas, overthrow and govern the world, how does one arouse and channel them in the proper direction? Comte had suggested the imposition of new political and religious sytems, but the English writers rejected this suggestion as too authoritarian. They did, however, accept Comte's other suggestions. The first was for the Positivist to concentrate on encouraging the growth of the sympathies by the individual's experience within the family, the most "natural" of social organizations. The second was by providing vicarious experiences through a new kind of literature. The ethical evolutionists' emphasis on the major role of the family is of particular importance in understanding Hardy's handling of the plots and characters in his novels and will be discussed later. But the emphasis on the role of literature is of general importance in understanding his aims and therefore requires some explanation here.

Comte had suggested that one of the best ways of bringing about the sociological phase of man's development was by a new kind of poetry. Epic poetry had always dealt with man's history and had conveyed the highest values of the culture: in the past, however, it had reflected the earlier stages of man's history; what was needed now was a new kind of poetry based upon reason and science. The new poetry could reflect man's present state, and, by contrasting it to the past, illuminate his future. Moreover, it had the advantage over science in that it could appeal to man's feelings as well as his intellect. "Next to direct culture of the heart, it is in ideal art that we shall find the best assistance to become more loving and more noble" (*GV,* p. 353). According to Comte, poetry was superior in its moral effects even to experience, for it could select those aspects of experience most conducive to arousing and reinforcing the social sympathies. For Comte, the new literature was to be the handmaiden of sociology.

Although Mill himself had attempted to affect "the minds and destinies of his countrymen generally" by his political actions and his essays, he felt that neither of these activities had as great an effect in bringing about change as literature. "Literature is a province of exertion upon which more, of the first value to human nature depends, than upon any other. [Writers] form the opinions and shape the characters of subsequent ages" ("Civilization," p. 65). Stephen reiterated Comte's two major criteria for literature: he believed that it should contain "a scientific system of thought" and that it should "give strength to our sympathies, something which will make us better specimens of the human race, and more fitted to discharge any of the duties which lie before us."[9] Hardy's view of the function of literature is the same as Comte's and Stephen's. Art, he said, is "science with addition." The addition is, apparently, the appeal to the moral feelings. While fiction must contain scientific truths, it must appeal to the "emotional reason," for, he says, it is "by their emotions men are acted upon and act upon others."[10]

But if Stephen and Hardy followed Comte in limiting the function of literature to the revelation of scientific truths and the evocation of moral feelings, they both disagreed with him about the way in which the moral feelings should be aroused. Where Comte had emphasized happiness, both Stephen and Hardy stressed sorrow. Since they both considered pain and sorrow as the chief means by which man was to become more moral,

ETHICAL EVOLUTION

it was the obligation of the poet to demonstrate this truth. Stephen, therefore, praised Wordsworth for having taught "the necessity of transmuting sorrow into strength" and pointed to his "Happy Warrior" as an example of the kind of poetry which expresses such truth. In that poem, Wordsworth idealizes "the man who . . . is made more compassionate by familiarity with sorrow, more placable by contest, purer by temptation, and more enduring by distress" (*HL* III, p. 167).[11] (Not accidentally, such a description would also be applicable to Hardy's characterization of the "pure" woman, Tess.) Thus, Hardy's stated belief that altruism would come about "by the pain we see in others reflected in ourselves" coincides with Stephen's. His admission that his works were concerned with the exploration and recognition of reality "with an eye to the best consummation possible, briefly, evolutionary meliorism" indicates that Hardy was attempting to embody this belief in his literature. And indeed, each successive novel demonstrates Hardy's "bitter pill" theory more dramatically. Ever more emphatically, he allows his characters no possibility for happiness and no possible way of retreat from "the inevitable movement onward." Eventually, the reader is forced into the position Hardy had worked out for Elizabeth Jane, who, through her experience with Michael Henchard, eventually recognizes that "happiness was but the occasional episode in the general drama of pain," and who has become habituated to "making limited opportunities endurable."

Once we are aware of what Hardy's aim was, we can understand, to some extent at least, why he was so reticent about making it explicit. In the first place, to make his readers aware that he was intentionally arousing their social sympathies would negate the emotional effect of the work itself. Rather than eliciting their sympathetic responses, he would, if he were to admit his aims, arouse his readers' conscious defenses. In the second place, he must surely have been aware that his position was hardly tenable. For a writer to stimulate altruism in others by causing them pain, even if such a method imitated the processes of nature and history, is undeniably an odd form of unselfishness. In addition, to assume, as Hardy seems to assume, that one is intellectually and morally more advanced than others smacks of the very kind of egotism Hardy himself attacked in his novels. Clym Yeobright and Angel Clare reveal somewhat the same sense of moral superiority, and from his treatment of these characters it would seem that Hardy was aware of his own dilemma and foresaw its consequences. Clym Yeobright and Angel Clare, like his other, less advanced egotists, are made to suffer the consequences of their egotism. The efforts of Jude and Sue, his last fictional characters to transcend their egotism, fail. Hardy makes them aware that, to some degree, their failure is the result of their own limitations. But he also has them place the blame

25

on society's inability to understand or accept them.

As an author, Hardy himself took the latter position publicly. It was society, not he, that was at fault. Society was not "advanced" enough to accept the "ideas and emotions" he had expressed in the novels. In one sense, society's failure to understand him was reassuring, for it proved that he was, indeed, one of the advanced few who were bound to suffer the consequences of braving convention. Ignoring the financial success and critical acclaim that his novels brought him, he saw his fate as a novelist as precisely what Stephen and Spencer had predicted for all those who were in advance of their time: Stephen had said that "every reformer who breaks with the world, though for the world's good, must naturally expect much pain" (*SE*, p. 418). Spencer predicted not only pain but failure: "The young convention breaker eventually finds that he pays too heavily for his non-conformity."

But the role Hardy played publicly was not his only response. The hostile reaction to his novels indicated that the public had understood him only too well. Their hostility was in some sense justified, for like Tess they had been the innocent victims of Hardy's moral arrogance. Interestingly enough, he reacted in precisely the same way as his most "altruistic" fictional character. Like Clym Yeobright, he turned the tables and made himself into an example of suffering. In lyric poetry, the poet, conventionally, becomes the sufferer and the reader is put in the superior position as sympathizer. In this way, the notion that altruism would be brought about "by the pain we see in other reflected in ourselves" is still maintained. It is simply inverted. The pain is no longer that of the "others" — either the fictional character or the reader — but of the altruist himself. The result is that Hardy, like Clym, can engage the reader's sympathy without arousing his hostility. (Interestingly enough, this has been precisely the reaction to his poetry. It has never called forth the hostile reactions that his novels did.) As a novelist, Hardy had considered himself only as an agent of change in others. As poet he was both agent and victim at once.

If this is so, we must read his poems as we do those of Yeats, for example, not as simple and direct statements but as dramatic utterances. Such a reading certainly merits further study. For the present, however, it is necessary to focus upon the novels where his ideas about ethical evolution worked themselves out. For, despite the fact that he may have failed either to manipulate the reader's values in the precise way that he wished or to reveal the "scientific" validity of his moral beliefs, the novels are anything but failures. Indeed, a large part of their success is based on his ideas about ethical evolution, for these beliefs give the novels their form and meaning.

ETHICAL EVOLUTION

NOTES

1. When, for example, critics ascribed the anonymously published *Far From the Madding Crowd* to George Eliot, Hardy explained that their terminology was similar because he had been "reading Comte's *Positive Philosophy*" prior to writing the novel (Jan. 1874, p. 98). Quite rightly, as Bernard Paris's *Experiments in Life* (Detroit, 1965) makes clear, Hardy associated George Eliot with Positivism. Her death "set him thinking about Positivism," and the following remark indicates that he, too, considered it to contain at least the "germs of a true system": "Thousands decry what in their heart of hearts they hold to contain the germs of a true system" (Nov. 20, 1880, p. 146).

He seemed to adopt Comte's view of history as a "looped orbit," using it in a passage in the "Apology" and in the following one:

". . . the periodicity which marks the course of taste in civilized countries does not take the form of a true cycle of repetition, but what Comte, in speaking of general progress, happily characterizes as 'a looped orbit': not a movement of revolution, but — to use the current word — evolution" ("Candour in English Fiction," Orel, p. 127).

2. In *The Life of Leslie Stephen* (London: 1906) F. W. Maitland quotes Hardy's comment that he had read an article of Stephen's in the current *Fortnightly Review* and that Stephen had thanked Hardy for praising it. This article, according to Maitland, was Stephen's "Are We Christians?" which appeared in the March 1873 issue of the magazine and was reprinted in *Freethinking and Plainspeaking* (New York: 1908). It is from the book that the subsequent passages are taken (Maitland, p. 272).
3. Hardy's description of Mill, as well as his comment about knowing "On Liberty" by heart, appeared in a letter to the *Times*, May 21, 1906, and can be found in *The Life*, p. 330.
4. J. H. Bridges, trans., *A General View of Positivism*, by Auguste Comte (London: 1865), pp. 159-163. Harriet Martineau's translation, *The Positive Philosophy* (London: 1853), of Comte's *Cours de Philosophie Positive* (Paris: 1830-42) was the version most likely read by the English writers.
5. Leslie Stephen, *The Science of Ethics* (London: 1882), p. vii.
6. The following passage characterizes this belief: "We learn from the theory of evolution that as the individual organism is composed of mutually dependent parts, and that its existence involves the maintenance of a certain equilibrium, so each organism supports itself as a part in a more general equilibrium, that its constitution depends at every moment upon the process of adaptation to the whole system of the world" (*SE*, p. 79). Burrow has shown that this idea of functional interdependence, deriving partially from Comte, was propounded in Mill's *System of Logic* and appeared again in Spencer's *Social Statics*. As Paris points out, this was also George Eliot's view, and accounts for her favorite metaphor of the spider's web (which Hardy also used).
7. John Stuart Mill, *Essential Works*, ed. Max Lerner (New York: 1961) "The Utility of Religion," p. 423.
8. Thomas H. Huxley, *Touchstone for Ethics*, ed. Julian Huxley (New

York: 1947) "Prolegomena to Evolution and Ethics," pp. 70-71, 66.

9. The first phrase comes from Stephen's essay on Wordsworth, *Hours in a Library*, III (New York: 1904), p. 136. The second appears in *Men, Books and Mountains* (Minneapolis: 1956), p. 44. Significantly, George Eliot, who was also influenced by Comte, expressed the same belief in the specific moral function of literature. The Comtean claim for literature is different from other claims in that it emphasizes new poetry reflecting new sociological truths and eliciting only *one kind* of reaction. Arnold's essay "Literature and Science" justly attacks this claim as too narrow. The "scientific view of human nature," he says, leaves out of account man's instinct for beauty and the literature which leaves this instinct out of account is also too narrow. For the Comtean, man's love of beauty was related to his desire to escape from pain and sorrow and was therefore a reflection of egotism. The Comtean would therefore reject beauty, as Hardy has his hero do in *The Well-Beloved* and he himself does in *The Return of the Native*.

The argument for basing the morality of literature on its emotional effect (and which is related to the "sentimentalism" of the eighteenth century) was countered by Ruskin in *Sesame and the Lilies* in 1865 and by J. A. Noble and Vernon Lee in 1885.

10. The first phrase comes from "The Science of Fiction," Orel, p. 134; the second from "The Profitable Reading of Fiction," *Selected Writings of Thomas Hardy*, ed. Irving Howe (New York: 1966), p. 142.

11. Arnold's essay on Wordsworth seems to be a direct refutation of Stephen's. Arnold contends that we admire Wordsworth for precisely the opposite reasons. We enjoy Wordsworth only when we ignore his moral philosophy, he contends.

Three

CHARACTER AS ETHICAL TYPE

One of the difficulties readers of Hardy's novels have encountered is the problem of how to deal with his method of characterization. John Holloway, for example, notes that Hardy's characters "lack rotundity in the literary figurative sense," but that "however much this may reduce their interest in isolation, it increases the power of the novels to give a single, unified effect."[1] Those critics who attempt to deal with the characters in isolation and who attempt to find psychological realism are disappointed at what they take to be Hardy's obtuseness. This difficulty is, apparently, not new; for, according to Kenneth Graham, even Hardy's contemporaries were "never quite sure by which standard, realist or non-realist, to appraise his stylized characters and incidents."[2]

Again it must be conceded that part of the difficulty is caused by Hardy's own apparent inconsistencies. His insistence on verisimilitude — as seen in his rigorous time charts and topographies — would seem to indicate that he was attempting to achieve realism; yet this is counteracted by his claims that "art must be more true than nature or history can be" and that art is "a disproportioning of realities."[3] This apparent inconsistency can be explained, however, if we understand Hardy's assumption, which seemed, perhaps, too obvious at the time for him to stress but which has become most difficult for the modern reader to comprehend. Hardy's assumption, like that of all the ethical evolutionists, was that morality *was* truth, and the function of art was to reveal it. Art is, he says, a "disproportioning of realities," to show "more clearly the features that matter in those realities." For Hardy, "the features that matter" are the moral ones. So, for example, his major concern in delineating character is in placing it within a moral hierarchy: in literature, he says, "the higher passions must ever rank above the inferior — the intellectual tendencies above the animal, the moral above the intellectual — whatever the treatment, realistic or ideal" ("PRF," p. 141).

Now this hierarchy of values is traditional in Western culture and had been the basic assumption of many writers prior to Hardy. But Hardy's treatment of it differs from, say, Fielding's or Jane Austen's in that he regarded it as having not only permanent and universal significance, but as being based upon scientifically demonstrated historic truth. For this view he was indebted to Comte, for Comte had taken the traditional hierarchy and presented it as a structure in time. For Comte, it was no longer a fixed structure of eternal truth, but a dynamic and evolving one. History could be seen as demonstrating man's progress from the physical to the intellectual stage of development, and from egotism toward altruism. Each stage was dependent upon the last and created conditions for the next.

This way of seeing morality historically has obvious advantages for the poet or novelist who wishes to reveal historic truth and at the same time to affect man's moral nature. By making a character correspond to a particular stage of moral history, the novelist could create a "type" that was neither strictly allegorical nor simply naturalistic. In the same way, by making the plot reveal the necessary relationship between cause and effect the novelist was not only satisfying moral and aesthetic demands but, because the plot also reflected the "laws of nature," revealing the truth. In adhering to "scientific" or "historic" truth, the novelist was being more moral than the strict allegorist or the creator of more imaginative fictions, for, according to Comte, only when man became more aware of his past and of the necessary relationship between cause and effect would he become intellectually "objective" enough to move to the next, altruistic stage of his development. The novelist who made men aware of these relationships was acting in the service of science. He was helping bring about the change which the Positivist philosophy predicted.

In creating literary types that were both historically true and morally instructive, the poet or novelist had one advantage over the moral philosopher or historian. That advantage was that he could also engage the reader's sympathies. For the literary type was not only a reflection of a particular stage in man's general history; it was also a reflection of a particular stage in the history of each individual. According to Comte, each individual repeats the general history of the race. Intellectually, "every man is a theologian in his childhood, a metaphysician in his youth, a philosopher in manhood." Morally, each man also passes through the same successive stages that mark the progress of the race — the personal, the domestic, and the social stage. By tracing the history of the race, the Positivist poet could, according to Comte, "awaken our sympathies and revive the traces which each individual may recognize of corresponding phases in his own history" (*GV*, p. 330). In other words, the reader could identify with a literary type representative of an earlier stage of development and infer his future from those types representative of stages beyond his own development.

Although Comte made his suggestions to future epic poets, his theory of the correspondence between the history of the individual and the history of the race can be seen as readily adaptable to the novel, since the novel conventionally deals with the personal and the domestic areas of man's life. Comte himself had thought that the proper development within these two stages was crucial for any further progress. He had advised the Positivist to consider the domestic stage as "his best resource in attempting as far as possible to reach the normal state; subordination of self-love to social feeling" (*GV*, p. 68). He saw marriage as the crucial pivot between the personal and the domestic stage. The relationship between husband and wife, based originally upon selfishness, becomes, ideally, transformed into "the only association in which entire identity of interests is possible." Marriage "completes and confirms the education of the heart by calling out the purest and strongest social sympathies." And just as the sexual instincts lead to marriage, so the conjugal tie leads to the next stage, the domestic one. For Comte, as for Stephen and Spencer, the family is "the basis of the social spirit." Filial affection gives the child his first tie to the whole past history of man; parental affection calls forth even greater altruism and binds the parent to the future.

The English writers, particularly Stephen and Spencer, placed even greater emphasis on the role of marriage and the family than Comte had; for Comte had believed that the future Positivists needed only see to it that these institutions remained fixed and stable and should concentrate their energies on creating a third form of social and political institution that would have a dynamic effect on the final, "social stage" of man's development. Rejecting Comte's theory that only new political and social institutions could create further change and reasserting their belief in the freedom of the individual, the English ethical evolutionists saw marriage and the family as dynamic forces rather than simply as stabilizing ones. A change in these institutions could make, they believed, a radical difference in man's future moral growth. It was, perhaps, for this principle that Mill urged greater freedom of divorce and argued for the emancipation of women. Stephen openly asserted his belief that the nature of the family unit determined the structure of society. He saw "the present stage of monogamy and comparative social equality" as "one of the greatest conceivable changes in social growth" (*SE*, pp. 133-135).

Hardy himself opposed "present marriage laws" because, he said, "they account for at least half the misery of the community."[4] In his novels, however, he is not so much interested in changing the laws as in changing attitudes that made the laws possible. "The eminently modern idea of a woman's not becoming necessarily the chattel and slave of her seducer impressed him as being one of the first glimmers of woman's enfranchisement; and he made use of it in succeeding years in more than one case in his fiction and verse" (Dec. 1882, p. 157). But in "making use" of this idea, Hardy was not simply reflecting a contemporary notion which he happened to agree with for, perhaps, personal reasons. By "opposing institutions to individuals," he was not, as he said, attacking the institutions, but rather attempting to change the fundamental moral nature of man. He "makes use" of the idea of woman's enfranchisement by creating character types such as Eustacia Vye, Tess, and Sue Bridehead that reflect the various stages of the struggle for freedom. Sue's attempt to escape from her own conventional notions of marriage and her failure to do so is not an attack on the institution of marriage itself but on a way of thinking which allowed the institution to exist in what was its present form. The reader is expected to see more objectively what the character, who is reacting more immediately and therefore more subjectively, cannot.[5] As a representative of a modern "type" Sue is to be sympathized with; she is not, however, to be emulated but rather transcended.

Hardy's treatment of "the marriage question" in *Jude the Obscure* is characteristic of his aims and methods in the other novels. Although the novel lends itself to situations involving marriage and the family, a novelist does not generally limit himself to those concerns. Significantly, however, Hardy does. *Every one* of Hardy's novels deals with the relationship between men and women before or after marriage and with the reciprocal effects of parents and children on the outcome of the marriage. To use the terms of the ethical evolutionists, Hardy limits himself to the personal and domestic stage of social evolution. If we accept his frequent assertions that the primary value of his novels is their moral effect, and his other assertions concerning his belief in altruism, we can understand why he limits himself to these relationships. If he believed, with Comte, Stephen, and Spencer, that the conjugal and filial relationships are the pivots between the egotistic and the altruistic impulses, then an improvement in these relationships is crucial for moral growth. Improvement of the family cannot be achieved by direct intervention; it can, however, be achieved indirectly by providing the reader with experiences representative of earlier stages of man's personal and domestic growth. In this way, the reader is emotionally and intellectually "brought up" to the present level. By making it clear that earlier stages are no longer possible, or indeed even desirable, the

CHARACTER AS ETHICAL TYPE

novelist forces the reader into a consideration of new possibilities.

In many ways, as we have seen, the theories of ethical evolution were distinctly adaptable to literary, and particularly novelistic, treatment. They had, however, as Hardy himself was to discover, some distinct disadvantages. Some of the disadvantages have already been suggested, but one disadvantage related to the construction of character types needs to be discussed here, for it presented a dilemma which Hardy grappled with in a variety of ways.

Comte had promised that in the future Positivist state, the poet would be able to reflect the highest ideals. He could create "types of the noblest kind by the contemplation of which our feelings and thoughts may be elevated." For the present, however, the poet was to restrict himself to what was immediately available. The poet of the present could not create the truly objective, altruistic type because, at present (with the possible exception of Comte himself), there was none. To put it another way, the poet who prided himself on being "scientific" was restricted to conveying the truths of history and science. He could not go beyond presenting values already revealed in the present. He could not, like Sidney's poet, create a golden world. He could, by reference to the past, *imply* man's future, but he could not make a model for it. "At all times the imagination must be subordinate to the laws of social development described by Positivist philosophy" (*GV*, pp. 314-316).[6]

In a curious note dated May 11, 1900, several years after the publication of *Jude,* Hardy revealed his own awareness, as well as Stephen's, of the dilemma of the poet who wished to characterize new values on the basis of those available in the present: "Leslie Stephen says, 'The old ideals have become obsolete, and the new are not yet constructed. We cannot write living poetry on an ancient model. The Gods and heroes are too dead, and we cannot seriously sympathize with . . . the idealized prizefighter' " (p. 308). He may have been thinking of his current work, his "epic-drama," *The Dynasts.* He solved the problem in this work by using historic figures as his "types": Napoleon representing the antagonist, nationalistic egotism, and the English leaders representing the protagonists, engaged in cooperative efforts to save the Allies from destruction. But he had already attempted to solve the problem in other ways in the novels, where he had created characters representative of various stages of intellectual and moral evolution.

Readers of Hardy need hardly be reminded that he was, indeed, prone to describe his characters as types. Only a few examples should recall this habit. Angel Clare, for example, is "a sample product of the last five-and-twenty years" — being "shaded by his own limitations." The "constitution" of Stephen Smith in *A Pair of Blue Eyes* is described as "one which, rare in the springtime of civilizations, seems to grow abundant as a nation grows older, individuality fades, and education spreads, that is, his brain had extraordinary receptive powers, and no great creativeness." Swithin St. Cleve, of *Two on a Tower*, is "a scientist, and took words literally. There is something in the inexorably simple logic of such men which partakes of the cruelty of the natural laws which are their study." It should be remarked here that, although each of these characters represents a modern "type," Hardy does not restrict himself to representing only the most recent stage of development. As the subsequent chapters will show, he also presents characters representative of earlier stages of evolution. These earlier types provide a kind of historic perspective to the major characters or act as catalysts affecting the progress of the modern type.

As his descriptions of Angel Clare, Stephen Smith, and Swithin St. Cleve make clear, Hardy tended, like the other ethical evolutionists, to see the modern type as predominantly intellectual. As intellectuals, they tend to be more objective than their more romantic predecessors. (The contrast between Donald Farfrae and Michael Henchard is an example.) They may also, like Clym Yeobright and Angel Clare, be intellectually aware of the need for a change in social or religious values. But how can they also foreshadow the *next* stage, where moral feeling rather than intellect dominates? How can they, as reflections of the modern type, engage the reader's sympathies and, at the proper time, disengage them?

Since he could not present "ideal" types representative of the future, how could Hardy imply the future in the presentation of his modern types? Hardy's solution was to take the negative way — to show the modern types as "shaded by limitations," as lacking in moral feeling, and to show the effect of these limitations on their own lives as well as the lives of others. As a result of their limitations they suffer, or cause others to suffer, greater unhappiness than the less advanced characters. Sue Bridehead is Hardy's most extreme example of this method. While she is advanced intellectually, she is also markedly lacking in genuine moral feeling. Although she wants to be loved, she confesses herself incapable of returning it. Her actions testify to the validity of her statements. She leaves Jude at the very time when he needs her most, and allows him to walk away from her at last, knowing that he is walking to his death. She is willing to sacrifice him in order to satisfy her own need for moral salvation. Hardy had written the novel, he asserts, with particular regard to the ending and had been convinced that it would "make for morality." He had presented the novel, he declares, "not without hope that certain cathartic, Aristotelian qualities might be found therein."[7] By presenting Sue at the beginning in a most attractive light as an intellectually advanced free spirit, Hardy at first engages the reader's sympathies. But by shading her with limitations of increasingly apparent seriousness, he gradually disengages that sympathy until, ultimately, like Jude, the reader rejects Sue. Apparently Hardy hoped that by leading the reader to reject Sue he would effect a catharsis of egotism within the reader himself.

Sue, like most of Hardy's "advanced" types, is a hortatory, as well as an exemplary type. But the fact that he presents her as a hortatory type does not mean that he has an anti-modern, anti-intellectual bias, or that he is revealing a profound desire to return to a more stable world embodying the homely comforts of a simple rustic life. (He makes his position clear by contrasting Sue with an earlier egotistic type, Arabella.) Rather, he would infer from the limitations of the present the needs of the future. He would, as he says in the preface to his later poetry, "take the reader forward even if not far, rather than backward."[8]

That Hardy's emphasis is always on "the inevitable movement onward" can be seen by the way in which he contrasts his modern character types to the earlier ones. If, by reference to the future, the modern types are "shaded by their limitations," by reference to the past they are made clearly superior.

Most of Hardy's modern characters oppose, in one way or another, situations or characters representing an earlier time. Jude and Sue are obvious examples, but Angel Clare is another, as are Donald Farfrae, Grace Melbury and Fitzpiers, Clym Yeobright, and Ethelberta. This list could be extended all the way back to the first published novel, *Desperate Remedies,* in which the younger and more enlightened Cytherea Graye and Edward Springrove are thrust into a situation created by a previous generation and made to work themselves out of it. In one way or another, these modern characters disturb the equilibrium, very often creating or suffering greater unhappiness than the less advanced characters. This disequilibrium and its consequent unhappiness is not, however, to be regretted, for it is a necessary accompaniment to moral progress: altruism, not happiness, is the goal of man, and altruism requires that man learn to give up those desires which satisfy his ego. It is perfectly true, as one critic has remarked, that few characters of Hardy are allowed to achieve their hearts' desires, but that is not to say that Hardy agreed that their hearts' desires should be satisfied. To say, as one critic has said, that "Hardy merely wanted people to be happy" is to miss the point entirely. He may have wanted them to be happy, but he preferred that they be good. And, in order to be good, he believed that they must change. Like Huxley, he believed that, in order to progress, "man must cast aside the notion that escape from pain and sorrow is the proper object in life." While it may have been possible to be both good and happy in a limited way in simpler times, by the nineteenth century the two values were mutually antagonistic. It was, indeed, no longer a matter of choice. By Hardy's day it was no longer possible for man to achieve happiness, or at least the kind of happiness which required the satisfaction of the ego at the expense of others.

Change and the necessity for change — that is the key point in understanding Hardy and the ethical evolutionists. For Hardy, a character's success is dependent upon his ability to adapt his desires to the needs of others. If, like Michael Henchard and Eustacia Vye, he is incapable of changing, of subordinating his egotistical desires for happiness to the needs of those around him, he is doomed to extinction. As long as he can, like Elizabeth Jane and Tess, learn to subordinate his egotism to the needs of others, he can survive. Each of Hardy's novels is an illustration of this point; each plot refutes the theory that Hardy yearned to return to a simpler and more stable world. The way in which he treats those characters who do attempt this retreat indicates that Hardy does not entirely identify with them. When, as in the case of Michael Henchard or Sue Bridehead, for example, the characters suffer a "relapse" to an earlier stage, the effect is usually catastrophic. After nearly twenty years of self-discipline after his first egotistic act of wife-selling, Henchard again commits a series of increasingly serious betrayals, beginning with his selling the townspeople faulty grain and culminating with his concealing the presence of her real father from Elizabeth Jane. Despite his attempts to control them, his selfish feelings again reassert themselves and cause reactions that lead to his destruction. Similarly, after having achieved a fair degree of freedom from convention in her relationship with Jude, Sue can go no farther. Only her jealousy of Arabella induces her to consummate their "marriage," and her fear of telling the "whole truth" to Father Time results in his killing himself and the other children. She admits to Jude's accusation that her return to Phillotson is a kind of reaction, a relapse to earlier values and beliefs. This "relapse" destroys not only herself but Jude.

Hardy not only shows the inevitable consequences of retreat into the past but he also shows the consequences of any attempt to escape from it. To attempt to ignore the past, as Tess does, for example, is equally disastrous. As Comte had insisted, Hardy believed that one must be aware of one's "filiation" with the past in order to find one's direction into the future. This is the function of history, and this "truth" operates on the private as well as on the public level. In order to show a major character's relationship to the past, Hardy usually provides a background of fixed and stable characters (very often, as in Tess's case, parents) representative of earlier stages of evolution. This background of minor characters provides the reader with some understanding of where the major characters have come from and what direction they should be working toward. The "good" and "simple" minor characters are never allowed to preempt the place of the more advanced major characters. Diggory Venn, for example, is never allowed to preempt the central position of Clym Yeobright. He has only a very limited appeal, precisely because he is a more limited, fixed, and stable character. Representing an earlier stage of altruism, his evolution has occurred before the story begins, and he acts "according to type" throughout the novel. Clym Yeobright, on the other hand, begins as an "intellectual type" but, during the course of the story, he begins to break out of this mold and to move toward another stage of development.

Whatever their moral and intellectual limitations, the major characters remain in the foreground as complex and dynamic. They are both the victims and the agents of change. Their unhappiness is not necessarily an indication that they are moving in the wrong direction. On the contrary, their very capacity for suffering signifies their greater moral and intellectual awareness and implies the direction of their change. They are incapable, however, no matter how advanced, of moving into the next stage because they are limited to reflecting man's current position. They are restricted to the present stage that their type represents. As he moves his characters out of their romantic illusions of happiness representative of past values into a more objective awareness of the limitations of the present, the author leaves them with a painful awareness of the difference between *what is* and *what ought to be*. But for Hardy, what ought to be lies not in some ideal past but somewhere in the future, in the kind of conscious intellectual and emotional responses that both sees and feels humanity to be "part of one body." The sense of disequilibrium at the conclusion of his last major novels becomes the catalyst for just such a response. For just as Eustacia Vye affects Clym's development and Tess affects Angel Clare's, so the reactions of these more modern characters elicit more advanced responses in the reader. By shading in the limitations of the present, the novelist would illuminate the future through the responses of his readers.

The subsequent chapters will show how, beginning with simple one-dimensional character types representing the egotist and altruist positions, Hardy develops his ethical perspective, rounds his characters with increasing psychological subtlety, and engages the ethical system within increasingly dynamic plot structures. By the last novel the ethical value system is so absorbed as to be evident only by reference to the previous works and by the novel's powerful evocative effects.

CHARACTER AS ETHICAL TYPE

NOTES

1. *The Victorian Sage* (London: 1962), p. 268.
2. *English Criticism of the Novel, 1865-1900* (Oxford: 1965), p. 39.
3. The first phrase is, of course, derived from Sidney's "An Apology for Poetry." It appears in Hardy's essay "On the Profitable Reading of Fiction" (Howe, p. 144). The full text for the second phrase is as follows: "Art is a disproportioning — (i.e., distorting, throwing out of proportion) — of realities, to show more clearly the features that matter in those realities, which, if merely copied or reported inventorially, might possibly be observed, but would more probably be overlooked. Hence, 'realism' is not art" (*The Life*, p. 239).
4. Orel, p. 252. This essay was a contribution to the series "Laws, the Cause of Misery," in *Nash's Magazine*, March 1912, p. 683.
5. J. Hillis Miller, in *Thomas Hardy: Distance and Desire* (Cambridge, Mass.: 1970), sees this technique as characteristic of Hardy's method: "Each of Hardy's characters lives out his life moving toward an incomplete illumination.... The character ultimately glimpses a covert design in his life which has been invisible while he has been living that life. The artist brings that design into the full light of day" (p. 269).
6. Apparently Stephen assimilated Comte's theories of literary types and applied it to his criticism of the novel. Character in the novel, he said, should embody "the great currents of thought and feeling of the time." He praised Sterne's Uncle Toby as "the projection in concrete form of certain ideas which had affected Sterne's imagination" and which represented the best thought of the age. Uncle Toby was "the incarnation of the sentimentalism of the eighteenth century" (*HL* III, pp. 296-300). Hardy seems to have shared Stephen's fondness for Uncle Toby as well as his theory of types. Asserting his belief that the best fiction "is more true than nature or history can be" since it need not take into account inexplicable accidents or inconsistencies of character, he uses Uncle Toby as one of his examples. "Nobody ever met an Uncle Toby who was Uncle Toby all round.... What is called idealization of characters, is, in truth, making them too real to be possible" ("PRF," p. 144).
7. Orel, p. 34. This comment first appeared in a "Postscript" to *Jude the Obscure*, Wessex Edition III, 1912.
8. Preface to *Time's Laughingstocks*, published in 1909 (Orel, p. 44). Hardy even seemed to consider "idealizing" particular emotions if they represented "a higher consciousness and a deeper insight." The date as well as the content of the following note from *The Life* indicates that he may have been thinking of Sue Bridehead: "Courage has been idealized; why not Fear? — which is a higher consciousness and based on a deeper insight" (April 25, 1893).

Four

THE EARLY NOVELS

A review of Hardy's early novels indicates that the development of his value system and techniques was gradual. Not until *The Return of the Native* do they emerge in full scale within a structure complex and dynamic enough to contain them. That is not to say, however, that his general ethical attitudes are not present from the first. They are present in incipient form, but they lack focus and dimension. At first, like the characters themselves, they seem one-dimensional, dominated by the exigencies of plot. From time to time, however, character, value, and action fortuitously combine, and these moments foreshadow the great effects in the later fiction.

Hardy's first novel is a social satire. *The Poor Man and the Lady* pits the egotism, "the frivolity, heartlessness, and selfishness of Londoners," against the "misery of the lower classes."[1] The second novel, *Desperate Remedies,* is less generalized, pitting the egocentricity of some of the characters against the misery of two young lovers. In this novel Hardy establishes a basic pattern: the evolution of altruism in one character as a reaction to the egotism of other characters. In this case the heroine, Cytherea Graye, is confronted with a crucial ethical choice, a choice which defines and then questions the conventional notion of altruism: should she sacrifice herself and thereby "give happiness to at least two hearts whose emotional activities were still unwounded?" She decides to do so, but the novelist makes it clear that this kind of altruism is limited and self-deceptive: it is too passive, the result of a "willful indifference to the future."[2] Cytherea is made to see the limitations of this response when her lover, the ailing Springrove, shows a real need for her and calls forth a more genuine response. At this point she questions the conventional social imperative that disregards the life being sacrificed. The kind of altruism she envisions would be more long-lasting, more reciprocal, more significant. In a passage remarkably prophetic of Tess's after the death of her child, Cytherea considers the future significance of her act of self-sacrifice. She sees herself regarded in the future as "but a thought, easily held in two words of pity, 'Poor Girl!'" The significance of her sacrifice, the "hours, minutes, and peculiar minutes" of her suffering will have no permanent effect on the lives and attitudes of those who have known her. It will not create the kind of responsiveness that such a sacrifice should engender; in short, what is so tragic about the situation is the failure of empathy: "nobody can enter into another's nature truly, that's what is so grievous" (pp. 278-279). At this point Cytherea has reached an awareness of the need for what Hardy means by the term altruism: "the pain we see in others reacting on ourselves as if we and they were one body."

In his treatment of Cytherea Graye, Hardy sketches in broad outline what he will develop with increasing depth and subtlety in his later novels. He introduces his character at "the extreme posterior edge of a tract in her life in which the real meaning of Taking thought had never been known," and through a series of painful situations develops that character's feelings and attitudes in characteristic ways. Cytherea's love for Springrove becomes protective; she sees herself in relation to past and future and is aware of the "grievousness" of the failure of empathy.

While Cytherea's ethical development ends here, Hardy picks up its evolution in another character, Edward Springrove. The way in which his attitudes are transformed is more explicit. By the end of the novel his "passion" for Cytherea has turned into a "longing to cherish"; his admiration, to "warm fellowship"; and his possessive love to disinterested concern (p. 296). In short, Springrove becomes the altruist response for which Cytherea yearns.

In *Under the Greenwood Tree* (1872) Hardy provides somewhat greater depth to the values he establishes by setting his young lovers in a more congenial historic background. In this case the young lovers attempt to establish their individualistic and romantic values against the older rural values of Mellstock. In an outcome that is rare in Hardy, the lovers manage to achieve the best of both worlds. The Mellstock Quire graciously gives way to the "isolated organist" after hearing Mr. Maybold's explanation that "it is not that fiddles are bad but that an organ is better," and when they learn that one of their own, Dick Dewy, has fallen in love with the organist, Fancy Day. But in order to make such a harmonious adaptation possible, the lovers must also learn their own lesson of renunciation. Dick Dewy learns to behave as his less romantic parents behave: he becomes patient, tolerant, and practical. And Fancy Day learns that if she is to have Dick Dewy she cannot also have other lovers. As Dewy learns to see and accept the imperfections of his beloved, Fancy Day also recognizes that she must limit her desires for complete freedom and happiness. The character who orchestrates this harmonious reciprocity between the lovers and between the past and present is Maybold. He not only persuades the choir to give place to the organist but himself renounces his desire for Fancy Day. This deus ex machina then disappears from the scene, never to return in a Hardy novel; for while such a character is possible in a pastoral romance, he cannot appear in realistic fiction. There, as the young Jude observes, "nobody comes," because in real life, as the novelist remarks, "nobody ever does." For Hardy it is not the absence of God but the absence of the altruist response in man that makes present life unbearable.

A Pair of Blue Eyes (1873) deepens in ethical perspective by the introduction of a new element embodied in a new character type, the intellectual altruist. While the earlier novels had dealt with romantic young lovers, rural types, and stage villains, this novel provides the romantic young heroine with a lover more advanced than herself. The introduction of this new element in Hardy's fiction is especially significant at this time, since it is possible to conjecture that it coincides with Hardy's introduction to Leslie Stephen, "the one contemporary whose philosophy was to influence him the most" and who was to become the publisher of his next novel and a personal friend for a number of years. Since this novel, in its treatment of the Elfride Swancourt-Stephen Smith relationship, is generally regarded as partially autobiographical, deriving from Hardy's own romance at Cornwall with Emily Lavinia Gifford, it is possible to speculate that the character Harry Knight, literary critic, editor, and social philosopher, also had a real-life prototype and that that prototype was Leslie Stephen. Certainly it is clear that Hardy had read and admired Stephen's essays by the time he was writing *A Pair of Blue Eyes*.[3] One episode in particular suggests that Hardy had Stephen in mind when he created Harry Knight.

But before dealing with Harry Knight, it is necessary to see how Hardy prepares his heroine for Knight. It would seem at first glance that she is like his previous romantic heroines. Like Cytherea Graye, Elfride Swancourt is haunted by an ancestral pattern from which she longs to escape. Unlike the earlier heroine, however, she sees her romance from a double perspective. Although she experiences the spontaneity and enthusiasm of first love in her romance with Stephen Smith, she also has a sense of déjà vu. She sees herself as the intellectually and socially superior lady of the courtly love tradition and Smith as her faithful and adoring knight. Furthermore, while she is playing her role of La Belle Dame Sans Merci she is in the process of writing a similar romance, *The Court of King Arthur's Castle: A Romance of Lyonnesse.*

Having distanced herself from Smith by space as well as by time, Elfride falls in love with Smith's mentor and her own literary critic, Harry Knight. His objectivity allows her to further distance herself from the past. She comes to see her romances, both fictional and real, as juvenile. She prefers Knight's coolness to her younger lover's youthful ardors. Like most of Hardy's heroines, Elfride begins to rank the "intellectual tendencies above the animal." The novelist, however, goes a step beyond, ranking the "moral above the intellectual." While Elfride perceives her new lover to be intellectually superior, the novelist makes him ethically superior. Indeed, Knight's ethical superiority diminishes the stature of the young lovers: the "thoroughness and integrity" of the older man "illuminated his features with a dignity not even incipient in the other two."[4] In short, Knight realizes the vague aspirations that had made Elfride discontented with her former lover, Stephen Smith.

The introduction of Knight allows Hardy to provide, for the first time, an intellectual basis and perspective for his ethical values. Knight's conversations with Elfride reveal the Positivist position. When she asks the essayist why he contents himself with brief reviews rather than undertaking some mighty work, he replies in a vein characteristic of both Stephen and Hardy that "a chance limitation of direction is often better than absolute freedom." For both Stephen and Hardy the desire for absolute freedom is the mark of the romantic egotist blind to the past and future and oblivious to the relationship between cause and effect. Similarly, Knight's comments at the Luxellian tomb reveal the Positivist perspective. Knight sees ancient social and political power being replaced by intellectual power. On the other hand, "one has a sense of wrong . . . that such an appreciative breadth as a sentient being possesses should be committed to the frail casket of a body." Rejecting the idea of immortality, the intellect recognizes its own limitations. Knight's reaction to this perception is, like Stephen's, primarily ethical: "what weakens one's intentions regarding the future like the thought of this?" However, the thought is temporarily dismissed, for "there's a great deal to be done yet by us all" (p. 299).[5]

The high point of the novel occurs when Knight confronts his own death. While the scene has been admired by readers and critics, its similarity to Stephen's own fictional account of a similar situation has not been recognized. In "A Bad Five Minutes in the Alps" Stephen uses a cliff-hanging situation to make a brief historical survey of the various ethical and philosophic approaches to life and death.[6] Hardy uses the same predicament as the climax of his novel, placing Knight face to face with a dead fossil and having him retrace human and biological history to its beginnings. As Knight clings precariously to the cliff, tortured by both his awkward position and the pelting rain, he begins to think of himself as an innocent victim of "a hostile and cosmic agency." Gradually, however, he takes a more objective view of the significance of his own suffering and death. He is no Prometheus, though he believes his intellect is above average and his death would be "a deliberate loss to earth of good material" (p. 245). Both in tone and sequence, Knight's reactions are remarkably like Stephen's.

Although Stephen ends his essay by extricating himself from the predicament, the conclusion of Hardy's episode is close to Stephen's system of values as they appear in *The Science of Ethics*. The way in which Hardy concludes the episode is significant, for it shifts the emphasis from intellectual objectivity to moral feelings. As the earlier episode at the Luxellian tomb had suggested, the broad mental perspective and objectivity expressed by Knight, though admirable, is shown to be ultimately limited. The capacity for seeing oneself in retrospect offers some comfort for the present moment, but, as Knight himself remarks at the Luxellian tomb, provides very little hope or faith for the future. If one faces the finality of death with scientific objectivity, what motivates one to continue struggling to live? This is the question Stephen asks himself in "A Bad Five Minutes in the Alps," and it is the question Hardy answers in this scene. Knight transfers his faith and hope from Divine Providence to Elfride, and it is Elfride's charity that saves him, not for the next life but for this.

Knight's intellectual perspective had led him only to a calm and dispassionate contemplation of death. In close proximity to death and absolute isolation from other human beings, Knight for the first time recognizes his dependence on another human being. Upon seeing Elfride return, Knight's eyes express what he feels keenly for the first time: "the whole diapason of eloquence, from lover's deep love to fellow-man's gratitude for a token of remembrance from one of his kind" (p. 246). It is this "gratitude for ... remembrance from one of his kind" that is a deeper kind of love than the lover's romantic exclusivity. It is the kind of response Cytherea Graye had yearned for, and it will be what Tess and Jude require and fail to evoke in their partners. The kind of mutuality that Knight and Elfride achieve momentarily on the cliff as they attempt to save each other is, for Hardy, both the means and end of life, the "altruism" which both sustains life and gives it meaning. The moment on the cliff becomes the perspective by which the later actions in the novel are measured.

If the scene on the cliff embodies the values Hardy prized most highly, the dénouement reveals the technique he will henceforth use to create his most evocative effects. As the space in an arch is defined by the stone that surrounds it, and the letters on stone by the hollows engraved upon it, so Hardy defines the altruist response by its absence. In this case, having brought Knight to experience "the whole diapason of feeling" that would complement his cool objectivity, he has him forget it. Knight is the first to portray the *failure* of the altruist response. For Knight, "truth is too clean and pure a thing to be so hopelessly churned in with error" as he finds it to be in Elfride's case.[7] And so Knight rejects Elfride as Elfride had rejected Stephen Smith.

But while this gratuitous reenactment of the past is destructive of Elfride, it is instructive to Knight, for it provides him with the experience of "going wrong" for the first time. As a result, he himself experiences the sense of loss and guilt he had not been able to understand in Elfride. Hence, by the end of the novel the relationship is once again reciprocal: just as Knight had affected Elfride's intellectual development in the first part of the novel, so Elfride affects his emotional development in the second. But the reciprocity is not mutual and instantaneous, as on the cliff; rather, it is one-sided and temporal, the evolution of Knight requiring the death of Elfride. While such a pattern may be necessary on the natural level, it is shown to be gratuitous because unnecessarily repetitive and destructive on the human one. On the other hand, the evolution toward the altruist response is shown to be inevitable. If it is avoided in one way, it is developed in another, slower, more painful way.

In the preface to *A Pair of Blue Eyes* Hardy says that this novel presents "the romantic stage" of ideas he was to develop more fully in his later novels. This is true of his technique as well. By juxtaposing characters representing a hierarchy of values — romantic-intellectual-ethical — he establishes the basis for the more dynamic structures of his later novels. And despite the contrived plot and somewhat superficial treatment of characters, Hardy's values come through clearly. The episode on the cliff, melodramatic though it may be, represents what Hardy considered the highest stage of human development: the blend of objective perspective regarding oneself in relation to the past and future that is achieved by Knight, and the fellow-feeling evoked by the presence of Elfride. This blend of intellectual perspective and social sympathy is what Hardy called altruism. It is the goal toward which his characters move and the point by which their success or failure is measured.

THE EARLY NOVELS

NOTES

1. Quoted by Harvey Webster in *On A Darkling Plain* (Chicago: 1947), p. 59.
2. *Desperate Remedies* (London: 1951), p. 257.
3. According to Carl Weber, Hardy began work on the novel before the end of July, 1872, and the final installment appeared in July, 1873 (*Hardy of Wessex* [Connecticut: 1962] p. 61). According to William Maitland, with whom Hardy collaborated on Stephen's biography, the novelist had read Stephen's essays in *The Fortnightly Review* prior to their being reprinted in *Freethinking and Plainspeaking*. That the two corresponded during the period of time is confirmed by Maitland in *The Life of Leslie Stephen* (London: 1906), p. 272. Maitland dates their meeting as 1874, but comments in *The Life* indicate that it was 1873 (p. 128) and may have been as early as 1872 (pp. 36-37). Hardy's characteristic reticence about revealing autobiographical aspects of his work suggests that the confusion of dates may have been deliberate. The physical description of Knight corresponds to photographs of Leslie Stephen, and Hardy's characterization is very similar to that given by James Bryce and Herbert Paul, reprinted in the later edition of *Freethinking and Plainspeaking* (New York: 1905), pp. ix-xiv.
4. *A Pair of Blue Eyes* (London: 1952), p. 299.
5. Such ideas are expressed in Stephen's essay "An Apology for Plainspeaking" in *Freethinking and Plainspeaking*, pp. 392, 404.
6. Stephen's essay "A Bad Five Minutes in the Alps" appeared in *Fraser's* in 1872 and was reprinted in *Freethinking and Plainspeaking*, pp. 177-225.
7. The idea that truth is "too clean and pure" to be mixed with lies is the theme that runs through "An Apology for Plainspeaking," p. 373, especially.

Five

FAR FROM THE MADDING CROWD

Hardy's next novel, *Far From the Madding Crowd* (1874), follows the patterns previously established in the earlier novels. As a result of her series of love relationships, the heroine, Bathsheba Everdene, changes from a vain, egotistical, and impulsive girl to a chastened, self-controlled, and practical woman.

The contrast between the initial picture of Bathsheba, as she glances at herself in the mirror while sitting among her plants and furniture in the moving van, and her later pantomime suggests just how far the novelist has brought his heroine. At the climax, after Boldwood has shot Troy, Gabriel Oak finds her

sitting on the floor beside the body of Troy, his head pillowed in her lap, where she had herself lifted it. With one hand she held her handkerchief to his breast and covered the wound, though scarcely a single drop had flowed, and with the other she tightly clasped his.[1]

The brief pantomime over, the *mater dolorosa* becomes a Florence Nightingale:

Deeds of endurance which seem ordinary in philosophy are rare in conduct, and Bathsheba was astonishing all around her now, for her philosophy was her conduct, and she seldom thought practicable what she did not practise. (p. 437)

The David to Hardy's Bathsheba, is of course, Gabriel Oak; and, as Roy Morrell suggests, Hardy's portrayal of this character should lay to rest notions that Hardy believed in passively accepting one's fate or even living "in accord with nature."[2] For Gabriel Oak is active rather than passive: he is the good shepherd who saves Bathsheba's farm first from fire and then from storm, and her sheep from death. Putting aside his own hopes for success, he works toward keeping Bathsheba's property and person secure. As Morrell points out, the scene in which both Oak and Bathsheba work together to protect the grain from the storm is "one of many in the novels that vividly suggest the need of the human pair for each other, the individual's comparative — sometimes complete — helplessness alone" (p. 63).

Like Elfride's relationship first with Smith and then with Knight, and Cytherea's relationship with Springrove, Bathsheba's relationship with Oak begins in the courtly love tradition, Bathsheba being the imperious and independent lady to the aspiring and loyal knight. Gradually, however, Bathsheba begins to rely more and more heavily on Oak's services and his judgment, and he rises in her esteem as well as in social position until the formerly imperious Bathsheba becomes Oak's suitor and supplicant.

That Bathsheba should look to Oak for direction is made understandable by the fact that Oak himself has undergone some of the experiences Bathsheba later endures. Having risen from shepherd to sheep-farmer, he loses his flock because of his own carelessness and his young dog's lack of restraint. Having been scorned by Bathsheba, as she in turn will be scorned by Troy, he endures his servitude without complaint, retaining nevertheless a degree of dignity and pride that prevents him from being abject.

Ultimately, like Elfride, Bathsheba measures Oak's capacities against those of her other lover, Boldwood, and against herself, and finds Oak's attributes superior. For Oak has those qualities of objectivity and perspective characteristic of the altruist that are lacking in both Boldwood and herself:

What a way Oak had, she thought, of enduring things. Boldwood, who seemed so much deeper and higher and stronger in feeling than Gabriel, had not yet learnt, any more than she herself, the simple lesson Oak showed a mastery of by every turn and look he gave — that among the multitude of interests by which he was surrounded, those which affected his personal well-being were not the most absorbing and important in his eyes. Oak meditatively looked upon the horizon of circumstances without any special regard to his own standpoint in the midst. That was how she would wish to be. (p. 338)

The contrast that Bathsheba perceives between Oak's objective perspective and Boldwood's egocentricity is reinforced by the novelist's treatment of the two suitors' reactions to Bathsheba's rejection of them. While

Oak sublimates his love, Boldwood allows his passion for Bathsheba to become all-absorbing.

In contrast to the strength and depth of Boldwood's all-absorbing passion for Bathsheba is Troy's light but fickle attraction to her. In contrast to both Boldwood and Oak, Troy is concerned only with his own pleasures from moment to moment. With Troy, Hardy makes his first extensive characterization of the intellectual and emotional limitations of the egotist.

Some of Troy's chief failings are his lack of concern with the past and the future, his failure to control his impulses, and his passivity in accepting untoward circumstances:

He was a man to whom memories were an encumbrance, and anticipations a superfluity. Simply feeling, considering, and caring for what was before his eyes, he was vulnerable only in the present. His outlook upon time was a transient flash of the eye now and then: that projection of consciousness into days gone by and to come, which makes the past a synonym for the pathetic and the future a word for circumspection, was foreign to Troy. With him the past was yesterday; the future tomorrow; never, the day after. (p. 190)

Although caricatured here, this inability to see one's proper relationship in time will become, in such tragic characters as Eustacia Vye, Michael Henchard, Tess and, to some extent, Sue, one of the failings which brings about their downfall. Like Troy, these characters are unaware of the "narrowing of higher tastes and sensations" which this "moral and aesthetic poverty" entails, as well as the destruction to which the absence of a sense of direction leads.

Associated with the lack of a historical sense is the egotist's passivity. Like Tess's, Troy's activities "were less of a locomotive than a vegetative nature," and "never being based upon an original foundation or direction, they were exercised on whatever object chance might place in their way." Unlike Oak, whose motions Hardy describes as having a slow and quiet deliberateness not without grace, Troy's actions are mercurial but uncontrolled (p. 11).

Hence, whilst he sometimes reached the brilliant in speech because that was spontaneous, he fell below the commonplace in action, from inability to guide incipient effort. He had a quick comprehension and considerable force of character; but being without the power to combine them, the comprehension became engaged with trivialities whilst waiting for the will to direct it, and the force wasted itself in useless grooves through unheeding the comprehension. (pp. 191-192)

Troy's relationship with Fanny Robin, whom he fails to marry because of an accident, demonstrates both Troy's unwillingness and his inability to control circumstances. But an even more dramatic example of his passivity in the face of circumstance is illustrated, as Morrell points out, in Troy's frustrated attempt to plant flowers on Fanny's grave. After he finds that the water from the rainspout has washed away his first weak attempt at reform, he gives up, believing that some power has intended to frustrate him.

The planting of the flowers on Fanny's grave had been perhaps but a species of elusion of the primary grief, and now it was as if his intention had been known and circumvented. (p. 364)

For the first time in his life, Troy experiences self-doubt: he can no longer see himself as the hero of a fictional romance. Unlike Oak, however, Troy does not allow such a shift of perspective to provide him with a new direction. If he cannot be a hero, he will be a victim. As Knight had done momentarily, and as Hardy's later tragic egotists, Eustacia Vye and Michael Henchard, will do, Troy shifts from self-love to self-hatred and despair.

He stood and meditated — a miserable man. Whither should he go? "He that is accursed, let him be accursed still," was the pitiless anathema written in this spoliated effort of his new-born solicitousness. (p. 364)

Like Jude, Troy falls into the deeper subjectivity of a more distant past, and curses himself and his lot.

As he will later do with Michael Henchard's belated attempts at reform, Hardy treats Troy's discouragement sympathetically:

A man who has spent his primal strength in one direction has not much spirit left for reversing his course.

But then, in characteristic fashion, Hardy juxtaposes Troy's point of view with a more objective perspective of his actions. Troy's reasons for giving up his attempts seem plausible at first:

Troy had, since yesterday, faintly reversed his [course]; but the merest opposition disheartened him. To turn about would have been hard enough under the greatest providential encouragement; but to find that Providence, far from helping him into a new course or showing any wish that he might adopt one, actually jeered his first trembling and critical attempt in that kind, was more than he could bear. (pp. 364-365)

At this point, Hardy shifts the focus from within Troy's mind to outside of it, and we are made to see his actions with greater detachment:

> He slowly withdrew from the grave. He did not attempt to fill up the hole, replace the flowers, or do anything at all. He simply threw up his cards and foreswore his game for that time and always. (p. 365)

The next scene underscores the difference between what Troy *ought* to have done and what he *does*, for when Bathsheba visits the grave, she does easily what Troy found so impossible: she restores the grave, replants the flowers, and has the rainspout directed in another way. In allowing the reader to see what Troy does not see, Hardy emphasizes Troy's blindness. Such blindness is reinforced by the presence of the abandoned Bathsheba at Fanny's grave. Although he has been overcome by grief and guilt at having abandoned Fanny, Troy is not aware that he is repeating the same pattern in now abandoning Bathsheba. Hardy will use this technique of contrasting the actions and attitudes of one character with those of another in subsequent novels. As we shall see in *The Return of the Native,* the blindness of the egotist's responses and the narrowness of his perspective will be made clear through the perceptions and actions of the other characters. The desire to make the reader see the narrowness of his characters' perceptions accounts for one of Hardy's characteristic techniques: his use of dramatic irony. We are made to see, through the subtle gradations in perception and attitude of his characters, more of the pattern than any one of the actors.[3] For Hardy, this kind of perspective provides a moral, as well as an aesthetic richness.

In sum, what Hardy does in *Far From the Madding Crowd* is to develop new and more subtle ways of expressing his values. In his heroine, Bathsheba Everdene, he traces the gradations of feeling that bring her from egotism to altruism. He also develops substantially the alternative lines of development in her suitors. Gabriel Oak's initial progress toward the altruist perspective foreshadows Bathsheba's, while Boldwood's concomitant decline and the consequences of Troy's limited perspective are fully delineated.

The contrapuntal movement of moral ascent and moral decline is further emphasized by juxtaposed scenes and actions. For example, the picture of the early Bathsheba preening herself is juxtaposed to that of the later Bathsheba ministering to the dying Troy; and Troy's actions at Fanny's grave are contrasted to those of Bathsheba at the same scene. Furthermore, the contrapuntal movement is maintained in the novelist's handling of a given character in a particular situation, as he first describes the character's reactions subjectively, from within, and then observes his reactions objectively, from without. Thus Troy's fatalism is first treated sympathetically and then ironically. These techniques make *Far From the Madding Crowd* more dramatic, and hence more effective, than the earlier novels with their sensational plots and static characters had been; but the drama is still based on Hardy's ethical values, the tensions arising from the conflict between what a character *ought* to do and what, in fact, he *does*.

NOTES

1. *Far From the Madding Crowd* (New York: Harper & Brothers, n.d.), p. 437. All future references are to this text.
2. Thomas Hardy: *The Will and The Way* (Singapore: University of Malaya Press, 1968), ch. 5, pp. 59-72.
3. J. Hillis Miller, in *Thomas Hardy: Distance and Desire* (Massachusetts: 1970) sees this technique as characteristic of Hardy's fiction, although he sees it as a purely aesthetic one (p. 269, *passim*).

Six

THE HAND OF ETHELBERTA

Although Hardy acknowledges in the preface that this novel is "a somewhat frivolous narrative produced as an interlude between stories of a more sober design,"[1] it is interesting for what it further reveals about his values and his developing fictional techniques.

Hardy's treatment of his major character in this novel suggests that he may have asked himself, after completing his story about Bathsheba's ethical ascent, "How would I treat a similar character's ethical decline?" For Ethelberta begins much in the way of Bathsheba, having a potential for development in either direction. She is practical but sensitive, socially ambitious yet in love with a poet and sensitive to the needs of her family. Conscious that she can move in either direction, Ethelberta ultimately opts for social ascent, which means, in this case, ethical decline.

Ostensibly a social satire, the novel traces the progress of Ethelberta, the daughter of a butler, into the upper classes. The "hand" referred to in the title has a double meaning, for it refers not only to the various proposals offered by a succession of suitors, but also to the increasing control and power that Ethelberta exerts over others. For in marrying Lord Mountclere, Ethelberta gains control not only over the life and estate of the old reprobate but over his entire social sphere and her own family as well. Furthermore the synecdoche of the title suggests what the story develops: the "hand" of Ethelberta takes such increasing precedence over her heart, and indeed over her entire personality, that it ultimately becomes the only accurate description of Ethelberta herself.

In his characterization of Ethelberta, Hardy, like Mill, reveals the reductionism and materialism implicit in the utilitarian philosophy and suggests, by his juxtaposition of Picotee against Ethelberta, a more satisfactory alternative, an alternative in which feelings balance reason, flexibility balances will. In contrast to his previous treatment of his heroines, he presents in Ethelberta a narrowing of possibilities for development. Instead of gaining greater insight and deeper feelings in the course of her experiences, Ethelberta's perspectives narrow and her feelings wither until she becomes as hard and cold as the diamond that glitters on her hand.

That Ethelberta is aware of the course of her development is made clear at the moment when she decides to marry Mountclere. At that moment, she has a perception of her past and the direction that she is to take in the future:

In looking back upon her past as she retired to rest, Ethelberta could almost doubt herself to be the identical woman with her who had entered on a romantic career a few short years ago. For that doubt she had good reason. She had begun as a part of the Satanic school in a sweetened form; she was ending as a *pseudo*-utilitarian. Was there ever such a transmutation effected before by the action of a hard environment? It was not without a qualm of regret that she discerned how the last infirmity of noble mind had at length nearly departed from her. She wondered if her early notes had had the genuine ring in them, or whether a poet who could be thrust by realities to a distance beyond recognition as such was a true poet at all. (p. 321)

In response to Ethelberta's self-doubts, the novelist provides his objective perspective. Her progress is regarded as having evolved through a series of historical stages:

Yet Ethelberta's gradient had been regular: emotional poetry, light verse, romance as an object, romance as a means, thoughts of marriage as an aid to her pursuits, a vow to marry for the good of her family; in other words, from soft and playful Romanticism to distorted Benthamism. (p. 321)

Hardy concludes the summary of his heroine's "history" by focusing the reader's attention on the fundamental question implicitly raised in each of his "histories of character": "Was the moral incline upward or down?" The dénouement of the novel answers the question. Ethelberta's progress is not complete: it is arrested at the utilitarian level of development, and hence is no better than the romanticism that had preceded it.

Despite the fact that the novel fails as a social satire primarily because Hardy's own hand is too heavy for comedy, it is interesting in revealing how his ethical values are related to his fictional technique. While he had formerly developed his heroines in terms of the growth of their ethical values, with Ethelberta he introduces a character who fails to develop, stagnates, and declines. He will continue this pattern in his characterizations of Eustacia Vye, Tess, Michael Henchard, and Sue Bridehead. Like Angel Clare, these later characters will be "shaded by their limitations," their romanticism and/or moral obtuseness preventing them from developing the full range of feeling and perspective characteristic of what he perceived to be the highest stage of psychological and ethical development.

Hardy's treatment of Ethelberta is also interesting in that it shows the novelist becoming more self-conscious about his fictional techniques. In many ways, Ethelberta is a parody of the conventional fictional heroine. Her situation, her stratagems, and her linguistic skills correspond to those of an earlier heroine, Pamela, in her relationship with Lord B. Ethelberta, however, is more consciously utilitarian than her romantic forebear. She resembles the less romantic fictional heroine, Becky Sharp, much more closely. Like Thackeray's heroine, she begins as a governess, marries secretly into an upper class family, relies on superlative dramatic performances for social recognition, and aims ultimately for a relationship with a corrupt lord.[2] (The similarities between Lord Steyne and Mountclere suggest that Hardy's character derives either from Thackeray's or from the original, the Marquess of Hertford.) But what makes Becky Sharp's situation pathetic makes Ethelberta's absurd. The accidental meeting between Steyne and Crawley, which destroys all Becky's hopes, seems to be caricatured by Hardy's scene in which he brings Ethelberta's three suitors together to discover that they have all been betrayed and compromised by Ethelberta. But instead of being overcome by the situation as Becky is, Ethelberta makes the most of the situation, eliciting a proposal of marriage from Mountclere and later eliminating his jealousy, as well as all of her former and future rivals. Ethelberta's unqualified success deprives her of the haze of pathos that surrounds Becky Sharp's weak attempts to recoup her losses. By the end of the novel Ethelberta evokes no response. Like Christopher Julian, we too dismiss her as no longer worthy of our interest or our concern.

It can be said, in this case, that Hardy's ethical treatment of his character is what makes her fail as a fictional creation. But what makes her also fail as a character is our sense that she is not quite real. She is too much a fiction based on other fictions. On the other hand, Hardy makes the most of this artifice by deliberately showing her to be an imitation. Ethelberta is herself a maker of fictions and imitations.

While Ethelberta's stories are poorly constructed and manifestly false, the manner of her delivery makes them seem like truth. The novelist makes it a point to approve of Ethelberta's having taken DeFoe as her model, since "he had the most amazing talent on record for telling lies" (p. 120).

THE HAND OF ETHELBERTA

But just as Hardy eventually rectifies Ethelberta's "distorted Benthamism," he corrects her penchant for telling "lies" by having her finally give a true accounting of herself. The last story she tells is a recapitulation of her own experiences.

Ethelberta's shifting from the imitation of former fictions to an honest recounting of her own experiences will become a pattern of Hardy's later characters who are also forced, at crucial moments, to surrender their romantic notions of themselves and others and repeat their histories accurately without romantic illusion. For example, as a means of doing penance and providing illumination, Clym will repeat his history to the natives of Egdon Heath. Similarly, Tess will repeat her history to Angel Clare, Jocelyn Pierston will expose his age and failings to Avice Caro, and Sue will explain her motives to Jude.

This ability to shift from the stage of romantic illusion to a "just appraisal" of the self is one of the attributes of the altruist. It was precisely from this position that Hardy believed himself to be working. As he had done with Troy and as he does with Ethelberta, he will increasingly "defictionalize" his characters, casting their romantic notions of themselves in an ironic light. From a position in advance of his characters, he will trace the stages of their progress or decline by what he regarded as the perspective of historical truth. With Ethelberta, he shows the self-deception of romanticism and the limitations of utilitarianism, and, through the actions of Picotee and the perceptions of Christopher Julian, the necessity for a more fully developed ethical position.

NOTES

1. *The Hand of Ethelberta* (London: 1951), p. v. All future references are to this text.
2. Any consideration of social satire would probably suggest Thackeray's *Vanity Fair* as a model. (See Weber, *Hardy of Wessex*, pp. 38-39.) However, the fact that Hardy's publisher and friend, Leslie Stephen, was married to Thackeray's daughter may have reinforced the suggestion. Hardy's appreciation of DeFoe is precisely the same as Stephen's as it appears in his essay on DeFoe written in 1868.

Seven

EUSTACIA VYE: THE ROMANTIC EGOTIST

We have already seen how Hardy contrasts one generation with the next, the romantic values against the communal, and how he traces the "stages" of his character's history. In his characterization of Eustacia Vye he goes beyond what he had done previously, however, taking great pains to "place" her in her proper historical setting, and by so doing, making her development and decline seem necessary, and, indeed, inevitable. As he had done in *A Pair of Blue Eyes* and *Far From the Madding Crowd*, he juxtaposes the decline of one character with the ascent of another. In this case, he juxtaposes Eustacia Vye's decline with the ethical ascent of the more advanced Clym. In this novel the contrapuntal pattern is more dynamic, however, for it is not only by the contrast between the characters but also by their interaction that the effect is achieved.

In the chapter "Queen of the Night," Hardy establishes Eustacia in her exact place along the evolutionary scale of development. Like Troy, and to some extent Ethelberta, Eustacia Vye is made to seem like the heroine of fiction and drama. At the same time, the heroic aspect of the character is cut down by the ironic commentary that follows. Eustacia Vye is set among the goddesses of the past. Her passions and instincts "form the raw material of a divinity." While these attributes make her "a model goddess," they do not, however, make her "a model woman," for unlike her divine counterparts, Artemis, Athena, and Hera, Eustacia is aware that her power is limited, and "the consciousness of this limitation biassed her development."[1]

Mentally and emotionally, Eustacia is at the romantic stage of development and is unable to adapt to her present circumstances.

EUSTACIA VYE

... in Eustacia's brain were juxtaposed the strangest assortment of ideas, from old time and from new. There was no middle distance in her perspective — romantic recollections of sunny afternoons and an esplanade ... stood like gilded letters upon the dark tablet surrounding Egdon. (p. 74)

Philosophically, Eustacia is still at the subjective stage of development, projecting her own feelings upon the outer world. Comte would have said that she belonged to the "theological" phase of development. "She could show a most reproachful look at times, but it was less directed against human beings than against certain creatures of the mind, the chief of these being Destiny" (p. 75). Also symptomatic of her individualistic stage of evolution is her admiration for the destructive, morally questionable figures in history; her heroes are Strafford, Napoleon, and Pontius Pilate.

Her attitude toward love is also distinctively romantic: "She seemed to long for the abstraction called love more than for any particular lover" (p. 75). "Having got beyond the vision of some marriage of inexpressible glory," she could still not adjust to the idea of a "meaner union." Even after her unhappy experience with Clym, she still expects a union, if not a marriage, of "inexpressible glory." After having decided to leave Egdon Heath with Wildeve, she hesitates, questioning Wildeve's heroic stature: "'Can I go, can I go?'" she moaned. 'He's not great enough for me to give myself to — he does not suffice for my desire! ... If he had been a Saul or a Bonaparte — ah! But to break my marriage vow for him — it is too poor a luxury!'" (p. 354)

In order to make sure that the reader knows exactly what to think of Eustacia's romanticism, Hardy makes the following comment:

To have lost the godlike conceit that we may do what we will, and not to have acquired a homely zest for doing what we can, shows a grandeur of temper which cannot be objected to in the abstract, for it denotes a mind that, though disappointed, forswears compromise. But, if congenial to philosophy, it is apt to be dangerous to the commonwealth. In a world where doing means marrying, and the commonwealth is one of the hearts and hands, the same peril attends the condition. (p. 79)

By making such a comment, Hardy places Eustacia in perspective and at the same time prepares the reader for her tragic end. Not wishing to break the spell entirely, he concludes that she is "not altogether unloveable," but to make certain that we see her as a figure belonging to the past, he concludes his description with the following prediction: "In heaven she will probably sit between the Heloises and Cleopatras" (p. 77).

Even before placing his romantic heroine temporally in the mytho-

57

logical and historical past, the novelist had presented her in comparable spatial terms. She is first viewed from a distance, standing at the highest summit of the barrow overlooking the heath, transposed to a figure from a far earlier time. The figure that Diggory Venn sees against the sky "seemed the last man among [the Celts] musing for a moment before dropping into eternal night with the rest of his race." She is the element which gives a momentary artistic completeness to the ancient scene. "There the form stood, motionless as the hill beneath. Above the plain rose the hill, above the hill rose the barrow, and above the barrow rose the figure. Above the figure was nothing that could be mapped elsewhere than on a celestial globe" (p. 20). As she stands on the barrow, she is given a degree of importance far outweighing that of the other characters. Although she is quickly succeeded by a procession of more ordinary creatures, "the imagination of the observer clung by preference to that vanished, solitary figure, as to something more interesting, more important, more likely to have a history worth knowing than these newcomers" (p. 21). Her fire burns brighter and longer, for example, and it has been made with a different, more deliberate and personal intent.

But these first appearances, which distinguish Eustacia Vye in such sharp physical and historical outline, also foreshadow her imminent decline. Her first appearance on the barrow is impressive, but brief. It is quickly supplanted by the arrival of the more ordinary natives. As they approach the barrow to the right, Eustacia disappears down the left "with the glide of a water-drop down a bud" (p. 20).

Eustacia Vye's relationship to the past is further reinforced by the disguise she chooses to adopt in order to see Clym. The ploy itself is compared with that used by Venus, the "Queen of Love," before her son, Aeneas. The particular choice of disguise is itself revealing of Eustacia's character and, consequently, her dénouement. Like her fire, the glory of her role as Turkish Knight is brief, for after killing the Valiant Soldier, the pagan Knight is in turn killed by the Christian Saint George.

Like Troy, however, Eustacia is not concerned with the consequences of her actions but only with the expression of her will at the moment. Like the knight whose part she plays, Eustacia is concerned with wielding power. At first this will exerts considerable force. Her fire, for example, does succeed in drawing Wildeve back to her. It extends to her firetender, Johnny Nunsuch, who "seemed a mere automaton, galvanized into moving and speaking by the wayward Eustacia's will. He might have been the brass statue which Albertus Magnus is said to have animated just so far as to make it chatter, and move, and be his servant" (p. 65). She is easily able to persuade Charley to let her take his role as Turkish Knight. She is able to meet, to charm, and to marry Clym. But here her power ends. She cannot persuade him to leave the heath or to give up his ambitions of school-teaching. In Clym she confronts qualities she cannot overcome, and the second half of the story traces Clym's rise as it follows her decline.

But it is not her confrontation with Clym alone that causes her decline; her decline is also caused by characteristics inherent in the romantic heroine herself. Her very choice of disguise reveals an essential passivity and destructiveness. Like Troy's, her initial energies are poorly directed and quickly dissipated. Her plan to disguise herself in order to meet Clym is shown to be lacking in foresight and hence self-defeating, since it prevents her from her real purpose: making herself known to him.

Even before Eustacia meets Clym, however, her passivity is revealed in a "trivial incident" reminiscent of the scene in which Bathsheba meets Troy. As she waits for Wildeve, Eustacia's skirts are caught by a bramble. Her attempts to extricate herself are proleptic of her future course:

The pedestrian noticed nothing just now, and a clue to her abstraction was afforded by a trivial incident. A bramble caught hold of her skirt, and checked her progress. Instead of putting it off and hastening along, she yielded herself up to the pull, and stood passively still. When she began to extricate herself it was by turning round and round, and so unwinding the prickly switch. She was in a desponding reverie. (p. 62)

Another early example of Eustacia's passivity is her reaction to Venn's offer to find work for her at Budmouth so that she can escape the heath. Her reaction to Venn's offer is almost comic.

"I should have to work, perhaps?" she asks. [When Venn protests that she would have very little to do, she replies,] "I knew it meant work," and droop[s] to langour again. [She sums up her position with the following remarks:] "It is to wear myself out to please her! and I won't go. O, if I could live in a gay town as a lady should, and go my ways, and do my own doings, I'd give the wrinkled half of my life. Yes, reddleman, that would I." (p. 99)[2]

But what is here presented comically is presented later in increasingly serious tones, until at the climax Eustacia's passivity has enormous consequences. When she discovers that Clym is bent on going out to find his mother alone, although she fears the consequences, she does not resist him. She responds, "Let it be as you say, then." This response is followed by the novelist's objective comment on her passivity: Eustacia is "one, who, though willing to ward off evil consequences by a mild effort, would let events fall out as they might sooner than wrestle hard to direct them."[3]

A corollary to Eustacia's passivity is her willingness to shift responsibility from herself to others. When she is ignored by the natives, she complains that "Nobody here respects me." Once again, this perspective is "corrected" by the objective commentary: Eustacia was "unable to dismiss a slight as unwittingly shown" and, what is more important, "of her own causing" (p. 149). Later, she confesses to Clym that she had often felt "an agonizing pity for myself that ever I was born" (p. 200).

Once again, these seemingly trivial reactions and weaknesses become major weaknesses at the crucial moment. For Eustacia that moment occurs when she decides not to answer Mrs. Yeobright's knock at her door. And instead of assuming the responsibility for having consciously rejected her mother-in-law, she shifts the responsibility to fate. Once again the novelist contrasts this subjective response with objective commentary:

... nothing could save her from censure in refusing to answer the first knock. Yet, instead of blaming herself for the issue she laid the fault upon the shoulders of some indistinct, colossal Prince of the World, who had framed her situation and ruled her lot. (p. 298)

Like Troy, Eustacia ultimately prefers to be a victim if she cannot be the heroine of her own drama. Her last speech goes to the farthest reaches of egotistic self-pity. Only if one disregards all that has gone before can one take Eustacia's quite seriously.

"How I have tried and tried to be a splendid woman, and how destiny has been against me! ... I do not deserve my lot!" she cried in a frenzy of bitter revolt. "O, the cruelty of putting me into this ill-conceived world! I was capable of much; but I have been injured and blighted and crushed by things beyond my control! O, how hard it is of Heaven to devise such tortures for me, who have done no harm to Heaven at all!" (p. 354)

The prior actions and attitudes of Eustacia form an ironic commentary on the heroine's romantic outburst.

Eustacia's death is an adequate culmination of the novelist's dramatic treatment of his romantic heroine. Its ambivalent nature (was it a suicide or an accident?) derives from the skillful blending of the two characteristics of her nature, her passivity and her self-pity. If her passivity were uppermost, her death would be accidental; if her self-pity were dominant, then suicide would be the way for the heroine to do something dramatic and heroic. The fact that the question is left unresolved underscores the double nature of the novelist's approach to her. Even her dead face reflects "a momentary transition between fervour and resignation."

Hardy's emphasis on his romantic heroine's place in the historic past and her blind attempts to escape from the present is reinforced by his final remarks: "The stateliness of look which had been almost too marked for a dweller in a county domicile had at last found an artistically happy background" (p. 293). In death, Eustacia takes her proper place in the past.

From the beginning, Hardy makes Eustacia an anomaly in the present, not only by revealing her exalted notions about herself and about destiny, but socially as well. Her egocentricity is clearest in her relationship to others. Although she claims to have done "no harm," her blindness to the suffering of others is obvious. For example, when Venn argues that in reclaiming Wildeve she is making Thomasin suffer, she responds with possessive obstinacy, "I will never give him up — never!" The objective comment that follows "places" Eustacia's reactions on the scale of ethical values: "As far as social ethics was concerned, Eustacia's approached a savage state ..." (p. 180). Later, the "greediness" of Eustacia's passion for Clym is contrasted with Venn's disinterested (and altruistic) concern for Thomasin. The conversation in which Venn and Eustacia negotiate the terms of Eustacia's surrender of Wildeve reveal their differences in attitude. Like Troy, Eustacia is incapable of apprehending "higher" modes of feeling, and hence does not feel her own "moral and aesthetic poverty."

"I suppose you think to serve Thomasin in some way by it. Are you as anxious as ever to help on her marriage?" Venn was a little moved. "I would sooner have married her myself," he said in a low voice. "But what I feel is that if she cannot be happy without him I will do my duty in helping her to get him, as a man ought." Eustacia looked curiously at the singular man who spoke thus. What a strange sort of love, to be entirely free from that quality of selfishness which is frequently the chief constituent of the passion, and sometimes its only one! The reddleman's disinterestedness was so well deserving of respect that it overshot respect by being barely comprehended; and she almost thought it absurd.

Despite her lack of comprehension, Eustacia agrees to give Wildeve up, acting out of enlightened self-interest since she will be assured of Clym in return. She concludes the negotiation with Venn with a remark that once again reveals her blindness to the differences between Venn's altruism and her own egotism. "Then we are both of one mind at last," she says (p. 159). The contrast between Eustacia's obtuseness and the clearly perceptible differences between the values of the two makes for the irony of effect.

But if Eustacia is contrasted to Venn on one side, she is also contrasted to Clym on the other. When the more ethically advanced Clym asks her to join him in his plans for teaching, she replies, "I don't quite feel anxious to. I have not much love for my fellow creatures. Sometimes I quite hate them" (p. 190). This lack of fellow-feeling, seemingly trivial here, becomes crucial in her later rejection of Clym and his mother. Her insistence upon achieving her own personal freedom and happiness first isolate her and them doom her to extinction.

That the "grandeur of temper" exhibited by Eustacia "is apt to be dangerous to the commonwealth" is evident from subsequent events of the novel; for Eustacia destroys Thomasin's happiness, is instrumental in Mrs. Yeobright's death, draws Wildeve to his death with herself, and nearly destroys Clym. In terms of social evolution, the destruction of the romantic egotist is both necessary and inevitable.

But while Hardy shows Eustacia's decline and ultimate extinction as both necessary and inevitable, he treats his romantic heroine with a good deal of sympathy. While he had treated his earlier romantic egotists such as Troy and Boldwood as villains in his comedy, he treats Eustacia Vye, if not as the conventional tragic heroine, certainly as the subject of interest and sympathy. Such treatment is consistent with the position of the ethical evolutionist, who saw social and intellectual values in relative rather than absolute terms.[4] Such values as individualism and theology, which were good and useful in the past, are now no longer necessary, and indeed, if maintained without change, impede future progress. They become, however, the sub-strata upon which new values are built; and indeed, as we have seen before, a just recognition of one's relationship to the past is one of the essential components of the altruist position. For Hardy, as for the other ethical evolutionists, the past can neither be dismissed nor sustained, for it is by the past that one takes one's direction for the future.

Hardy's fictional treatment of Eustacia Vye coincides with this view, for he shows her to be not only a victim of past values but also an agent of change in the present, for her effect on Clym completes his education as an altruist. And just as the novelist treats Eustacia from a double perspective — that is, by her subjective responses and his own objective commentary, so he contrasts Clym's ethical absolutism toward Eustacia with his own sympathetic treatment of her. In other words, he develops what he had begun in *A Pair of Blue Eyes:* he mirrors the blindness of the heroine in the blindness of the more advanced hero, ironically undercutting the hero's perceived superiority by a more sympathetic presentation of the heroine. As a character, Eustacia functions both statically and dynamically. Incapable of change herself, she initiates change in others. As "Queen of the Night," she seems to draw out the egotism of such characters as Wildeve, Mrs. Yeobright, and Clym. By her suffering and death, however, she releases the opposite kind of response.

Hardy's sympathetic treatment of his romantic egotist has led to a good deal of critical confusion. Because she is handled sympathetically, it is easy enough for the reader to disregard the "authorial intrusions" and ironic commentaries and to identify with Eustacia's romanticism, seeing the action from her subjective point of view. Such a position, however, disregards a good deal of action occurring outside of Eustacia's frame of reference and leads the reader away from the novel to unanswerable questions about Hardy's "fatalism" or "pessimism."

On the other hand, those critics who do take into account the ironic commentaries that "objectify" Eustacia conclude that Hardy expresses an unresolved ambivalence toward his heroine. Seeing her actions and attitudes as caricatures of the romantic response, and Eustacia as a spoiled adolescent, one might well ask why the novelist fails to pass judgment on his romantic egotist. Such a question is answered by the novelist's treatment of his more advanced hero, Clym, who does, in fact, express this kind of reaction and pass this kind of judgment. By showing the consequences of Clym Yeobright's moral absolutism toward Eustacia Vye, Hardy answers the question of why he treats his romantic heroine with sympathetic detachment. In terms of Hardy's ethical values, such moral absolutism is as repressive and destructive as the belief in Divine Wrath or the Dark Prince of Destiny, for it assumes those powers in oneself that had been formerly assigned to the gods. It is a form of egotism that isolates and desensitizes, blinding one to the relationship between the self and the other, the past and the future, and one's "true" relationship to the social world.

What Hardy does with Clym shows that, rather than being Eustacia's opposite, as he perceives himself to be, he is more similar than different, and that, while his ideas and attitudes are in advance of hers, they mirror, rather than contradict, her own. As Clym consciously resists the parallels, they are increasingly forced upon him, until at last he confronts that aspect in himself that he would reject in her. The fellow-feeling that Hardy valued most highly implies kinship with the past rather than rejection of it. It is not without significance that Clym's first sermon treats of the interdependence between mother and son.

NOTES

1. *The Return of the Native* (New York: 1959), pp. 73-74.
2. Robert Evans in "The Other Eustacia," *The Novel* (Spring 1968), notes those passages which make Eustacia seem more like a spoiled adolescent than a romantic heroine; and David Eggenshiller's stylistic analysis, "Eustacia Vye, Queen of the Night and Courtly Pretender," *Nineteenth Century Fiction* 25 (March, 1971), pp. 444-458, indicates that much of the heroic rhetoric is actually mock-heroic or parody.
3. A note in *The Life* dated six months before publication of *The Return of the Native* seems particularly relevant to this interpretation:

Note: a Plot of Tragedy, should arise from the gradual closing in of a situation that comes of ordinary human passions, prejudices, and ambitions, by reason of the characters not taking trouble to ward off the disastrous events produced by said passions, prejudices and ambitions. (April 1878, p. 120)

4. According to Comte, ethical absolutism stands in the way of the development of altruistic feelings: "Now to judge others without immediate reference to self, is a process which may possibly result in strong convictions, but so far from calling out right feelings, it will, if carried too far, interfere with and check their natural development" (*GV*, p. 111).

Eight

THE EVOLUTION OF CLYM YEOBRIGHT

*To Sorrow
I bade good morrow,
And thought to leave her far away behind;
But cheerly, cheerly,
She loves me dearly;
She is so constant to me and so kind.
I would deceive her,
And so leave her
But ah! she is so constant and so kind.*

This last stanza of the Indian Maid's song, which prepares Endymion for his choice of mortal, rather than ideal love, appears on the title page of *The Return of the Native,* setting the stage for the action that follows.

It has already been noted that Hardy, like Leslie Stephen, believed that sorrow or pain was, perhaps, the only means by which altruism could be brought about, and we have already seen how an earlier intellectually advanced type, Harry Knight, was brought to a level of feeling commensurate with his intellectual perceptions through his experience of "going wrong" in his judgment of Elfride Swancourt. Hardy does much the same thing in his treatment of Clym Yeobright, although with a good deal more psychological subtlety and depth.

The contrast between Eustacia Vye's passions and Clym Yeobright's intellect is clear to the most casual reader. What may not be so apparent is how fully the novelist bases the contrast on his own system of values and how he reveals these values in his treatment of Clym's reactions to Eustacia Vye.

If Eustacia Vye can be said to represent the egotistic type, Clym can be said to represent the more advanced altruist. While Eustacia is self-indulgent, having explored the "secret recesses of sensuousness," Clym is self-disciplined and ascetic. While she is "raw feeling," he is mostly intellect. While her education has been acquired at the romantic resort of Budmouth, his has been gotten in the commercial and intellectual world of Paris. (The Comtean influence on Clym is suggested by the comment that "much of his development he may have owed to his studious life in Paris, where he had become acquainted with ethical systems popular at the time." [p. 176]

THE EVOLUTION OF CLYM YEOBRIGHT

Their social attitudes and values are, perhaps, their most important difference: while Eustacia's social ethics are "barbaric," Clym's are advanced. While Eustacia "quite hates them" Clym "loves his kind" (p. 176), and while Eustacia is ambitious for personal and social success, Clym is ambitious to do good: "He had a conviction that the want of most men was a knowledge of the sort to bring wisdom rather than affluence." Perhaps the comment that most clearly distinguishes between Clym's modern altruistic values and Eustacia's heroic ideals is the following: "He wished to raise the class at the expense of individuals rather than individuals at the expense of the class." Recognizing that the rise of one necessitates the destruction of the other, Clym "was ready to be the first unit sacrificed." This attitude is, of course, directly opposite to that of Eustacia, who would raise her own individuality to prominence no matter what the sacrifice to others, and who is a most unwilling sacrificial victim.

That Clym is presented not only in contrast to Eustacia but also in advance of her in terms of ethical evolution is also made clear. For, on the one hand, while she looks back to a heroic past, he looks forward to "a providential future." Their respective attitudes are reflected in their physical appearance. Eustacia's beauty is the kind that will soon cease to be appreciated, while "in Clym Yeobright's face could be dimly seen the typical countenance of the future" (p. 171). Clym's facial expression reveals a greater degree of perceptiveness and a more qualified expectation of happiness: according to the novelist, such an expression will come to assume aesthetic value in the future. It will be valued not for its natural beauty but for the human history that it records (p. 172).

Clym's face is proleptic not only of the general future but of his own as well. It is this bright hint that attracts and "troubles" Eustacia in the first place:

As for his look, it was a natural cheerfulness striving against depression from without, and not quite succeeding. The look suggested isolation, but it revealed something more. As is usual with bright natures, the deity that lies ignominiously chained within an ephemeral human carcass shone out of him like a ray.

The effect upon Eustacia was palpable. The extraordinary pitch of excitement that she had reached before-hand would, indeed, have caused her to be influenced by the most commonplace man. She was troubled at Yeobright's presence. (p. 144)

Like Harry Knight, Clym is also aware of his superiority and makes a point of his greater experience and wisdom. For example, when Eustacia complains about Egdon Heath, he comments that he, too, had felt the "same longing for town bustle," and suggests that "five years in a great city would be a perfect cure for that" (p. 191). And when Eustacia complains that instead of singing at his furze-cutting he should be cursing his lot, he replies with a complacent sense of superiority:

"Now, don't you suppose, my inexperienced girl, that I cannot rebel, in high Promethean fashion, against the gods and fate as well as you? I have felt more steam and smoke of that sort than you have ever heard of. But the more I see of life the more do I perceive that there is nothing particularly great in its greatest walks, and therefore nothing particularly small in mine of furze-cutting. If I feel that the greatest blessings vouchsafed to us are not very valuable, how can I feel it to be any great hardship when they are taken away?" (p. 257)

There is, however, a crucial difference between Hardy's treatment of his "advanced" character and Clym's perception of his own superiority. For while Clym perceives himself as having reached the end of the scale in terms of evolution, the novelist reveals that he has not yet reached its limits, and that, while he is in advance of Eustacia intellectually, he still mirrors some of her failings.[1] Although Clym is not aware of the parallels, they are made clear to the reader.

One of the natives suggests a match between the two because of their similarities in background and education. But there are also other, less obvious similarities between Clym and Eustacia. Because of their social backgrounds, both are isolated from the rest of the natives. Neither cares to conform to custom, Clym having passed beyond it and Eustacia "having hardly crossed the threshold of conventionality" (p. 100). They meet at a time when each is undergoing a kind of spiritual crisis. Eustacia "had reached that stage of enlightenment which feels that nothing is worthwhile" (p. 77). Clym "had reached the stage in a young man's life when the grimness of the general human situation first becomes clear; and the realization of this causes ambition to halt awhile" (p. 192). Both wish to escape from the circumstances in which they are placed — Eustacia from Egdon Heath, Clym from his position with the diamond merchant in Paris. Although Eustacia's efforts to escape are more sporadic than Clym's, he also is subject to a passivity akin to Eustacia's. Later, he accepts furze-cutting with too good a grace to indicate mere stoic resignation: "The monotony of his occupation soothed him, and was in itself a pleasure. A forced limitation of effort offered a justification of homely courses to an unambitious man, whose conscience would hardly have allowed him to remain in such obscurity while his powers were unimpeded" (p. 254). Part of his love for the heath derives from its passive aspect which corresponds to that in his own nature. "He indulged in a barbarous satisfaction in noting the ferns and furze tufts stubbornly reasserting themselves despite the farmer's ambitious attempt to cultivate the waste" (p. 178).

Clym is as blinded by his obsession with the future as Eustacia is blinded by her obsession with the past. That this obsession is also an escape from the present is indicated in a scene when Clym is waiting to meet Eustacia. He gazes at the moon and wishes he were there:

> In returning to labour in this sequestered spot he had anticipated an escape from the chafing social necessities; yet behold they were here also. More than ever he longed to be in some world where personal ambition was not the only recognized form of progress — such, perhaps, as might have been the case at some time or other in the silvery globe then shining upon him. His eye travelled over the length and breadth of that distant country — over the Bay of Rainbows, the sombre Sea of Crises, the Ocean of Storms, the Lake of Dreams, the vast Walled Plains, and the wondrous Ring Mountains — till he almost felt himself to be voyaging bodily through its wild scenes, standing on its hollow hills, traversing its deserts, descending its vales and old sea bottoms, or mounting to the edges of its craters. (pp. 198-199)

Coupled with Clym's escapist tendency is his unawareness of the stages of social and historical progress. It is this unawareness of the evolutionary nature of this progress which dooms his "education scheme" to failure. In trying to impose his system on Egdon Heath, Clym ignores the intermediate stage which the natives must yet pass through.

> In passing from the bucolic to the intellectual life the intermediate stages are usually two at least, frequently many more; and one of those stages is almost sure to be worldly advanced [sic]. We can hardly imagine bucolic placidity quickening to intellectual aims without imagining social aims as the transitional phase. (p. 176)

Having apparently given some thought to what makes for successful social propaganda, the novelist remarks that ideas will only be heard when they express what has already been felt by their listeners.

Successful propagandists have succeeded because the doctrine they bring into form is that which their listeners have for some time felt without being able to shape. A man who advocates aesthetic effort and deprecates social effort is only likely to be understood by a class to which social effort has become a stale matter. To argue upon the possibility of culture before luxury to the bucolic world may be to argue truly, but it is an attempt to disturb a sequence to which humanity has been long accustomed.

He concludes that by ignoring the necessary historical and social sequence Clym dooms his education scheme to failure.

> Yeobright preaching to the Egdon eremites that they might rise to a serene comprehensiveness without going through the process of enriching themselves was not unlike arguing to ancient Chaldeans that in ascending from earth to the pure empyrean it was not necessary to pass first into the intervening heaven of ether. (p. 177)

Clym's blindness to the intermediate stage of social ambition is revealed in his personal relationship with his mother and Eustacia Vye, both of whom represent this intermediate stage. It is in these personal relationships that he reveals his limitations most clearly. For while he is intellectually advanced, he is still an egotist in terms of feeling. If Eustacia is at the "theological" stage of development, seeing malignant or beneficent forces ruling her destiny, Clym is at the metaphysical stage, seeing life in terms of abstractions, without taking note of particular circumstances.

This tendency to rely on reason alone is revealed by Clym's response to his mother's reactions to his arguments: "He had despaired of teaching her by argument; and it was almost a discovery to him that he could reach her by a magnetism which was as superior to words as words are to yells" (p. 193). Later, he thinks of his mother in terms of her obligations to him as a son, as he will think of Eustacia in terms of his obligations as a husband. In other words, he thinks in terms of moral imperatives, such as duty in the abstract, rather than responding to the particular situation from a spontaneous sense of interdependence and fellow-feeling.

Clym's attitudes toward Eustacia Vye follow a sequence that should by now be familiar. He first thinks of her as useful for his education scheme; later, when he hears of Susan Nunsuch's attack on her, he thinks of her as "a romantic martyr to superstition." By the time they are engaged, however, some of her utilitarian value and romantic charm have worn off. She is now "no longer the goddess but the woman to him, a being to fight for, support, help, be maligned for." Unlike Edward Springrove, who acts upon this new insight, Clym hesitates, however, feeling himself not quite ready to assume the obligation: "He would have preferred a less hasty marriage" (p. 211).

A subsequent chapter will show how, after his marriage, Clym pursues a course of self-destructiveness and passivity similar to that of his mate, Eustacia Vye. In both his over-zealousness and his furze-cutting, he blinds himself to the needs of both his mother and his wife.

The shock of his mother's death has both a positive and negative effect on him. Remorse at his former neglect humbles him and upsets his former complacency. He can no longer think himself as superior, as he once did. He recognizes that his insensitivity to his mother accorded badly with his high ideals, and he compares his former passivity with the actions of the simpler Thomasin:

"You laboured to win her round; I did nothing. I, who was going to teach people the higher secrets of happiness, did not know how to keep out that gross misery which the most untaught are wise enough to avoid." (p. 313)

On the other hand, like Troy, his remorse is itself egocentric. He becomes "too deeply absorbed in his remorseful state to notice" Eustacia's suffering. Ironically, it is Eustacia who points out the effect of his remorse upon her. She suggests the sense of interdependence necessarily accompanying the married state:

"Single men have, no doubt, a right to curse themselves as much as they please; but men with wives involve two in the doom they pray down."

Absorbed in self-hatred, Clym disregards Eustacia's words:

"I am in too sorry a state to understand what you are refining on," said the wretched man. "Day and night shout at me, 'You have helped to kill her.' But in loathing myself I may, I own, be unjust to you, my poor wife. Forgive me for it, Eustacia, for I scarcely know what I do." (p. 310)

Although Clym is more objective than Eustacia in blaming himself rather than Destiny for what has happened, he is still far from the detachment necessary for the altruist position. Although he is aware of the cause-effect relationship of past events, he considers himself the central figure of the drama and, blinded by the egocentricity of this position, is incapable of seeing the proper direction for his future actions. Like Eustacia, he becomes trapped by a perspective of the past in which he figures, if not as the hero, then as the villain.

Unable to support the heavy burden of guilt and self-hatred for long, however, Clym searches for a scapegoat to assume the burden and finds it in Eustacia. When he discovers that she had turned his mother away, he shifts the burden of guilt entirely to her and rages at her in the manner of an Othello or a Hamlet. (Eustacia's coolness and the reader's awareness of the parallels between Clym and Eustacia heighten the artificiality and defensiveness of Clym's overly dramatic posturings.)

Clym's reactions substantiate Comte's warnings regarding moral absolutism: "Now to judge others without immediate reference to the self, is a process which may possibly result in strong convictions, but so far as

THE EVOLUTION OF CLYM YEOBRIGHT

calling out right feelings, it will, if carried too far, interfere with and check their natural development." In judging Eustacia, Clym enmeshes himself in the past even more deeply. His self-righteousness is more vicious because it is a more conscious form of cruelty than that which he castigates. In ignoring his mother's first knock, Eustacia had assumed that Clym would let her in. In sending Eustacia away, Clym allows for no such alternative. He deliberately "turn[s] his eyes aside, that he might not be tempted to softness" (p. 331). Hence, Clym recapitulates both his own and Eustacia's former actions but in a more conscious and deliberate way.

More quickly than he had done with his mother, however, Clym repents of his action. He writes, asking her to return, saying, "I must obey my heart without consulting my reason too closely" (p. 346). But, as in the first case, because he had trapped himself in the past for too long, Clym's forgiveness comes too late to save Eustacia. He has set forces in motion over which he no longer has any control.

When Clym reappears after nearly drowning in his attempts to save her, he sees their relative positions as reversed: "It is I who ought to have drowned myself. It would have been a charity to the living had the river drowned me and borne her up" (p. 376).

Eustacia's suffering and death have transformed him. He appears as one resurrected from the dead, "a thin, pallid, almost spectral form, wrapped in a blanket and looking like Lazarus come from the tomb" (p. 375). His abstract idealism and rigid self-righteousness are transformed into those of the new dispensation, his face fulfilling the prophecy it had formerly predicted. It is now "pensive and lined," old for a man whose years "still numbered less than thirty-three."

The latter-day Christ's new Sermon on the Mount somewhat resembles the old, being "sometimes secular, and sometimes religious, but never dogmatic." However, rather than suggesting transcendence or even "abstract creeds and systems of philosophy," it concerns only "the opinions and actions of all good men" (pp. 405-406).

Progress, according to Comte, was to be brought about by the interaction between the old and the new: "the destruction of the old elements being the means of disclosing the new; the motive force of one period naturally imparting itself to the next" (*PP* II, p. 305). Through his interaction with Eustacia and by her death, Clym has achieved a new level of feeling and a new perspective. The sorrow brought about by the deaths of the two women has created a new kind of altruism that had previously existed only in the abstract.

By the end of the novel Clym has become, as his face had forecast, the type of future altruist. Having begun as naturally ascetic, and having been educated by the "advanced" social theories in Paris, he returns to the heath to complete his "education." Through his experience with his mother and Eustacia Vye (the most immediate members of his family and therefore the most conducive to moral growth), he comes to recognize the "filiation" between past and present. His growing recognition of his own part in that past and present induces him to accept his role in the future. Having lost whatever little desire he had had for personal happiness, he accepts his condition of suffering, disciplining his sorrow to socially useful ends. He would have others benefit from the lessons of his experience, and therefore assumes his role as "teacher" of the natives.

The scene which closes the novel forms the "proper artistic setting" for what has gone before. The contrast between the opening and closing scene is explicit:

From a distance there simply appeared to be a motionless figure standing on top of the tumulus, just as Eustacia had stood on that lonely summit some two years and a half before. But now it was fine warm weather, with only a summer breeze blowing, and early afternoon instead of dull twilight.

Instead of being dull twilight it is full day, and instead of being alone and isolated as Eustacia was, Clym is accompanied by others.

The scene has been drained of the romance, drama, and intensity that Eustacia had brought it; but a new equilibrium has been reached, a new kind of relationship between the individual and the group has been established. "Those who ascended to the immediate neighbourhood of the Barrow perceived that the erect form in the centre, piercing the sky, was not really alone. Round him upon the slopes of the Barrow a number of heathmen and women were reclining or sitting at their ease" (p. 404).

There is, however, a degree of irony in the situation, for while Clym himself is fully conscious of the relationship between past and present and the interdependence between parents and children, husbands and wives, he is still not altogether conscious of the differences between speaker and listener, words and actions. For his listeners do not respond with the degree of attention or assent that he expects. They are unconvinced by his words, some finding them commonplace, others finding them lacking in theological rigor. Still others remark that "it was well enough for a man to take to preaching who could not see to do anything else." But while his words do not convince them intellectually, his presence and example do evoke the kind of feelings he seeks to evoke by his words: "Everywhere he was kindly received, for the story of his life had become generally known."

In terms of Hardy's own artistic development, Clym is, in one way, a unique creation. He is the only character who fully symbolizes what Hardy believed to be the future type of man. He becomes aware of the interdependent nature of society and of the relationship between past and present, and present and future. He is also the only character who exhibits far-reaching altruistic tendencies. He shows a concern for other members of society outside of his immediate circle. In this way, he is the most revealing of Hardy's characters, for he reflects Hardy's own beliefs and attitudes.[2]

As this study has established above, Hardy's aim as an artist was to make society conscious of the interrelationship of its parts and of its general direction. The method he chose, however, was to be different from Clym's. Rather than direct sermonizing, he would evoke feelings and attitudes indirectly, by the method suggested by Comte — that of implied contrast. He would, as the study of his handling of Eustacia and Clym demonstrates, indicate the contrast between the past and the present: in the future, however, he would only suggest by implication the need for a sense of interdependence and fellow-feeling. In treating Clym's sermons sardonically, Hardy forecasts a shift in his own technique as a novelist. In the major novels that follow *The Return of the Native,* Hardy tries for more subtle effects, drawing the reader into the kinds of experience conducive to altruistic feelings and attitudes. Convinced that the novels which "most conduce to moral profit" are those that "impress the reader with the inevitableness of character and environment in working out destiny," he asserted that "a didactic novel teaches nothing but the impossibility of tampering with natural truth to advance dogmatic opinions" ("PRF," pp. 144-145). He remained convinced, however, that art should be "edifying," although "the edified should not perceive the edification." He prided himself on his own art, which, he felt, "concealed art" (Easter 1890, p. 225).

As two notes in *The Life* indicate, Hardy became more and more interested in dramatizing the "evolution" of individual consciousness in the novel:

A sensation novel is possible in which the sensationalism is not casualty, but evolution; not physical but psychical.... The difference between the latter kind of novel and the novel of physical sensationalism — i.e., personal adventure, etc., is this: that whereas in the physical the adventure is itself the subject of interest, the psychical results being passed over as commonplace, in the psychical the casualty or adventure is held to be of no intrinsic interest, but the effect upon the faculties is the important matter to be depicted. (January 14, 1888, p. 204)

The next year, at the time of Browning's death, he quoted one line that he admired: "'Incidents in the development of a soul! little else is worth study'" (December 13, 1889, p. 223).

THE EVOLUTION OF CLYM YEOBRIGHT

Although Hardy was increasingly interested in portraying the evolution of consciousness in the novel, he never again allowed that consciousness to develop as explicitly or as extensively as Clym's. He never, in other words, attempted to present a "future type" but instead restricted himself to presenting past or present "types." He became increasingly concerned with presenting the tragic consequence resulting from the inability of these characters to achieve the degree of awareness and self-control that Clym had achieved. He probably felt, and with some reason, that his presentation of Eustacia had been more evocative than that of Clym, and he was increasingly concerned with this kind of evocative effect. He wished to "impress the reader with the inevitableness of character and environment in working out destiny." In giving the reader "a full look at the worst" he expected to evoke responses similar to the ones he had created in Clym through the suffering of his mother and Eustacia. Because he was convinced that the "higher sentiments" superseded rationality, he had to go beyond the rationalistic methods of presentation that he had used in creating Clym. More and more his interests began to lie "at the difference point between rationality and irrationality" (1901, p. 309). Art, rather than philosophy, was to be the pivot for the transition toward the next stage in man's development. By tracing man's development up to the present, it could imply the direction of the future. One of the ways of indicating that future was, as the previous chapters have demonstrated, through comparison and contrast. By "placing" his characters along a historical line, Hardy could reveal the moral truths that the "scientific" view of history had discovered. The next chapter will demonstrate how, by placing his minor characters still further back in history, he makes the contrast between the past and the present, the unconscious and conscious, even more evident.

THE EVOLUTION OF CLYM YEOBRIGHT

NOTES

1. The title of the chapter which describes Clym's mental state, "My Mind To Me a Kingdom Is," refers to the sixteenth-century lyric by Sir Edward Dyer. It is used as an ironic commentary on Clym's intellectual complacency. The difference between Clym's perception of his advanced intellect and Hardy's is what accounts for some critical confusion regarding Hardy's attitude toward "intellectual modernism." By paralleling Clym's egotism with Eustacia's, he shows that rather than having gone too far, Clym has not gone far enough. In order to reach the most advanced stage, one must not only recognize the need for altruism in the abstract but be capable of sympathetic responses to the particular. It is this latter quality that is developed through Clym's relationship with Eustacia Vye.
2. In correcting proofs for the Wessex Edition, Hardy notes, in a letter to a friend, that "I had got to like the character of Clym before I had done with him. I think he is the nicest of all my heroes, and *not a bit* like me." (April 22, 1912, *The Life*, p. 301) The first part of this statement confirms the notion that Clym reflects Hardy's own values. The second part suggests a significant distinction that will become increasingly clear during the course of this study: the distinction between what one is and what one ought to be. Hardy's professed values were not the expressions of an achieved personality, but rather reflections of qualities he perhaps found lacking in himself.

75

Nine

HISTORICAL PERSPECTIVE: THE MINOR CHARACTERS

One of the major difficulties that readers concerned with Hardy's ethical values encounter is the fact that he seems to place his "good" characters in the past and his egotists in the present. This apparent method would seem to suggest that Hardy, like his heroine Eustacia Vye, yearned for a simpler, less complex time. Such a conclusion, however, is based more on our own perceptions and values than Hardy's and reflects our preference for stasis rather than disequilibrium, conclusiveness rather than open-endedness, and our much simpler notions of altruism. For Hardy, "evolutionary meliorism" did not suggest simply some vague hope that somewhere, somehow, things would be better than they are now. It certainly did not mean that man would be freer or happier but, rather, the reverse. For Hardy, ethical evolution was a continuous event; it was a painfully slow, tragically wasteful process by which men were learning through pain both to accept limitations on their personal freedom and happiness and to see themselves in relation to the entire historical and social spectrum. For that reason, the sense of disequilibrium is preferable, for it represents a fundamental shift in perceptions and values toward a conscious awareness of the diminution of the ego in relation to the over-all design.

This state of mind and feeling is what the ethical evolutionists called "altruism"; it is clearly quite different from the simple "unselfishness" that the term generally connotes. This distinction is important, for it accounts both for Hardy's treatment of his "simpler" characters and for the critical confusion concerning them. Such characters as Diggory Venn and Thomasin are altruists of the simpler kind, and Hardy makes it clear that their simple-minded devotion to one other person is both limited and obsolete.

HISTORICAL PERSPECTIVE

Diggory Venn is presented as a diminished Gabriel Oak. Like Oak, he has vowed himself to an "active devotion" to his beloved's "cause." Throughout the novel Venn functions as Thomasin's guardian spirit, alert to protect her from all possible mishaps and dangers. To some extent he is successful, for he recovers her money from Wildeve, keeps Wildeve away from Eustacia, and, on the night of the storm, guides the lost Thomasin home again. Unlike Mrs. Yeobright, who insists that Clym follow her direction, Venn is "determined to aid [Thomasin] to be happier in her own way." In doing so, Venn denies his own self-interest: his love is "generous" (p. 86).

Venn's actions and attitudes toward Thomasin are shadowed by Charley, who stands in the same relation to Eustacia Vye. For Charley, "having once really succored Eustacia and possibly preserved her from the rashest of acts, mentally assumed in addition a guardian's responsibility for her welfare" (p. 337). Like Charley's, however, Venn's attempts to protect Thomasin ultimately fail. Venn cannot secure Thomasin from pain and sorrow, nor can he secure Wildeve for her permanently; the pseudo-Providential character drops into obscurity (in the first ending) or emerges an altogether commonplace farmer (in the second). While Venn's devotion to Thomasin is pure, it is made clear that his altruism is of the most limited kind.

The first indication that Venn is self-limited is his choice of vocation. Like Clym, Venn has placed himself in the past by his choice of occupation. By becoming a reddleman he has made himself an anachronism:

He was one of a class rapidly becoming extinct in Wessex, filling at present in the rural world the place which, during the last century, the dodo occupied in the world of animals. He is a curious, interesting, and nearly perished link between obsolete forms of life and those which generally prevail. (p. 16)

Venn is an anomaly even to the heath, for there is little opportunity there for plying his trade — heath-croppers, rather than sheep, being the local form of animal life.

And just as his social ambition is retrogressive, his emotional and ethical development is static. Unlike Gabriel Oak, Venn does not grow by his self-sacrifice and suffering. His feelings never fluctuate, his vision is not enlarged by his experience. The contrast between Clym's development and Venn's failure to develop is shown in their two crucial encounters. When Venn attempts to console Clym after his mother's death, Clym's response goes beyond Venn's capacity to understand, and Venn can only reply,

"Trouble has taught you a different vein of talk than mine" (p. 318). Later, when he again attempts to console Clym after Eustacia's death, he cannot see as deeply as Clym into the nature of the latter's remorse. He can only comment that "your aim has always been good. Why should you say such desperate things?" (p. 377).

Venn's incapacity to feel and to suffer is also juxtaposed to Eustacia's larger capacities. It is for this reason that Hardy has given Venn a stature inferior to hers. The contrast is made first on the physical level; Eustacia, standing on the hill, dominates the scene as Venn regards her from the foreground. Even earlier, however, he is first presented as "the single atom of life" moving slowly against the immense background of Egdon Heath. The trouble is that Venn is unaware of the significance of this perspective: he is unconscious of the relation of part to whole and automatically follows the rhythms of the heath. He does things "musingly and by small degrees" and thus seems in perfect harmony with his environment. But the novelist contrasts the apparent torpor of Egdon with the vital forces underlying it, forces which can be apprehended only by a consciousness lacking in Venn.

To do things musingly, and by small degrees, seemed, indeed, to be a duty in the Egdon valleys at this transitional hour, for there was that in the condition of the heath itself which resembled protracted and halting dubiousness. It was the quality of the repose appertaining to the scene. This was not the repose of actual stagnation, but the apparent repose of incredible slowness. A condition of healthy life so nearly resembling the torpor of death is a noticeable thing of its sort; to exhibit the inertness of the desert, and at the same time to be exercising powers akin to those of the meadow, and even of the forest, awakened in those who thought of it the attentiveness usually engendered by understatement and reserve. (p. 19)

By contrast to Eustacia, Venn seems "dull and lucid, like a flame in sunlight." Unlike hers, Venn's actions are hidden, unobserved and unrecognized, slight and inconsequential. Because her energies and powers are outside of his comprehension, he cannot, ultimately, cope with Eustacia, and his single-minded effort to secure Wildeve for Thomasin and to protect her from harm ultimately fails.

In some respects what limits Venn is the "ideal woman" he has chosen to pursue, protect, and cherish; for Thomasin is herself limited. By degrees, she learns self-discipline by reconciling herself to Wildeve and her aunt. And her love for her child allows her to pass unharmed through the same storm that drives Eustacia to her death. The contrast between Thomasin's more "objective" mental state and Eustacia's is made explicit:

HISTORICAL PERSPECTIVE

To her there were not, as to Eustacia, demons in the air, and malice in every bush and bough. The drops which lashed her face were not scorpions, but prosy rain; Egdon in the mass was no monster whatever, but impersonal open ground. Her fears of the place were rational, her dislikes of its worst moods reasonable. At this time it was in her view a windy, wet place, in which a person might experience much discomfort, lose the path without care, and possibly catch cold. (p. 363)

Such objectivity, does not, however, prevent her from getting lost. She is presented consistently as birdlike, with a narrower range of feelings and interests than those of either Eustacia or Clym. The "happy-ending" sequel makes the contrast even more emphatic: Thomasin's complacency and provinciality are caricatured, as she tends her baby and flirts with Venn. Even in the "happy ending" Thomasin's fate is restricted by the limitations of her perspective. She has learned enough for survival, but not enough for progress. At the end of the novel, she suggests the pattern of determined and ambitious maternity earlier established by Mrs. Yeobright.

Of all the minor characters, Wildeve is perhaps the most interesting because he is less static and more ambivalent and functions as a kind of pivot between the minor and the major figures. His impulses alternate between the selfish and the generous. He is first presented as a typical "lady's man" with a weak will and shifting passions. Like Venn and Yeobright, he has abandoned his vocation, but he has done so without their reasons. He seems, at first, a kind of Eustacia in diluted form. Like her, he tends to find most valuable what he cannot have. He is, however, unlike Eustacia, "tender-hearted." He is also capable of generosity. Her suffering, for example, calls forth his most generous impulses. Like Clym, he is ultimately pained by her situation, and assumes all the guilt and responsibility for it (p. 341).

Wildeve's chivalry, however, is too chimerical. He is not, Eustacia feels, "good enough" to break her marriage vow for. That his remorse and proffered restitution should precede Clym's only makes Clym's neglect more cruel and Eustacia's suffering more intense. That he should follow her into the weir, to be followed in turn by Clym, symbolizes the nature of his relationship to the major characters. He is found clinging to Yeobright, "his fingertips scarified in his dying endeavours to obtain a hold on the face of the weir wall" (p. 376). Even at the moment of his greatest self-sacrifice, he is torn by his contrasting impulse simply to survive.

Betweeen these minor figures and the natural world is a still slighter group of figures representing a still more limited and earlier stage of moral and intellectual evolution. They represent older, less conscious forms of fear and aspiration. Grandfer Cantle, for example, in recalling the days of his military glory and in his love of song and dance, is a kind of reductio ad absurdum of Eustacia's romantic dreams of the past and her hopes for a whirling social life in Paris. His timid, "maphrodite" son Christian is ashamed of his father's unabashed pursuit of pleasure, but is too irresponsible, weak, and frightened to advance beyond him. Christian is as much a disappointment to his father as Clym is to his mother.

Johnny Nunsuch's superstitious fears of the reddleman represent an even earlier intellectual stage of "theological" thought than Eustacia's. In his relationship to her, he shows a curious parallel with Clym. At first he is "charmed" by Eustacia into feeding her fire; he later becomes the immediate cause of her downfall by telling Clym of her part in turning his mother away. In his attendance upon Mrs. Yeobright during her return from Alderworth, he is more concerned with her than Clym had been, but not concerned enough to save her. Hardy describes Johnny's ambivalent feelings in some detail, emphasizing their childish nature:

Before quite leaving her he threw upon her face a wistful glance, as if he had misgivings on the generosity of forsaking her thus. He gazed into her face in a vague, wondering manner, like that of one examining some strange old manuscript the key to whose characters is undiscoverable. He was not so young as to be absolutely without a sense that sympathy was demanded, he was not old enough to be free from the terror felt in childhood at beholding misery in adult quarters hitherto deemed impregnable; and whether she were in a position to cause trouble or to suffer from it, whether she and her affliction were something to pity or something to fear, was beyond him to decide. He lowered his eyes and went on without another word. Before he had gone half a mile he had forgotten all about her, except that she was a woman who had sat down to rest. (p. 389)

Johnny's fear of Mrs. Yeobright is akin to Eustacia's. His indifference is similar to Clym's. His reactions are implicitly contrasted with theirs, however, for Johnny is a child, and the ability to sympathize is "beyond him." Clym seems to identify with Johnny, however, when he learns of his actions. He first responds accusingly, "And then you left her to die." But he quickly shifts the blame from Johnny (and indirectly himself) to Eustacia. "What he did is a trifle to what he saw" (Eustacia's face in the window). Clym understands that Johnny is not culpable, for he was unconscious of the effect of his actions. He believes, however, that Eustacia *is* guilty, for he thinks her actions were the result of deliberate malice. What Clym does not recognize until later is that Eustacia's act was as unconscious a reaction to fear as Johnny's, and that his own earlier indifference and procrastination were as culpable as her fear.

Susan Nunsuch's maternal protectiveness is a cruder form of Mrs. Yeobright's. She defends her son's actions against Clym's accusations: "No. He did not leave her to die. She sent him away" (p. 323). She considers Eustacia a witch who has harmed her child, and she practices a spell calculated to bring "powerlessness, atrophy, and annihilation" upon her. Such a practice, Hardy notes, "is one that is not quite extinct to the present day" (p. 355). Susan's act is only a more barbaric form of cruelty than Mrs. Yeobright's social snobbery and Clym's more "advanced" moral indignation. It is this more modern form of cruelty which does Eustacia actual harm, although it is less visible and is condoned by present social conventions and moral attitudes.

After Clym accuses himself of having killed his mother and his wife, he complains that "for what I have done no man or law can punish me!" (p. 377). The "more advanced" form of crime is punished by a "more advanced" form of punishment. Clym's punishment is self-inflicted and internal. His crime cannot be expiated by a single act. His punishment is a sense of continual remorse, a constant sense of pain. It is this sense of pain, however, this sensitivity to his relationship with the past, which moves him beyond his abstract idealism and moral absolutism. His "sorrow" is, therefore, as the poem prefacing the novel indicates, both "constant" and "kind."

Before discussing Hardy's purpose in comparing and contrasting the minor characters with the major ones, there is one final similarity that should be noted, because it accounts for critical analyses which treat Hardy's characters, or groups of characters, as separate, distinct, and isolated entities. The reason that these critics see the characters as distinct and isolated is that this is the way that the characters see themselves. Susan Nunsuch, for example, is so concerned with curing her son that she practices her witchcraft with the assurance that what she is doing is perfectly justified. Although Susan's actions seem like a single instance of hostility, all of the other characters illustrate similar tendencies in subtler forms. Even the early altruists are limited in their perspective. In their exclusive concern for one individual, they are indifferent to or unconscious of the effect of their actions on other characters. In Diggory Venn's concern with restoring the money to Thomasin, for example, he neglects to note that half the portion is due to Clym, and thus contributes to the series of events that lead to the destruction of Mrs. Yeobright and Eustacia. In Mrs. Yeobright's concern for Clym's future, she treats Eustacia with hostility and evokes a corresponding response. When she sees Eustacia's face in the window, she is unaware that it reflects the fear and hostility her own attitude has engendered. Clym's excessive remorse at his mother's death frightens Eustacia into concealing her part in it. In their desire for the happiness of themselves or one other person, each of the characters acts blindly, unaware of the consequences of his actions on the lives of the other characters.

Eustacia Vye epitomizes this total lack of concern for the consequences of her actions. Only Clym becomes aware of the effect of his previous actions, of the relationship between cause and effect, of the interdependence between one generation and the next. As a result, he blames neither Fate nor Eustacia for his destiny. Rather, by comparing his own actions with Eustacia's, he finds hers relatively innocent and forgivable. Her error had been simply her desire to be happy. His had been a more recently acquired one, a trait he shared with his mother — that of moral absolutism. It is also a trait that he shares with several other of Hardy's "modern" heroes, including Harry Knight and Angel Clare. Like them, Clym finds this moral absolutism more destructive than their protagonists' simpler desires for happiness. As a result of seeing the effect of this moral absolutism, Clym achieves a degree of intellectual and emotional flexibility.

It is for the purpose of establishing just such moral relativism in the reader that Hardy juxtaposes his major characters with his minor ones. Thus, for example, Eustacia's impulses and actions are presented as a more exaggerated form of each character's desire for happiness. Because we sympathize with these impulses when they are exhibited in a lesser degree, we cannot entirely condemn them when they appear in quintessential form in Eustacia. Similarly, by describing Johnny Nunsuch's reactions to Mrs. Yeobright as childish, Hardy reduces the culpability of Eustacia's and Clym's reactions; Eustacia's fears of Mrs. Yeobright and Clym's insensitivity to her seem only the more exaggerated forms of the child's unconscious reactions. In the same way, Mrs. Yeobright's pride seems relatively mild and inoffensive when contrasted with Eustacia's; yet, when the two are yoked together, Eustacia's pride becomes more understandable. In their one direct confrontation, we see how Eustacia's anger is fed by Mrs. Yeobright's stiffness and how each is locked into a rigid position by the same feelings of self-righteousness and moral indignation. Since both err in the same way, no final moral judgment of either is allowed. Rather, we tend to see their self-righteousness as a limitation rather than as a positive evil. Each character tends to illuminate the limitations of the other.

This technique of using characters to illuminate the limitations of each other is fairly consistent in most of Hardy's novels. It corresponds, in its literary way, to the use that the ethical evolutionists make of historical relativism. Significantly, there are no villains in *The Return of the Native* and few, if any, in all of Hardy's novels. Rather, there are characters who are limited to a greater or lesser degree by the energy with which they pursue their own ends. As in the confrontation between Mrs. Yeobright and Eustacia, the conflicts arise as the result of each character's pursuing his own happiness without regard to the needs of the other. The claim of

HISTORICAL PERSPECTIVE

each character has a degree of legitimacy, and we can do no more than sympathize with each, even when we see that the full expression of the one character's desire must necessarily conflict with that of the other.

But to say that Hardy establishes a kind of moral relativism by indicating similarities between the minor characters and the major ones is not to imply that he is unconcerned with marking the differences between them. In making these parallels and contrasts, Hardy is placing his characters along an evolutionary scale. The differences, though only of degree, are therefore equally important, for they indicate the successive stages of ethical evolution. As the minor characters differ from the rustics, so the major characters differ from the minor ones. Each group exhibits a greater degree of feeling and consciousness. Thus, for example, Johnny Nunsuch is not aware of his responsibility to Mrs. Yeobright, Eustacia is more aware of hers, and Clym is overwhelmed by his. Similarly, Susan Nunsuch sees nothing wrong with practicing witchcraft on Eustacia in order to cure her son; Mrs. Yeobright has misgivings about her behavior toward Eustacia; and Clym cannot forgive himself for his cruelty toward her. Thomasin is incapable of responding to Wildeve's infidelity with the same degree of feeling with which Clym responds to Eustacia's because her relationship to Wildeve is of obviously lesser intensity than that between Eustacia and Clym. Diggory Venn's altruism, while more "generous" than Mrs. Yeobright's, lacks the kind of perspective which Clym finally achieves. The actions and impulses of the minor characters are consistently more limited, more habitual, and more automatic than those of the major characters. The equilibrium gained by the minor characters is the result of a more limited range of feeling and perspective. It is achieved at the expense of any further growth.

What we have seen in this study of the roles of the minor characters is how, by juxtaposing them, the novelist shows them to be parallel and complementary rather than self-contained and contradictory. Each of the characters is defined, not only by his own past but by his "filiation" with other characters. And while each seems to be acting independently as a discrete entity from his own perspective, we see them as interrelated and as operating within parallel value systems. While each is unaware of the consequences of his well-intentioned actions, the reader is allowed to see the consequences and to understand their effects on the other characters. While each character sees himself as acting within an immediate present, we see them as falling within an historical continuum — a continuum that is not in the present but in the constantly receding past.

What makes Hardy's technique somewhat different from Scott's or Dickens's is that the historical continuum is only gradually visible: it becomes clear only after the perspective of each character is focused upon and distanced. In other words, we are made to participate in a point of view that emerges only gradually. The structure of Hardy's novel is organic, but organic in a special way: it is hierarchical and progressive, imitating the process and pattern that he saw in history.

The characters in *The Return of the Native* express the full spectrum of the evolutionary pattern including "theological," "metaphysical," and "sociological stages" of thought and feeling; they convey the contrasts between earlier and advanced altruism and egotism, and by their unconscious interactions with each other they reveal the interdependence and interrelatedness between one stage and the next. The sense of disequilibrium and open-endedness that concludes the novel indicates the "inevitable movement onward" that Hardy sought to evoke for the reader by having worked out the consequences of earlier modes of thought and feeling in his characters.

What this technique means in terms of how we read the novel is important, for it differs somewhat from our conventional notions of organic form. For although most novels have a cumulative effect, it is often possible to extract an episode and find within it a microcosm of the novel's entire structure and to determine quite accurately the novelist's point of view. One can, for example, take the opening chapter of *Pride and Prejudice* and know quite clearly just what Jane Austen's attitudes and values are. While her values are hierarchic, her point of view is constant. We know that Mrs. Bennet will always be Mrs. Bennet and Jane Austen's attitude toward her will remain constant. Similarly, while the perspective of Elizabeth shifts, the distance between the heroine and the novelist remains constant. On the other hand, while Hardy's scale of values is also hierarchic, his point of view is not constant. Since the actions and attitudes of each of the characters is presented from his own perspective, it is more difficult to extract one particular passage and determine the novelist's attitude and values. It is not possible, for example, to extract the passage describing Clym's furze-cutting and assume that, because Clym is happy and the passage is moving, Hardy approves of the action. We have to know what precedes and what follows this action; we have to see the reactions of Eustacia Vye and Mrs. Yeobright before we can get the scene in proper perspective. Only gradually do we see the way a single episode falls into the larger frame.

But to say that Hardy's point of view shifts with that of his characters is not to say that Hardy is a modern relativist either. Although he treats each of his characters sympathetically, he does not give them equal weight, as, say, Faulkner does in *As I Lay Dying*. For while each character's point of view is shown to be relative and complementary, it is measured by an absolute frame of reference. Thus, for example, Thomasin is

HISTORICAL PERSPECTIVE

not given the same weight as Eustacia Vye, nor Diggory Venn the same emphasis as Clym Yeobright. The characters are placed in a historical and ethical hierarchy, the diminution of one character serving as stimulus for the enlargement of the next. In Hardy, the movement is linear and sequential rather than circular, as it is in Faulkner or Joyce. Thus, just as the point of view is not constant but emergent, so the structure is not self-contained but evolutionary and open-ended, corresponding to the way Hardy viewed both history and the life processes.

It is precisely this open-ended and evolutionary pattern in such novels as *The Return of the Native* and the ones that follow it that most disturbs us as modern readers. When we see such clear patterns as we do in Hardy, we expect to find the other characteristics of organic form; that is, we expect to find a consistent point of view, and/or a self-contained and hence aesthetically satisfying structure. Hardy's later novels provide neither. His point of view is visible only in the total design of the work and in our reactions as readers. What happens when we read *The Return of the Native* and later novels is that we, as readers, are taken into the fictional frames and are made part of the on-going process. Having gone through frame after frame, we are left at the end with Hardy's own point of view, which is neither aesthetically nor emotionally satisfying. Our own values have been displaced and we are left with others which we would prefer to reject. In *The Return of the Native* we have seen both the dissolution of the romantic heroine and the diminution of the "more advanced" hero who would take her place. But before blaming our discomfort on Hardy's unresolved conflicts and/or artistic failure, we should be aware that it is this very state of disequilibrium which Hardy most valued as essential to man's future progress. A sense of disequilibrium is the effect of change of perspective. It is the result of shifting one's focus from self to other, from seeing the individual as the center of the world to seeing him as coming at the end of a much larger spatial and temporal design. It is the psychological and ethical equivalent of the scientific shift from the Ptolemaic to the Copernican view of the universe.

For Hardy, as we have seen, this shift of perspective was painful but necessary. It was, to him, the only thing that would allow man to survive in the future. He indicates, in *The Return of the Native,* that there is no escape in the past, in nature, or in fiction. He shows any such hope to be an illusion. For Eustacia Vye there is no spatial escape: there is no place which offers the kind of freedom and happiness that she desires. For Clym there is no temporal escape, either by going "back to nature" or by retreating to a rustic community that will allow him the place he believes he deserves. The hopes and desires of the characters are shown to be fictions; the course of their lives, defictionalizing processes. As readers, who identify with these needs for freedom, happiness, and ego gratification, we also are thwarted. As the movement goes forward, our desires are blocked. We participate in action which, by the end of the novel, has become a pattern that is shown to be irreversible. There is no way to go but forward. What makes our position even more difficult is that Hardy provides us with no model for the future. We cannot project the pattern of the past onto the future because, as we have seen during the course of our reading, a pattern is visible only in retrospect. We are left in the uncomfortable position of having to create our own pattern. We are left to ourselves without the help either of Providence or of a reliable narrator.

However much we may dislike this position, our uncomfortable reaction as readers is an indication of the success of Hardy's design. By the end of the novel, the defictionalizing process is complete for us, as well as for the characters.

Subsequent chapters will show how Hardy structures the later novels by using his same scale of values but with greater psychological subtlety. Such an analysis should help us distinguish between the responses that Hardy evokes and our own defensive reactions to them.

Ten

TWO ON A TOWER

After having fully expressed his system of values by placing his characters along an evolutionary spectrum continuous with the natural background in *The Return of the Native,* Hardy seems to have reached a plateau in the development of his fictional techniques. His next two novels, *The Trumpet Major* and *The Laodicean,* show no further development either in terms of technique or expression of value. In *Two on a Tower* (1881), however, he seems to shift his focus deliberately from the temporal and ethical to the spatial and psychological dimension, and rather than dealing with a vast array of major and minor characters, he focuses on only two.

In the preface he states that "this slightly built romance was the outcome of a wish to set the emotional history of two infinitesimal lives against the background of the stellar universe."[1] As for the relative importance of these two perspectives, he would "impart to the readers the sentiment that of these contrasting magnitudes the smaller might be the greater to them as men."

Besides wishing to "impart a sentiment," he further wishes that "some few readers ... will be reminded ... in a manner not unprofitable to the growth of social sympathies, of the pathos, misery, long-suffering and divine tenderness which in real life frequently accompany the passion of such a woman as Viviette for a lover several years her junior" (p. vi).

This comment bears looking into, for it reveals a conscious attempt to evoke a particular effect — "the growth of the social sympathies" in the reader. That is, Hardy would make the ethical values revealed in his fiction continuous with real life, by evoking those responses in his readers that he believed were the most promising for the future. In this case he chooses to evoke such an effect by describing the particular feelings – "the pathos, long-suffering and divine sympathy" – of a woman in a particular kind of love relationship, that between an older woman and a younger man.

This concentration on the feelings of an older woman and their effect on the reader reveals a significant shift of focus, for he had heretofore dealt with younger, more conventionally romantic heroines who, by their relationship with their "more advanced" lovers, themselves evolve from their initial subjectivity and egotism to more objective, altruistic feelings and attitudes. This is the way he had presented the stories of Cytherea Graye, Bathsheba Everdene, and Elfride Swancourt. In *The Return of the Native* he had shown, by Eustacia Vye's relationship to Clym, the tragic consequences of the romantic heroine's failure to make the necessary adaptation. While there is some suggestion in these novels that the effect of the evolution of the romantic heroines on their lovers is, or should be, reciprocal, the major emphasis is primarily on the evolution of the young romantic heroine from egotism to altruism.

In *Two on a Tower,* however, Hardy begins where he had formerly left off – at the end of the evolutionary spectrum rather than in the middle. He focuses on the effect of Lady Constantine's altruism on her younger lover. Lady Constantine begins as an altruist, and the novel traces the further refinement and sublimation of her feelings as she interacts with St. Cleeve. While the novel fails to achieve the desired evocative effect, it is nonetheless interesting in revealing more fully all that Hardy meant by the term "altruism."

But what makes the novel even more interesting is that, in focusing primarily on the values associated with altruism, Hardy reveals the psychological basis for these values. In developing the "emotional history" of two lives, he consciously explores the psychological sources of their feelings and values. Just below the surface of this strange love story runs a concurrent psychological pattern that is nearly explicit and that is recognizable and familiar to the modern reader.

The story concerns the increasing interest that an upper-class woman, bound by strict vows of isolation during the absence of her estranged and jealous husband, takes in a younger man of a somewhat lower social class. Swithin St. Cleeve, the focus of her attention and increasing devotion, is a youth of sublime innocence and beauty. Lady Constantine first sees the young Adonis in his occupation as a modern astronomer, engaged in "what may be called a very chastened or schooled form of that first and most natural of adorations" – the worship of the sun. From first to last, Viviette is torn between encouraging St. Cleeve to follow his natural scientific bent in studying "stellar Venuses" and drawing his devotion to herself.

From the first, Viviette acts as the young man's patroness, purchasing both lens and telescope for his further study. On the other hand, she takes great pains to conceal both her actions from others and her feelings from him. Only when she learns of her husband's death does she reveal these feelings. St. Cleeve, in turn, awakened at last by the gossip of their neighbors, returns her passion, and, after much subterfuge, the couple are secretly married. Even here, however, Lady Constantine is forced to take the initiative, procuring the license and making the necessary arrangements for the ceremony.

Because of their difference in age and social position, the couple agree to keep their union secret, St. Cleeve following the directions of his mistress almost automatically. Viviette soon decides that the young scientist should be confirmed in the Anglican church; and as a result of that decision (as well as her older brother's desire that she remarry), a third character is introduced. The Bishop, having been a friend of the young man's dead father, a parson who had married beneath him, becomes both St. Cleeve's spiritual father and Lady Constantine's suitor.

The presence of the Bishop drives St. Cleeve away from Viviette. Prevented from acknowledging their marriage by both Lady Constantine and the terms of his great-uncle's will, St. Cleeve is sent off to pursue his studies at the South Pole with the understanding that he will return after five years when his success and age will make their positions more nearly equal.

In the meantime, however, finding herself pregnant, Viviette agrees to marry the Bishop in order to protect her child and to free St. Cleeve to pursue his career. St. Cleeve returns five years later to find the Bishop dead and Viviette, with their child, waiting for him. After momentarily hesitating upon seeing the older and now clearly maternal Viviette, St. Cleeve, in a burst of reciprocal feeling, acknowledges and returns Viviette's love. The strain of waiting, however, has been too much for Viviette, and "with a shriek of amazed joy" she falls in his arms, dead. The novel ends with the following sentences: "Viviette was dead. The Bishop was avenged."

Even a cursory review of the plot reveals to the modern reader its strong oedipal overtones. The focus here, however, is primarily on the Jocasta, rather than on the Oedipus. The wife, in the absence of her husband, focuses her sexual impulses on the son, and he becomes, in effect, both her son and her lover. Meanwhile, the third figure in the triangle, the husband and father, hovers in the background threatening to prevent, reveal, or destroy the incestuous nature of the relationship.

What is most interesting here, however, is that the pre-Freudian Hardy makes the psychological aspects of the case so explicit. Both Viviette's guilt and her desire to keep her feelings secret, even from St. Cleeve, are emphasized, and the conscious sublimation of her sexual feelings with the concomitant reinforcement of her maternal feelings is also made explicit. That this process is described in both psychological and ethical terms indicates a greater degree of awareness, on Hardy's part, of the psychological basis for his ethical values.

Earlier, the romantic heroines had been only dimly aware of the changes within them and had been unconscious of their effect on their intellectual lovers. In this novel, Viviette goes one step beyond this level of perception, becoming increasingly conscious of her feelings and deliberately "schooling" them until she becomes a conscious and explicit symbol of a kind of love that is both altruistic and objective. The effect of her evolution on her intellectually advanced lover is also explicit.

That Hardy should choose a woman rather than a man to symbolize the altruist values is not unusual. Both Comte and Stephen had done so, too. Like Stephen, apparently Hardy saw the ideal altruist as a type of mother, all giving, responsive, self-sacrificial. But Viviette is no more the typical mother than she is the typical mistress; rather, she is an amalgam of the best features of both. She has the concerns of the mother combined with the sensitivity, responsiveness, and sexual attractiveness of the mistress, but with neither the possessiveness of the one nor the potential destructiveness of the other. In this she represents the next stage, which Hardy conceptualized as "altruist," but which he here presents in more recognizable form. In choosing this type of woman to embody his altruist values, Hardy is, perhaps, revealing the psychological basis for his own ethical values. In portraying Viviette, he is, perhaps, projecting those attributes of which he himself, like his intellectually advanced heroes, is in most need.

The way in which Hardy develops his ideal altruist type would suggest that Viviette might be a projection of that aspect in himself which he cannot, in reality, achieve. For Viviette is engaged in processes similar to that of the novelist: she disguises her feelings until she is forced to confront them, and, as soon as she does, she forces them to conform to her newly determined ethical values. The conflict in Viviette is between the conscience and consciousness. When she is forced to confront the real feelings which she has concealed under a conventional code of social behavior, she creates a new code of values more appropriate to her needs. In no previous novel is Hardy's emphasis on the sublimation of sexual instinct so strong, and in no previous novel is that which is deliberately repressed so clearly revealed.

From the first, Viviette's feelings for St. Cleeve are "maternal, sisterly, and amorous," but she conceals her amorous feelings in convenient fictions. As Elfride had done with Stephen Smith, she consciously follows the courtly love tradition, beginning by lightly playing the role of "Queen" to her "royal astronomer." She soon takes her function as patroness more seriously, however, purchasing first a lens and then full telescopic equipment and housing both St. Cleeve and the instruments in the tower on her husband's estate. Pretending to no more than benign concern with his intellectual pursuits, she restrains her desire to pursue her Adonis through the woods and secludes herself in her husband's manor.

Such seclusion is not enough, however, to sublimate her desires entirely, and so she decides to quell all hope of union with him by finding a substitute for herself. She takes upon herself the role of queenly matchmaker. Inside the church, accompanied by the sounds of Tabitha Lark's organ-playing, she looks at her position more objectively, and from a distant perspective "register[s] a magnanimous vow" to match St. Cleeve to "an ideal maiden." She will endow the girl with money, "and the interest of her ... life" will be "in watching the development of love between Swithin and the ideal maiden" (p. 85).

News of her husband's death breaks the idealistic vow, however, and forces Lady Constantine to confront the amorous feelings she had attempted to sublimate entirely. But the sexual relationship between the two is very brief, and after the honeymoon Lady Constantine, having been accidentally slashed on the cheek by the whip of her unknowing brother, with a degree of shame returns to her former position as mistress of the manor.

Brief and occasional meetings with St. Cleeve seem to make Viviette increasingly aware of his childlike nature and her own culpability; and, as if to do penance for the marriage and almost reverse the process, she insists that St. Cleeve be confirmed. Sitting in church as his sponsor, she watches St. Cleeve accompanied by younger people undergo the ceremony that marks "the age of discretion" and that usually precedes matrimony by at least ten years. The presence of the Bishop and her older brother heightens her awareness of the differences between them. The presence of the Bishop as her suitor and her brother as his agent serves to further quell her amorous feelings.

What Viviette becomes increasingly aware of is that the sexual feeling that had first attracted her to St. Cleeve, and that she had for so long artifically repressed, is, indeed, what she had feared it might be — destructive of her lover. She begins to notice that their marriage, rather than reinforcing his scientific pursuits and focusing his ambition as they had hoped, has blunted his purpose and dissipated his energies. In other words, Viviette perceives that the expression of that instinct which is most self-assertive and self-fulfilling is also most destructive of the mate.[2] At this point she begins to feel genuinely what she had formerly merely imitated. From having pretended to being queenly patroness, she has become St. Cleeve's mistress. Now, however, she moves from mistress to sublime mother. While the transition has been slowly and subtly developed, the moment when she becomes conscious of the necessity of making this transition is dramatic. At this point Viviette undergoes a kind of death and resurrection.

Already filled with guilt and self-doubt, when she learns that their secret marriage is illegal, having occurred before the actual death of her husband, Viviette questions whether she should repeat the act. With the picture of her husband's suicide freshly in her mind and the damning letter of St. Cleeve's great-uncle before her, she is overcome by a "conviction against self." "Mortified" by the idea that St. Cleeve might later regard her as destructive and convinced that the old man's "cynical view of her nature" is "virtually right," she feels a "wish for annihilation" that comes from "a despair that arises when we, our best and firmest friend, cease to believe in our cause" (p. 255). Like Tess when she is rejected by Angel and Jude when he is rejected by Sue, Viviette gives up the desire for life. It is at this point, that Viviette decides not to marry St. Cleeve.

It is another Viviette entirely who emerges from this mortification and despair. No longer possessed by sexual desires, and therefore having no need to conceal or disguise them, her conflicts rise to an ethical and intellectual level. She is torn between doing what is socially correct (that is, marrying St. Cleeve) and what is ethically right (that is, freeing him from herself). She must decide between the "egocentricity" of her possessiveness and a more "sympathetic attitude." And the artificial pattern that she had formerly established now impels her forward: "The self-centred attitude natural to one in her situation was becoming displaced by the sympathetic attitude." Having lost the instinct for her own self-preservation, she cannot much care for it on the social level. What had been "artificially fostered" is now becoming natural; altruistic feelings are now replacing egotistic instincts. What had formerly only caused pain now gives her some pleasure: she begins to feel "a certain sweet sense that she was rising above self-love" (p. 258).

In deciding to "sink" her self-love in order to "raise" her lover, Viviette is more than conventionally self-sacrificial and maternal, for her concerns go beyond even St. Cleeve. She will not, "to save her narrow honour, waste the wide promise of his ability," for "there was no telling what good might not result to mankind at large from his exploits." Once again, she finds the idea of "immolating herself" and leaving St. Cleeve "free to work wonders for the good of his creatures" to be "consoling by its breadth . . . even while it tortured her by making herself the scapegoat or single unit upon whom the evil would fall" (p. 257).

The comment that concludes Viviette's ruminations summarizes the process by which her "maternal, sisterly, amorous" feelings have been winnowed, and identifies the maternal element as the source of the altruistic values:

That maternal element which from time to time evinced itself in her affection for the youth and was imparted by her superior ripeness in experience and years appeared now again, as she drew nearer to the resolve not to secure propriety in her own social condition at the expense of this youth's earthly utility. (p. 258)

The "maternal element" as it now appears is reinforced and expanded to include not only St. Cleeve but "mankind at large." The judgment of Viviette's attitude and feelings is explicit: "In loving St. Cleeve so far better than herself as this was to surpass the love of women as conventionally understood and as mostly existing" (p. 258).

The way in which Viviette finds intellectual justification for her feelings brings her to an ethical position exactly congruent with that of the novelist. Looking back to the past for a pattern of historical evolution, she discerns "a line of conduct which transcend[s] mere self-preservation: 'Save thyself' was sound Old Testament doctrine and not altogether discountenanced by the New. But was there a line of conduct which transcended mere self-preservation? And would it not be an excellent thing to put it in practice now?" (p. 256) After considering another kind of charity than that which begins "at home," Viviette turns to a consideration of the evolution of love between man and woman:

Love between man and woman, which, in Homer, Moses, and other early exhibitors of life is mere desire, had for centuries past so far broadened as to include sympathy and friendship; surely it should in this advanced stage of the world include benevolence also. (p. 257)

Following this line of reasoning, Viviette concludes that "it was her duty to set her young man free" (p. 257). She will not attempt what she had earlier thought she might do: "lime Swithin's young wings again solely for her credit's sake" (pp. 241-242).

Though the act of self-sacrifice resembles that of James's Milly Theale in *The Wings of the Dove*, the way in which Viviette arrives at her conclusions makes her recognizable as uniquely Hardyean.

In order to make the contrast between the "benevolence" and altruism of ideal maternity and more conventional maternal feelings even more clear, the novelist has Viviette undergo a temporary relapse when she discovers that she is pregnant. Then the "instinct for self-preservation" returns, "flaming up like a fire." "Her altruism in subjecting her self-love to benevolence, and letting Swithin go away from her" is "demolished by the new necessity, as if it had been a gossamer web" (p. 272). Swithin's absence and the Bishop's presence, however, short-circuit this renewed fire, for in marrying the Bishop she finds a way both to free St. Cleeve and to protect her child.

With the death of the Bishop the gossamer web becomes again apparent, and St. Cleeve is at last caught in it. Out of her guilt, secrecy, and self-immolation Viviette has created a new kind of feeling and attitude and is able, momentarily at least, to raise her former son-lover to her own level of feeling. Having forced St. Cleeve to repress his own sexual instincts for so long, she has created a different St. Cleeve. "The Swithin who return[ed] was not quite the Swithin who had gone away." Susceptible to her example, St. Cleeve recognizes "the purest benevolence" in Viviette's past actions. He acknowledges in her attitude the "'charity which seeketh not her own.'" Ultimately, he reciprocates her feelings of loving-kindness, acknowledging them to be "sentiments more to be prized than lover's love" (p. 312).

In tracing the evolution of Viviette from unconscious to conscious altruist, first by the revelation of her sexual instincts and then by her conscious sublimation of them, Hardy reveals a good deal of what his system of ethical values implies. By associating the sexual instincts with the desire for self-preservation and, hence, egotism, he suggests, through Viviette, that such instincts must be utterly destroyed before the "sympathetic attitudes" can fully emerge. The individual must, in effect, die and be reborn if his egotism is to be "sunk" and his altruism raised.

Hardy's treatment of St. Cleeve, though subordinate to that of his heroine, is nonetheless interesting, especially in the light of his psychological treatment of Viviette. For if Viviette is a projection of Hardy's hopes and desires, St. Cleeve may be a projection of his fears and his inadequacies. In some ways St. Cleeve prefigures Jude, both in his initial innocence and in his perceptions of the coldness of the universe. Devoid of the comforting illusions of Jude, he is nonetheless personally ambitious. And, like Jude, he is drawn to the very place that he finds most threatening, in this case the stellar universe. He sees the vast immensities of the universe as reducing human life to insignificance. Rather than seeing the sky as a "comforting concavity" or as a "vaulted roof fretted with golden fire" to provide a noble setting for human heroes, the modern scientist sees the vast empty spaces interspersed with dying fires and having no connection with man. In his first conversation, the scientific astronomer tells the romantic star-gazer that "whatever the stars were made for, they were not made to please our eyes." From this observation he draws the typical Hardyean conclusion: "it is just the same in everything: nothing is made for man" (pp. 31-32).

Viviette's "maternal solicitude" elicits the further confession that St. Cleeve is attracted by that which most horrifies him. He explains to her that "far more terrible than the monsters of shape" found in the seas "are the monsters of magnitude without known shape – the voids and waste places in the sky." These "coal sacks" are "deep wells for the human mind to let itself down into, leave alone the human body." The sheer magnitude of the stellar universe goes beyond the grandeur of nobility or the beauty of the sublime: it goes beyond the "awful" to the "ghastly." St. Cleeve then confesses that his own attraction to these vast empty spaces is morbid. "Such minds as exert their imaginative powers to bury themselves in the depths of that universe merely strain their faculties to gain a new horror." Like Conrad's Kurtz, however, St. Cleeve feels impelled to search out and enter this heart of darkness, and Viviette, like Marlowe, follows.

St. Cleeve continues his description of what he sees and how he feels by shifting from womblike metaphors to metaphors of the tomb. Besides being overcome by the depth and weirdness of these vast, dark, empty spaces, St. Cleeve also reveals his horror at their "quality of decay." He sees the stars burning out like candles. They are not, he says, as we suppose, either everlasting or eternal, but continually dying, and soon all stars will be extinguished. As horrifying as the empty spaces are now, they will be even more horrifying when the entire universe will be one dark eternal hole containing nothing but dead cinders.

Imagine them all extinguished, and your mind feeling its way through a heaven of total darkness, occasionally striking against a black invisible cinder of those stars. (p. 34)

The hell that the scientist contemplates creates more of a "metaphysical shudder" than that which an evangelist preacher could describe. It does so, perhaps, because it comes closer to the psychological truth in revealing regressive subconscious fears and desires.

The psychological basis for St. Cleeve's attraction and repulsion to the study of the universe is suggested by the description of his circumstances. Orphaned at an early age, he is cared for by his grandmother. Unself-consciously occupying her husband's tower to contemplate and confront a magnified mirror of his own situation in the universe, he takes comfort in Lady Constantine's sympathetic interest and physical support. His unawareness of her sexual attractiveness can only be explained as that of a child's similar attitude toward a parent. His concomitant attraction to what he fears as vast, dark, empty, and destructive suggests further reasons for his "blindness" to Viviette's sexual attractiveness.

When he is awakened suddenly to the sexual possibilities of the relationship, he returns Viviette's passion. But he continues the parent-child relationship within the sexual one, obediently following Viviette's instructions. The contrast between his intellectual maturity and his emotional infancy is explicit: "Stable as a giant in all that appertained to nature and life outside humanity" he is "a mere pupil in domestic matters" (p. 267).[3]

The mother-son relationship is emphasized when St. Cleeve is sent away by Lady Constantine to pursue his studies at the South Pole. He leaves his mistress "with a lightness of heart which most young men feel in forsaking old love for new adventure." Like his previous fictional forebears, St. Cleeve exhibits the egotism of youth: "the man was endowed with that schoolboy temperament which does not see, or at least consider with much curiosity, the effect of a given scheme on others than himself." He accepts the artificially contrived filial situation as natural for himself. Lady Constantine's pain at their parting "was forgotten in his feeling that she had done a very handsome and noble thing for him, and he was therefore bound to make the most of it" (p. 269).

Having accepted his filial relationship to her, he is shocked by the news of his fatherhood. Having first established a mother-son relationship and then aroused his sexual feelings, Viviette now awakens his conscience. He can no longer regard Viviette as a mother and himself as the innocent son; he is now more fully conscious of what has passed between them. Like Viviette's, St. Cleeve's reactions are described in psychological as well as ethical terms:

Swithin's heart swelled within him in sudden pity for her, first; then he blanched with a horrified sense of what she had done, and at his own relation to the deed. He felt like an awakened somnambulist who should find that he had been accessory to a tragedy during his unconsciousness.

The metaphor that St. Cleeve uses to describe what Viviette has done could not be more explicit in revealing St. Cleeve's relationship to her: "She had loosened the knot of her difficulties by cutting it through and through" (p. 296).

Having been cut off from Viviette entirely, St. Cleeve spends the remainder of his time at the South Pole pursuing his studies. But his activities, like those of Harry Knight when he has cut himself off from Elfride Swancourt, are described as mechanical and meaningless.

Although he is unaware of it, his absence from Viviette deprives him of the "food for the sympathetic instincts which create the changes in a life." From the "intersocial" point of view, he is merely "killing time" (p. 300).

His studies completed, St. Cleeve returns home with the desultory reluctance of a son returning to a mother. He postpones seeing Viviette immediately, taking a greater interest in the now fully-grown Tabith Lark.

But the course of St. Cleeve's *education sentimentale* is not complete. His third awakening occurs when he sees Viviette seated in the tower with their child at her feet. He is shocked and repelled by her "worn and faded" appearance. She seems "another woman" and not the original Viviette he had remembered. Unaware that such "chastened pensiveness" reveals "more promising material," he begins to retreat, the clearly maternal figure extinguishing his passion altogether. With a subtle stroke, the novelist here links Viviette with St. Cleeve's earlier pursuits, and suggests the link between his relationship to Viviette and his obsession with the stellar universe: "The masses of her hair which were darkness visible had become touched here and there by a faint gray haze, like the Via Lactea in a midnight sky" (p. 311).

Drawn back by such ties, St. Cleeve is reconciled to what he had both loved and feared, finding through Viviette's conscious sublimation of her passion the loving-kindness that had been absent in the empty universe and in himself.

The discovery is only momentary, however, and St. Cleeve is left once again alone. As he looks around for help, he sees only Tabitha Lark, "the only spot of colour and animation within the wide horizon," now distanced from himself in youth and feeling as he had been distanced from Lady Constantine. Taking his son's hand in his, he assumes the position Viviette had formerly occupied. Having been moved from the position of son to lover to parent, he has reached a kind of equality they had both sought, not one of age or of social position, but of feeling and attitude. At the conclusion of the novel the reader is made to see the relative and reciprocal positions of the lovers from both of their perspectives. With "a shriek of amazed joy" Viviette had recognized both her success and her successor, welcoming what she had, through her own sublimation and self-immolation, sought for and produced. And St. Cleeve, like Lawrence's Paul Morel, is bereft of what he now recognizes as the source and guide of his life. St. Cleeve's direction, as a result of his experience, like Paul's, is now back into life, rather than away from it.

NOTES

1. *Two on a Tower* (London: 1964) p. vi.
2. Pierre D'Exideuil, in *The Human Pair in the Works of Thomas Hardy* (New York: 1970), indicates that this view of the sexual relationship is characteristic of Hardy: "Everywhere . . . [the couples] show the same obstinate will to live and the same need for domination" (p. 70). Later, he indicates that such instincts are shown to "enslave" men to the natural laws and to reveal "a fatal egoism." He quotes the comment in *The Return of the Native:* "selfishness is frequently the chief constituent of . . . passion, and sometimes the only one" (p. 133). The comparison between Hardy's treatment of the libido and Freud's in his *Introductory Lectures on Psycho-Analysis* is worthy of attention. See page 195.
3. The comment that Hardy himself was a child till he was sixteen, a youth till he was five-and-twenty, and a young man till he was nearly fifty suggests a correspondence between St. Cleeve and the novelist. For commentary on the significance of this statement, which appears in *The Life*, see Havelock Ellis's introduction to *The Human Pair in the Work of Thomas Hardy*, p. xvi.

Eleven

THE MAYOR OF CASTERBRIDGE

Having explored the psychological concomitants of altruism in his characterization of the maternal Viviette, Hardy turns his attention to a further delineation of egotism in his characterization of the paternal Michael Henchard. In *Two on a Tower* he had treated the reciprocal relationship between mother and son: in *The Mayor of Casterbridge* (1886) he develops the reciprocal relationship between father and daughter. In this later novel, however, the psychological components are not stressed; rather, the relationship is dealt with almost entirely on the ethical level. It would be interesting to speculate as to the reasons why the novelist returns to this level of treatment and to ascertain just how conscious he was of using his system of ethical values to conceal the psychological basis for them, but such speculations would obviously be fruitless. What can be done, however, is to read the later novels with the oedipal pattern in mind and to see that a good deal of their effectiveness derives from this suppressed pattern. For the late major novels, beginning with *The Mayor of Casterbridge,* differ from the earlier ones only in this regard. That is, the ethical value system remains the same, but the psychological dynamics underlying the value system subtly reinforce it, and rather than depending on grotesque plots, stage villains, and heroines, or explicit ethical commentary, the novelist uses common familial conflicts that are congruent with the explicit value system. Partially as a result of the deliberate suppression of the psychological material and of the deliberate overlay of the ethical value system, the novels evoke their powerful effects. During these years when, as his essays reveal, Hardy was becoming increasingly aware of his role as an artist, of using his art "to conceal art" and to evoke particular responses in the reader, it is as if, like Lady Constantine, having discovered the psychological bases for his actions, he deliberately sublimated them in order to achieve certain desired effects. His treatment of Michael Henchard is the first example of this new technique.

Most readers have acknowledged that Michael Henchard is one of Hardy's finest tragic characters, but perhaps what is not so clear is how fully he is made to embody one aspect of Hardy's value system and the oedipal pattern underlying it. While his actions are described in purely ethical terms, his pattern of action resembles that of Paul's father in Lawrence's *Sons and Lovers*. Like Walter Morel, Henchard is self-exiled from the start; struggling to maintain his identity, he engages in bitter rivalry with the son, and at last, unable to maintain his ascendancy, in the bitterness of defeat he abdicates to the son. The presence of the stepdaughter, Elizabeth Jane, in Hardy's novel reinforces its oedipal base while at the same time distinguishing it from Lawrence's by reestablishing its ethical overlay. Hardy's treatment of the Henchard-Elizabeth Jane relationship is more like that of George Eliot than of Lawrence.

Since Hardy returns to the ethical level in his treatment of Michael Henchard, the novel will be dealt with primarily on those terms, although the oedipal pattern should also become apparent.

From first almost to last, Henchard is presented as the egotist who is unwilling or unable to make the necessary adaptation to the next stage of development. His first action clearly identifies him as an egotist. He tries to assert his identity by disengaging himself from his wife. Finding his wife a hindrance to his own advancement, he sells her and thereby abdicates his responsibility as her husband. Twenty years later he reappears at the height of his fortunes as mayor, remorseful of his former act of betrayal but revealing a similar tendency in selling the townspeople faulty grain.

As Susan and Elizabeth Jane stand outside the window watching him as leader of the party of dignitaries, they hear only his laughter, but the laughter is characteristic of the man: it is "not encouraging to strangers," for it reveals "a temperament which would have no pity for weakness but would yield ungrudging admiration for greatness and strength." The comment that follows clearly defines the man by his ethical values: "its producer's personal goodness, if he had any, would be of a very fitful cast — an occasional almost oppressive generosity rather than mild and constant kindness."[1]

Henchard's subsequent actions fulfill the prophecy of the laughter. He enthusiastically "adopts" Farfrae and only rather grudgingly accepts his returned wife and Elizabeth Jane. But his relationship with Farfrae, like his later relationship with Elizabeth Jane, follows the pattern he had established first with his wife and next with Lucetta. What begins as a friendly alliance quickly degenerates, and Henchard rejects Farfrae as he had rejected Susan and Lucetta. Because it is the most fully developed, Henchard's relationship with Farfrae is the most useful for illustrating how Hardy's ethical values are related to the psychological bases underlying them.

While Henchard had rejected Susan, his wife, as being altogether too passive, simple, and backward, and hence a hindrance to his own advancement, he embraces Farfrae as being more intelligent and forward-looking than himself. He sees Farfrae as being useful to him in his business, and as an extension of himself. For while he sees himself as having the necessary "strength and bustle" to establish a business, he sees the younger man as having the "judgment and knowledge" necessary to keep it going. He acknowledges himself to be a "rule o' thumb man," while Farfrae is "just the reverse" (p. 55). He embraces Farfrae as a younger brother, his poor opinion of the younger man's lack of "physical girth, strength and dash more than counter-balanced by the immense respect he had for his brains" (pp. 94-95). (In preferring Farfrae to Susan, Henchard reveals the same instinct for "more advanced" types that many of Hardy's earlier and later heroes and heroines reveal.)

At first the relationship between Henchard and Farfrae is friendly, their differences being regarded by Henchard as complementary rather than contradictory, and the relationship is almost that of father and son. This kind of complementarity between two generations is similar to that achieved in *Under the Greenwood Tree*. But in *The Mayor of Casterbridge* Hardy turns the complementarity into conflict by having Henchard resist both Farfrae's growth and his own concomitant decline. Unlike the men of the Mellstock quire, Henchard is unwilling to accept the rise of the young man's fortunes and the decline of his own. It is this resistance to change that causes his downfall. As he sees Farfrae rise in his employees' esteem, he himself becomes increasingly tyrannical and thereby renders Farfrae the "moral" master (p. 103). His rivalry in business extends itself into jealousy in love, and with the same results: Farfrae first wins Henchard's former mistress, Lucetta, and then his stepdaughter, Elizabeth Jane. Gradually, Henchard's impulsive generosity and hard-won self-discipline is worn away, and he reveals himself to be the same man that he had been from the first:

> Though under the long reign of self-control he had become Mayor and churchwarden and what not, there was still the same unruly volcanic stuff beneath the rind of Michael Henchard as when he had sold his wife at Weydon Fair. (p. 115)

In other words, Henchard's resistance to the external change that Farfrae represents ultimately reflects upon himself. His conflict with Farfrae exposes his essential nature. This inability to accept change is Henchard's flaw, as it was Knight's and Eustacia Vye's, and as it will be Angel Clare's and Sue's.

As Henchard loses more and more to Farfrae, his hatred grows until he tries to kill the younger man. His experiences do not change him, but rather actualize what had been only potential before – the destructive aspect of his egotism. He is "not only the same man but that man with his sinister qualities, formerly latent, quickened into life by its buffetings" (p. 236). In trying to destroy the man whom he had formerly seen as an extension of himself, he comes one step closer to his own self-destruction.

When Henchard shifts his paternal affections from Farfrae to Elizabeth Jane, who he thinks is his daughter only to learn immediately thereafter that she is not, he reacts in characteristic fashion: "Misery taught him nothing more than the defiant endurance of it." And rather than regarding such misery as the natural outcome of his previous actions, Henchard regards it as the result of "the scheme of some sinister intelligence bent on punishing him." Henchard is, "like all of his kind," superstitious (p. 128). That is, he is in the theological stage of development. Rather than regarding events as having "developed naturally," Henchard, like Troy and Eustacia Vye and then later Sue, reacts superstitiously, and his reactions are contrasted to the more objective reactions of the more advanced characters. Even at this point, however, the contrast between Henchard's readiness to adopt a complete stranger, Farfrae, and his unwillingness to accept Elizabeth Jane because she is not a blood relative is clear to the reader though obscure to Henchard himself.

In contrast to the increasingly clear destructiveness of Henchard's egotism, Farfrae remains stable. It is for this reason, perhaps, that he is less interesting to the reader. But he is clearly representative of the more advanced type. To the townspeople he is "like a poet of the new school who takes his contemporaries by storm; who is not really new, but is the first to articulate what all his listeners have felt, but dumbly, till then" (p. 60). He neither disregards the past nor is, like Henchard, trapped by guilt or remorse, but rather makes music out of his memories. Elizabeth Jane sees him as "no less thoughtful than cordial and impassioned," as one who, like herself, takes life seriously as a "tragical rather than a comical thing" but whose objectivity saves him from becoming a tragic hero himself (p. 61). The young stranger brings with him a way of restoring the faulty grain. Later, he avoids getting caught up in rivalry with Henchard. He does not seek vengeance after Lucetta's death, regarding its cause as neither sinister nor malicious, but as an "untoward accident" (p. 294). All of these characteristics are the marks of the more advanced altruist, and although Farfrae is not presented dramatically, his characteristics provide the perspective by which the reader sees Henchard.

Although Farfrae is a stable character, his counterpart, Elizabeth Jane, is not. Her development is the reverse of Henchard's. The continuity between Farfrae and Elizabeth Jane is established from the first. They appear in Casterbridge on the same day, and Farfrae is welcomed as friend and son by the same man from whom Elizabeth Jane is seeking protection and shelter. They are never, however, rivals, but rather complementary to each other. Farfrae is active, practical, and charming; Elizabeth Jane, like her mother, is passive and self-abnegating. Together they make up the amalgam of values associated with the altruist type. But while Farfrae remains as he is first presented, Elizabeth Jane becomes more clearly defined as a result of "life's buffetings." Her progress is the reverse of the direction of her father's.

From the first, Elizabeth Jane's chief characteristic, altruism, is in direct contrast to her father's egotism:

If there was one good thing more than another that characterized this single-hearted girl it was a willingness to sacrifice her personal comfort and dignity for the commonweal. (p. 51)

When she learns that she has lost not only her father's love but Farfrae's as well, she regards her position as commonplace, rather than tragic:

She had learnt her lesson of renunciation, and was as familiar with the wrench of each day's wishes as with the diurnal setting of the sun. If her earthly career had taught her few book philosophies, it had at least practised her well in this. Yet her experience had consisted less in a series of disappointments than in a series of substitutions. Continually it had happened that what she had desired had not been granted her, and that what had been granted her she had not desired. (p. 177)

Rather than succumbing to her fate or playing the role of tragic heroine, however, Elizabeth Jane persists, maintaining, like Harry Knight, a kind of mental and emotional objectivity about her situation. As a result, she regains both her father's love and Farfrae's, although not in the form she had once desired. In short, as a result of her altruistic characteristics, Elizabeth Jane succeeds where Henchard fails, and the novel traces the development of the altruist as it traces the decline of the egotist.

It must be granted, however, that Elizabeth Jane's virtues, like Farfrae's, pale before what can only be regarded as Henchard's vices. But Elizabeth Jane cannot be dismissed as an entirely superogatory and colorless character; like Cordelia in *King Lear,* her presence is crucial to the ultimate effect of the novel. For Elizabeth Jane serves not only to provide the necessary perspective for the portrayal of Henchard's character but also becomes an integral part of the tragic effect. It is Henchard's relationship with Elizabeth Jane, more than his relationship with his wife or Farfrae, that makes him a tragic character.

As we have already seen, Henchard's relationship with Farfrae merely exposes his latent self-destructiveness. His relationship with Farfrae makes him rather more rigid than he had been earlier. While it makes him more aware of his own limitations, it also makes him more stubborn in maintaining them. With Elizabeth Jane, however, his attitudes change. As his fortunes wane, his dependence on his stepdaughter grows. His need for her affection replaces the old vanities and ambitions. His "dependence on Elizabeth Jane's regard into which he had declined (or, in another sense, to which he had advanced), denaturalized him" (p. 298). In other words, Henchard's love for Elizabeth Jane is what ultimately humanizes him. It is this new feeling that makes his end seem tragic, for the new potential is not developed. When he returns to her wedding with the caged goldfinch, Henchard is far different from the vain and egocentric young man who had sold his wife at Weydon Fair. As he walks away for the last time, rejected because the change is not acknowledged, the situation is poignant because we are made aware of the possibilities for Henchard's future growth:

Externally there was nothing to hinder him making another start on the upward slope, and by his new lights achieving higher things than his soul in its half-formed state had been able to accomplish. (p. 313)

At the same time, the possibility for further growth is thwarted, for the "new lights" have come too late. Having directed his energies toward his material and social advancement, Henchard has little spirit left for further ethical growth.

Like Tess, Henchard, with little energy and less support, gives up the struggle and relapses into his former self, this time turning his guilt and remorse upon himself. He pronounces his own doom with the finality and harshness of the old dispensation.

As readers, however, we do not share Henchard's harsh judgment of himself, but rather we regard him with sympathetic understanding. Like Farfrae and Elizabeth Jane, we regard his end as both regrettable and inevitable. From a position of relative distance and safety we can admire the old values as ones we can no longer afford to embrace, and we view the end of the old tragic hero with a mixture of pity and relief. In terms of evolutionary ethics, this sympathetic response supersedes that of moral absolutism in the same way that altruism supersedes egotism. For Hardy, the only way out of the past is through a sympathetic awareness of it.[2]

NOTES

1. *The Mayor of Casterbridge* (New York: 1962), p. 40. All subsequent references are to this text.
2. Hardy's treatment of Henchard bears a striking resemblance to George Eliot's treatment of Bulstrode in *Middlemarch* as the evolution of Elizabeth Jane corresponds to the evolution of Dorothea Brooke. As Bernard Paris demonstrates, Eliot was working within a similar value system. See *Experiments in Life* (Detroit: 1965).

Twelve

THE EVOLUTION OF TESS

Just as Michael Henchard is Hardy's most powerful tragic male character, Tess is his most powerful female tragic character. No amount of explanation regarding Hardy's intellectual or artistic development can fully account for the creative energy and mastery that has created Tess. Like all masterpieces, Hardy's portrayal of Tess defies critical attempts to define, classify, or explain. And yet, while we cannot plumb the depths of the psychic process which creates such effects, we can attempt to delineate recognizable elements, if only to see how the artistry surpasses them.

Tess is at once the most natural and the most human of Hardy's creations. She is a living and palpitating being far different from Hardy's earlier stereotypic heroines. On the other hand, she embodies many of the values the earlier "types" had expressed, and part of her effectiveness as a character derives from the way in which Hardy successfully amalgamates characteristics he had previously dealt with separately. As Albert Guerard has noted, she possesses some earlier heroines' sensuousness and some of other earlier heroines' purity.[1] She is altruistic in the way Marty South is altruistic and yet almost as self-indulgent as Eustacia Vye and Suke Damson. Like Eustacia Vye and Michael Henchard, she is motivated by an "appetite for joy" that brings about her own destruction. Like them, her attempt to escape from the past fixes her more firmly in it. Like Elfride Swancourt, Eustacia Vye, and Grace Melbury, she is drawn to an intellectually and socially superior mate and is transformed by the process of interaction with her lover. This transformation in turn is reciprocal; for Tess, like Lady Constantine, ultimately becomes a maternal figure by which the lover must measure himself but from whom he is distanced forever.

THE EVOLUTION OF TESS

To describe Tess as "natural," as critics such as Roy Morrell and John Holloway do, is to reveal both her strength and her weaknesses.[2] For Hardy sees the natural world as somewhat circumscribed. While he views its processes as both necessary and inevitable, he also sees it as operating outside of the laws of cause and effect that it embodies. Nature, for Hardy, is both creative and destructive, the advance of one form of life being dependent on the death of another.[3] If one operates unconsciously on the natural level, one is either the destroyer or the destroyed, either the hero or the victim.

What happens in the case of Tess is that, beginning as a natural creature, full of the "appetite for joy that pervades all creation," she moves toward the human world that should discipline destructive instincts and protect the weak from the strong. She cannot, however, bridge the gap between the two worlds and is caught between them. Because of Angel's failure to respond, she struggles for awhile, but ultimately relapses into the natural world from which she has emerged. She becomes both victim and destroyer, a part of those very natural processes from which she has tried to emerge.

Perhaps more than any other character, Tess is defined by her place on the evolutionary scale. Each of her characteristics is described by its relationship to something in the past. Thus, for example, the young woman reveals her own history in her face: "Phases of her childhood lurked in her aspect, and despite her apparent womanliness, you could sometimes see her twelfth year in her cheeks or her ninth sparkling from her eyes; and even her fifth would flit over the curves of her mouth now and then."[4] She is first presented as just beginning her own individual history as a young woman: she is, at the beginning, "a mere vessel of emotion untinctured by experience." And yet she is also a part of the evolutionary scale, for she is distinctly related to the older generation from which she has sprung. The differences are at first most apparent. As Benjamin Sankey has noted, Tess's values are as sharply distinguished from those of her parents as from those which nature seems to endorse.[5]

> ... between the mother, with her fast-perishing lumber of superstitions, folk-lore, dialect, and orally transmitted ballads, and the daughter, with her trained National teachings and Standard knowledge under an infinitely Revised Code, there was a gap of two hundred years as ordinarily understood. (p. 34)

Despite her youth and rustic simplicity, Tess belongs as clearly to the present as her mother belongs to the past. "When they were together, the Jacobean and the Victorian ages were juxtaposed" (p. 34). Being "mentally older" than her mother, Tess regards Joan Durbeyfield's intelligence as "that of a happy child." When she tells her brother Abraham that "we live in a blighted world," she is not as fatalistic about it as her mother, for she is also aware that her parents' irresponsibility is at least partially responsible for their present condition. "She felt quite a Malthusian towards her mother for thoughtlessly giving her so many little sisters and brothers when it was such a trouble to provide for them." As a reaction to her mother, who is a "waiter on Providence," Tess has become "humanely beneficent toward the small ones" (p. 48). Sacrificing her own hopes of becoming a teacher, she becomes the physical and moral mainstay of her family and is looked upon as their best representative.

On the other hand, she still shares some of the traits of her parents, notably their natural passivity. For example, despite the fact that she thinks of Joan Durbeyfield as a child, she lets herself be persuaded to visit the D'Urbervilles and even to be dressed attractively. She gives her assent by "saying serenely, 'Do what you like with me, Mother'" (p. 66). She yields, after a small struggle, as passively to her mother (as she will later yield to Alec, to Angel, and to death) as Joan Durbeyfield yields to "nater." Unlike her mother's, however, Tess's passivity is mixed with a sense of responsibility. She goes to Chaseborough partly because she feels she must make reparation for having accidentally killed Prince, the family's only means of livelihoood. The death of Prince, on the other hand, is the result of Tess's falling into a "reverie" over the dreams of her parents. This reverie and the sleep that follows is the result of the same desire to escape from pain that impels her parents to visit Rolliver's Inn. At Rolliver's "troubles and realities took on a metaphysical impalpability"; one could "escape from the pressing concretions which chafed body and soul" (p. 33). Tess has been impelled to make the trip to market because her father has so successfully escaped from "the pressing concretions"; he is lying in a drunken stupor at home while Abraham and Tess sleep in the cart when the "accident" occurs.

It is this natural passivity, inherited from her parents, that is to be Tess's downfall. Each subsequent crisis is associated with Tess's sleeping. It is not without significance that her seduction occurs after she disdainfully leaves her drunken companions and falls asleep in the woods of The Chase. Later, on going to her room on the night of her confession to him, Angel finds her asleep, content to have at last shifted the burden of her secret to him. During his sleepwalking, she feigns death rather than awaken him, and she is asleep just before her apprehension at Stonehenge. Although she does not share her parents' predilection for liquor, and is, in fact, consciously abstemious, she can never overcome the impulse, at crucial times, to escape from the consciousness of pain.

Less passive than her father in attempting to achieve her goals, her attempts, like his, are never fully carried through. On the road to Talbothays, for example, she has fairly forgotten the past and is enjoying a sense of "high contentment" contemplating the future. At this point Hardy makes both the similarity and difference between father and daughter explicit: "Tess really wished to walk uprightly, while her father did nothing of the kind; but she resembled him in being content with immediate and small achievements..." (p. 120). It is this trait which prevents her from telling Angel of her past, from arousing him from his sleepwalking, and from completing her visit to the Clares. At the most crucial moments she becomes entirely passive. When, for example, Angel lays down the conditions for their separation, Hardy makes it clear that she could still have won him back and accounts for her total submission as stemming from that "pride ... which was perhaps a symptom of the reckless acquiescence in chance too apparent in the whole D'Urberville family..." (p. 271).

Beginning, then, as ethically and intellectually in advance of her parents but tied to them by the same natural passivity, Tess enters into life. For Tess, as for all of Hardy's characters who are capable of change, experience is a kind of refining or purifying process. Something is always lost, but something of greater value is gained. Experience is the means by which a character is moved from one phase of moral evolution to the next.

Although most readers cannot help but observe that Tess's "history" is described by "phases," what is not so clear is that these "phases" follow the pattern of ethical evolution. Hardy goes to great pains to describe Tess's changing attitudes toward nature, toward religion, toward morality and social convention, and toward herself. In the first and second phases Tess moves from the "theological" to the "metaphysical" stage of development. An understanding of her evolution through these stages is essential for an understanding of her later relationship with Angel. It is also important to see how great a role Hardy's system of ethical evolution plays in his treatment of this character, for it is with Tess's moral evolution that he is primarily concerned.

Tess's moral development begins with her family's economic and social exploitation of her. As a result of their dependence upon her, she assumes the responsibility of her family. Alec's sexual exploitation of her makes her more acutely aware of a sense of personal guilt. After the birth of her child, however, she becomes aware that such guilt has been induced by social convention and that "most of her misery had been generated by her conventional aspect and not by her innate sensations" (p. 107). As a result of this refining process, Tess loses the sense of a conventional social self and gains a sense of her own uniqueness very similar to that experienced by Cytherea Graye: "she was not an existence, an experience, a pas-

109

sion, a structure of sensations to anybody but herself" (p. 107).

Tess's attitude toward nature undergoes a similar change. When she returns to Marlott she no longer sees innocence and simplicity but a "terrible beauty" reflective of her own "fallen" state: "It was always beautiful from here; it was terribly beautiful to Tess to-day, for since her eyes last fell upon it she had learnt that the serpent hisses where the sweet birds sing, and her views of life had been totally changed for her by the lesson." Since "the world is only a psychological phenomenon," Tess sees a different Marlott, for she is "another girl than the simple one she had been at home" (p. 91). Later she seeks comfort in the natural world, and finds a correspondence between the wet day and her own grief. She believes that the wet day is "the expression of irremediable grief at her weakness in the mind of some vague ethical being whom she could not definitely classify as the God of her childhood and could not comprehend as any other" (p. 101). (The authorial comment makes it clear that this is still an anthropomorphic view and not a fully enlightened one.)

As Tess's experiences change her attitudes toward social conventions, moral responsibilities, and the natural world, they also change her attitudes toward God. She is appalled by the evangelical sign-painter's warning of damnation and tells him that his teachings are "horrible ... crushing ... killing!" She refuses "to believe that God said such things" (p. 97). Later, when she baptizes and buries her child she reasons that "if Providence would not ratify such an act of approximation she did not value the kind of heaven lost by the irregularity" (p. 111).

The "second phase" of Tess's development is fully completed after the death of her child. The child's death makes her own death real to her. Realizing the insignificance of her own life in the vast scheme of things, she determines to make what she can of it. Before leaving Marlott, she is resolved on one point: "there should be no more D'Urberville air-castles in the dreams and deeds of her hew life. She would be the dairymaid Tess and nothing more" (p. 115).

The novelist concludes this phase of Tess's development with the following remarks:

Almost at a leap, Tess thus changed from simple girl to complex woman. Symbols of reflectiveness passed into her face and a note of tragedy at times into her voice. Her eyes grew larger and more eloquent. She became what would have been called a fine creature; her aspect was fair and arresting; her soul that of a woman whom the turbulent experience of the last year or two had quite failed to demoralize. But for the world's opinion those experiences would have been simply a liberal education. (pp. 114-115)

But while one stage is concluded, it is also clear that another is beginning. "Mentally and sentimentally" Tess "has not finished growing." Because she is still young "it was impossible that any event should have left upon her an impression that was not in time capable of transmutation" (p. 120).

Although Tess leaves Marlott for the second time with renewed hope and a more liberal education, she goes forward more vulnerable than she had gone at first. For her changed attitudes deprive her of her former strength. Less certain than before of the existence of a Divine Providence, more aware of the destructiveness of the natural world, skeptical of social conventions, rejecting the attitudes and values of her parents, she has little to support her but her own sense of uniqueness and her determination to be "the dairymaid Tess and nothing more." Believing that she can begin anew, she is unaware of the freight of the past that she is carrying with her. It is this unawareness, perhaps, that makes her so vulnerable to Angel.

Having rejected the Old Testament God and hardly sure of the New, having rejected her father's pride and bereft of his protection, and having been repelled by the sexually exploitative Alec, she is unaware of the strong need to find a substitute for what she has rejected. Unable to find an adequate response for her needs either in the natural or religious or social world, she is ready to focus on one individual who will satisfy all of these needs together. By the time Tess arrives at Talbothays, she has, in terms of ethical evolution, left the theological stage of development and moved into the metaphysical. Through her experience she has reached the same level that Angel has achieved through his more formal education. Having by different avenues passed beyond the conventional belief in God and in social conventions, they tend to form idealizations and abstractions based upon their moral perceptions. In her first conversations with Angel, Tess indicates her contemporaneity: "she was expressing in her own nature phrases ... feelings which might almost have been called those of the age: the ache of modernism" (p. 140).

In falling in love with Angel, Tess falls in love with an abstraction rather than the man. He is a projection of her own needs. She begins by respecting him for what both her father and Alec had lacked: "a self-controlling sense of duty ... a quality she had never expected to find in one of the opposite sex" (p. 157). She regards him as "an intelligence rather than as a man" (p. 141), and he becomes "godlike in her eyes" (p. 199).

Tess's idealization of Clare is clearest in the following passage, which describes her state of mind during the engagement:

There was hardly a touch of earth in her love for Clare. To her sublime trustfulness he was all that goodness could be — knew all that a guide, philosopher, and friend should know. She thought every line in the contour of his person the perfection of masculine beauty, his soul the soul of a saint, his intellect that of a seer. The wisdom of her love for him, as love, sustained her dignity; she seemed to be wearing a crown. The compassion of his love for her, as she saw it, made her lift up her heart to him in devotion.... [She looked at him] as if she saw something immortal before her. (pp. 209-210)

What this passage reveals is that Tess's love for Clare is a reflection of her own nature, a projection of her need for an adequate kind of response to her own spiritual needs. As J. Hillis Miller points out, for Tess, as for Angel, love is, among other things, a covert religious quest.[6]

But Hardy is quick to point out that while beautiful, this metaphysical kind of love is wrong-headed. Shifting from Tess's point of view, the novelist comments that "Angel Clare was far from all she thought him in this respect; absurdly far, indeed...." Furthermore, he accounts for Tess's "excess of honour for Clare" by her "slight experiences" and "her indignation against the male sex" (p. 210). In other words, what Tess is doing in spiritualizing Clare is removing him from association with the males she has known in the past, just as she has removed herself. As she moves toward Clare in space, she would move outside of time.

Tess's desire for spiritual transcendence (a refined form of her parents' desire for social transcendence) had been hinted at earlier. She had talked of her own ability to project her soul out of her body by lying on the grass at night and looking at some bright star: "by fixing your mind on it, you will find that you are hundreds and hundreds o' miles away from your body, which you don't seem to want at all" (p. 136). Even earlier, she had loved the church music of Langdon, which, by its "god-like power" had led her "through sequences of emotion." Now, the sound of Angel's harp creates a similar hypnotic state:

Tess was conscious of neither time nor space. The exaltation which she had described as being producible at will by gazing at a star came now without any determination of hers; she undulated upon the thin notes of the harp, and their harmonies passed like breezes through her, bringing tears into her eyes. (p. 139)

She experiences a sense of synesthesia in which the pollen "seemed to be his notes made visible" and the "waves of colour mixed with the waves of sound."

Having listened for awhile "like a fascinated bird that could not leave the spot," she moves toward Angel, passing almost unconsciously through the rank grass and foul-smelling weeds as if she were moving backward through the fallen world toward an ideal one. Oblivious of "gathering cuckoo-spittle on her skirts," and of the thistle-milk and slug slime making "sticky blights" and "madder stains upon her skin," she moves toward Clare as she would move outside of time and space (p. 139). The same transcendent experience is repeated during their dawn meetings and their engagement period.

Freedom and happiness, union and ecstasy: these are the goals toward which Tess's experiences and her own natural impulse for joy have led her. And because we have followed this pilgrim's progress, we feel that Tess deserves such a reward.

On the other hand, we are made aware that the premise upon which her happiness is based is false; there is no way outside of time, no movement backward to Eden or above to the stars, and no one human being who can become the God for the mystical ecstasies of a modern Saint Theresa.[7]

For simultaneously with Tess's sense of escape the novelist presents a corresponding sense of entrapment. The passage in the garden suggests the entrapment. The natural world prevents Tess's passage to Eden and Angel's music traps her "like a bird." And as he describes her state of mind during the engagement, Hardy increasingly emphasizes Tess's loss of a sense of identity, her utter passivity, and a sense of retrogression:

Tess was now carried along upon the wings of the hours, without the sense of a will. The word had been given, the number of the day written down. Her naturally bright intelligence had begun to admit the fatalistic convictions common to field-folk and those who associate more extensively with natural phenomena than with their fellow-creatures; and she accordingly drifted into that passive responsiveness to all things her lover suggested, characteristic of the frame of mind. (p. 220)

Like Grace Melbury, Tess is haunted by the sense of time catching up with her as she approaches her wedding day:

Her affection for him was now the breath and life of Tess's being; it enveloped her as a photosphere, irradiated her into forgetfulness of her past sorrows, keeping back the gloomy spectres that would persist in their attempts to touch her — doubt, fear, moodiness, care, shame. She knew that they were waiting like wolves just outside the circumscribing light, but she had long spells of power to keep them in hungry subjection there. (p. 212)

As the wedding day approaches, Tess "walk[s] in brightness, but she [knows] that in the background those shapes of darkness were always spread" (p. 212).

Before the wedding ceremony, Tess attempts to pray, but God and Angel are so confused in her mind that "it was her husband who really had her supplication." She begins to fear her idealization as idolatry, and the idolatry itself as "ill-omened" (p. 232). She soon finds her fears more than justified; for having abandoned her own identity and transferred her hopes and fears as well as her responsibilities to Angel, she has placed herself entirely in his power.

The absolute power that Angel exercises over Tess is thus what she herself has given him. His response to her story is the reverse of what she had hoped for, the exaggeration of what she had feared. Like a Pauline God he pronounces his judgment on her. She is appalled by his coldness and his "grotesque laughter" "quite kills her" (p. 245). But because she still believes so strongly in his superiority, she submits to his domination completely, and willingly accepts the death he seems to want to inflict on her.

"No, I shan't do anything unless you order me to; and if you go away from me I shall not follow 'ee; and if you never speak to me any more I shall not ask why unless you tell me I may."

"And if I do order you to do anything?"

"I will obey you like your wretched slave even if it is to lie down and die." (p. 247)

And when Angel acts out his death wish in the sleepwalking scene, Tess gladly feigns death; "so easefully had she delivered her whole being up to him that it pleased her to think he was regarding her as his absolute possession, to dispose of as he should choose" (p. 265).

Tess's absolute passivity and self-abnegation seem to Angel at odds with the "past mood of self-preservation" that had previously prevented her from telling him her history. But from Tess's point of view the two impulses had been the same: her idealization of Angel had been a means of obliterating her past and her former self; her desire for transcendence had been an attempt to escape from the consciousness of pain. Such motives are translated into a love for Angel, and now through that love and her desire for transcendence is revealed a desire for death.

Though Hardy had earlier hinted at the dead end toward which idealistic love leads, he had never before so clearly related it to a death wish. He had come close to suggesting it in his treatment of Lady Constantine's self-immolation and Giles Winterbourne's altruism, but he had not made the point as clearly as he does here.

With the revelation of her story to Angel, the fourth phase of Tess's development ends. Having carried her metaphysical love to its farthest extreme, Tess has two alternatives left: to die or to change. Unlike the earlier romantic altruists, Tess momentarily chooses to live, and the long course of her devolution after her disillusionment with Angel is perhaps the most interesting in terms of the way Hardy relates the psychological development of his character with his ethical values, for from the moment of her disillusionment with Angel, Tess undergoes a subtle change. Moving away from the metaphysical stage of romantic illusion, she gropes toward a new series of responses and attitudes. The manner in which she moves is hesitant and groping, her failure more moving and psychologically convincing than her earlier successful passage from the theological to the metaphysical stage.

As in the earlier novels, as well as in Tess's earlier experience, a near brush with death changes Tess's direction. Just as the death of her child had changed Tess's attitude toward her own position in life, so Angel's near brush with death changes her once again. Tempted during the sleepwalking scene to "precipitate them both into the gulf," she is restrained by the idea that she has "no right to tamper with *his* life" (p. 266). From this moment on, she sees herself no longer as united with Angel but as distinct from him. She begins to see him more critically, as flawed rather than godlike. She is "appalled by the determination revealed in the depths of this gentle being she had married – the will to subdue the grosser to the subtler emotion, the substance to the conception, the flesh to the spirit." She herself had shared these same impulses; now being victimized by them, she feels the full force of their destructiveness. "Propensities, tendencies, habits, were as dead leaves upon the tyrannous wind of his ascendency" (p. 263). Although she agrees to the conditions he lays down, "because you know best what my punishment ought to be," she qualifies her acceptance by adding, "only—only—don't make it more than I can bear" (p. 271).

Angel's actions show him to be anything but the "chivalrous," "protective," and "compassionate" figure she had imagined him to be; she sees him now as "cold," "cruel," and "tyrannical." However, unlike Angel, who seems to cease loving once his illusions are destroyed, Tess's devotion and loyalty are strengthened. Just as her experience with Alec had transformed her religious and social attitudes, so her experience with Angel transforms and "purifies" her love. She becomes the ideal type, the "Apostolic Charity."

The firmness of her devotion to him was indeed almost pitiful; quicktempered as she naturally was, nothing he could say made her unseemly: she sought not her own, was not provoked, thought no evil of his treat-

115

ment of her. She might just now have been Apostolic Charity herself returned to a self-seeking modern world. (p. 259)

It is a somewhat different Tess that walks toward Flintcomb-Ash from the one that had walked toward Talbothays. No longer impelled by "an appetite for joy," she is rather sustained by a sense of pity for her fellow-sufferers. The contrast between the plight of the wounded birds and her own condition changes her perspective. Just as concern for her child had strengthened her independence from social convention and her concern for Angel's life prevented her from suicide, so now "the impulse of a soul who could feel for kindred sufferers as much as for herself" frees her from self-pity. Both she and the birds had been "mangled" by human cruelty, but while the birds are helpless, she is not. "I be not mangled, and I be not bleeding, and I have two hands to feed and clothe me." She realizes again, as she had realized after her experience with Alec, that "her gloom of the night [was] based on nothing more tangible than a sense of condemnation under an arbitrary law of society which had no foundation in nature" (p. 297).

With this realization, she continues her journey to Flintcomb-Ash. The difference between this journey and her early one to Talbothays is that this one is marked by her reduced hope for future happiness and her increased fortitude. Now, rather than attempting to forget the past, her memory of Angel and hope for his return sustain her. She disguises herself not to obliterate the past but to protect it. In terms of ethical evolution, she has clearly advanced beyond her former state. Willing to accept her past and giving up her idealization of Angel as she had earlier renounced her "D'Urberville air-castles," she moves forward toward the winter landscape of Flintcomb-Ash purified of her former illusions and willing to persevere in the world of space and time.

But Tess's progress from this point on is clearly downhill. Her dependence upon Angel is too strong to be broken. With nothing to replace her faith in him, she loses her way. The passage describing the early part of her journey to Flintcomb-Ash foreshadows the ultimate direction Tess will take:

... there was something of the habitude of the wild animal in the unreflecting instinct with which she rambled on — disconnecting herself by littles from her eventful past at every step, obliterating her identity, giving no thought to accidents or contingencies which might make a quick discovery of her whereabouts by others of importance to her own happiness. (p. 293)

Although Tess distinguishes her own human suffering from that of the wounded birds, her attempts to assert herself become increasingly weak. Focusing her faith, hope, and charity on a single man, Angel, she can find no direction for herself and merely marks time at Flintcomb-Ash. Her patience is "a blending of moral courage and physical timidity" (p. 303). Instead of taking significant action herself she relies on Angel, believing that "the magnanimity which she persisted in reckoning the chief ingredient in [his] character would lead him to rejoin her" (p. 305).

After learning of his offer to take Izz to Brazil, she becomes aware of the dangers of this passivity: "I have been very wrong and neglectful in leaving everything to be done by him!" (p. 312) She resolves to write, but quickly loses heart, contenting herself with wearing her wedding ring on her finger for the night. This symbolic act is enough to assure her that she is still his wife. Even her efforts the next day to visit his parents fail: "she went away without knowing that the greatest misfortune of her life was this feminine loss of courage at the last and critical moment" (p. 319). At Flintcomb-Ash, she keeps up her spirits, not as Marian does and her father would have done, by drinking, but in a more advanced, but equally ineffectual way — by practicing Angel's favorite songs. Tess is most aware of the uncertainty of the future on which her singing is based, and Hardy makes her position as pitiful in its helpless passivity as the dying birds' had been to her:

It would have melted the heart of a stone to hear her singing these ditties whenever she worked apart from the rest of the girls in this cold dry time; the tears running down her cheeks all the while at the thought that perhaps he would not, after all, come to hear her, and the simple silly words of the songs resounding in painful mockery of the aching heart of the singer. (p. 363)

Because Tess has placed all her hopes for the future in Angel, she becomes increasingly vulnerable. The returned Alec soon discovers her vulnerability and uses it. Alec observes that Tess's mind is "enslaved" to Angel's, and comments that her "simplicity of faith" could hardly have been deserved by the most perfect man, "much less her husband" (p. 340).

Tess proves her dependence on Angel by writing him as if he were the God of the New Testament, asking for kindness rather than justice, and reminding him of her fidelity, her beauty, and her need. When her prayers go unanswered, she at last rebels, saying that she can "never, never forgive him" and that she will "try to forget him" (pp. 376-377).

Having rejected Angel altogether, Tess tries to take the next step without him. No longer enslaved by illusions about Divine Providence or an idealized Angel Clare, she is ready to view herself and reality "objectively" and to concern herself only with the needs of her younger sisters and brothers without regard to her own personal happiness. Recognizing

117

that she cannot "leave them to Providence and their future kingdom," she decides "to be their Providence," assuming the role she had projected onto Angel.

Such a determination to move into the sociological stage is, however, spurious, for Tess is incapable of going forward alone. While intellectually she sees the direction she should take, emotionally she is incapable of taking it; for she is, by this time, both emotionally and physically spent. Finding no adequate response for her needs either in heaven or in earth, in the social world or the natural one, she lacks the support necessary for going on. So utterly have her faith and hope been focused upon Angel that when she rejects him and resolves to forget him, she ceases emotionally to live.

Of all the stages of ethical evolution that Hardy describes, this stage toward which Tess gropes is, perhaps, portrayed the most convincingly. It will become the ending toward which his next novel, *Jude the Obscure*, will focus, and it will also be expressed in his lyric poetry. The recognition of the necessity for moving beyond theological attitudes and metaphysical responses toward a more conscious awareness of the objective reality and specificity of the "other," is really at the heart of Hardy's evolutionary theory. But what this novel reveals is that while such a necessity can be grasped intellectually it cannot be achieved by the intellect alone. Nor can it be achieved by one individual, for the "altruist" or "sociological stage" is one of mutuality and interdependence: only another human being can fill the needs no longer fulfilled by a belief in Divine Providence or the beneficence of nature. What Hardy is best at doing he does here with Tess: he creates the sense of a universe bereft of meaning and the human yearning for a response that is not forthcoming.

Tess's rejection of Angel and her return to Alec mark the end of her period of mental and emotional stagnation and the beginning of her moral relapse and spiritual death. Her concern for the children is in terms only of their material future, and even this concern is passive rather than active; for no sooner does she take the role of Providence on herself than she passes it on to Alec. Clearly no spiritual or moral guide, Alec is providential only in the economic sense. By forgetting Angel and attempting to dismiss this part of her past, Tess begins to think only in material terms. For this reason she becomes increasingly persuaded that Alec is her only real husband, since he has been that in the physical sense.

The return of Angel merely emphasizes Tess's former spiritual stagnation, for her responses to Angel recapitulate her responses in the past. She experiences one last burst of energy, one last "impulse for joy." In returning to Angel she would, as she had done the first time, obliterate her past; and in the very attempt, she traps herself more firmly into it.

THE EVOLUTION OF TESS

What is apparent during the last episode is that all that is left of the former Tess is a kind of distillation. What is left is her love of Angel and her desire to be isolated with him in a world outside of time and space. Although each of her earlier experiences had advanced her emotional, spiritual, and moral development, the prolonged absence of Angel during her stay at Flintcomb-Ash had arrested it. By the time he returns, she is no longer capable of further progress. All she can do is enact the fruition of her past hopes.[8] Just as, during the courting, Tess had wished that time would stop, that "it would always be summer and autumn with Angel courting her," now she would remain at Bramston Manor, although she knows that to remain there is to invite death. Now she asks, "Why should we put an end to all that's sweet and lovely? All is trouble outside there; inside here content" (p. 411). At Stonehenge they are seemingly even more removed from space and time, and Tess wishes "there were no folk in the world but we two" (p. 415). The kind of love she feels toward Angel, like that of Giles Winterbourne, Marty South, or Diggory Venn, excludes concern for all others. At last Tess recognizes that the kind of happiness which her love of Angel had promised "could not have lasted." To expect it to last is to expect, as Angel had done, more than is possible in either nature or man. It is "too much." Recognizing that it is incompatible with the world of time and change, in a last desperate effort to preserve it, she hopes for its perpetuation in a future life. Angel's silence destroys even that hope.

Even within this brief idyll, however, the sense of freedom and happiness is not complete, for Tess can no more shorten the psychological distance between herself and Angel than she can escape from the pursuing police. For while she has been stagnating and now reverts to utter reliance upon Angel's former opinions, Angel has been moving forward and growing beyond them. This time it is Angel who is appalled by the destructiveness of this kind of exclusive love. He notes with horror that "her affection for him had apparently extinguished her moral sense altogether" (p. 406). Tess has become the mirror of his former self, yet his horror at her state indicates how far he himself has moved away from it.

Tess soon recognizes the difference between what she had been and what she has become: "How wickedly mad I was! Yet formerly I never could bear to hurt a fly or a worm and the sight of a bird in a cage used often to make me cry" (pp. 411-412). The return of her former feelings and attitudes toward Angel has extinguished her natural sympathy altogether. She has become less than what she had been formerly. With this recognition of the difference between her present state and her former self, Tess also becomes aware that, for all his new-found tolerance, Angel cannot condone the murder. She asserts that she does not wish to live to be again despised by him and deliberately delays their escape, knowing that such delays only increase the chances of her arrest. And although Angel denies her assertion that he will despise her, his willingness to accept her delays implies that he, too, accepts the fact that she has removed herself from any future life.

Tess comes at last to recognize that it is impossible to find "some nook which has no memories," and that the attempt to find such a nook is an attempt to escape from life itself.

With the recognition that the kind of happiness she had wanted for herself and Angel is not compatible with the world of time and change, Tess is left with the only alternative the ethical evolutionists considered available. She renounces her hope for happiness and extends her concern beyond herself. She asks Angel to care for her younger sister, Liza Lu. This kind of concern for others had been manifested earlier; it had appeared each time she had given up her own hopes for happiness. It had receded, however, each time the opportunity for happiness offered itself. Now she urges Angel to "train and teach Liza Lu" and to "bring her up for your own self." But the union she now urges is far different from the one she had sought for herself: it will be both better and worse than what she had desired. It will be better because "Liza Lu has all the best of me without the bad of me," and because Angel is now the "compassionate, chivalrous, protective" person she had earlier imagined him to be. It will be worse because the new union will not be an escape from time into a transcendent world of unalloyed happiness. It will be one brought about by a sense of shared loss, sustained not by joy but by a sense of sacrifice, by the memory of Tess's painful experience. It is the kind of future Tess herself is unwilling to face. If she cannot have happiness, she prefers to escape from life altogether.

In the last scene Tess is absent, but her memory is indelible in the minds of Angel and Liza Lu. They are united by the memory of Tess, whose "appetite for joy" had sustained, propelled, and finally destroyed her. Their state represents the final transformation which Tess had foreseen, but which she herself had been unable to undergo.

THE EVOLUTION OF TESS

NOTES

1. "The Women of the Novels," in *Hardy,* ed. Guerard (New Jersey: 1963), pp. 65, 67.
2. Morrell, *The Will and the Way,* p. 89, and John Holloway, "Hardy's Major Fiction," *Hardy,* p. 61.
3. F.B. Pinion, *A Hardy Companion* (New York: 1968).
4. *Tess of the D'Urbervilles* (New York: 1964), p. 26.
5. Sankey, "Character Portrayal in Tess," in *Hardy,* p. 97.
6. *Thomas Hardy: Distance and Desire* (Massachusetts: 1970), pp. 183-184.
7. Tess's name may have been suggested by George Eliot's remarks on later-born Theresas, who "with dim lights and tangled circumstance," try "to shape their thought and deed in noble agreement," but who are "helped by no coherent social faith and order which could perform the function of knowledge for the ardently willing soul." The conclusion of her introduction to *Middlemarch* is strongly suggestive of the plight of Hardy's Tess: "Here and there is born a Saint Theresa, foundress of nothing, whose loving heartbeats and sobs after unattained goodness tremble off and are despised among hindrances, instead of centring on some long-recognisable deed" (pp. 1, 2). Of course, it will be remembered that in Crashaw and Bernini, Saint Theresa's heart is pierced by the arrow of an angel.
8. Holloway describes this episode as "partly a psychological fugue, partly a kind of total recall, partly both" (*Hardy,* pp. 61, 62). And Arnold Kettle notes the "unreality" of the scene while also noting that "it *is* a fulfillment, a harmony, a completion of what Tess has been seeking" ("Introduction to *Tess of the D'Urbervilles,*" *Twentieth Century Interpretations of Tess,* ed. A.J. LaValley [New Jersey: 1969], p. 23).

121

Thirteen

TESS AS AGENT OF CHANGE

By tracing the trajectory of Tess's "history" along its evolutionary path, we have observed how she evolves and at what point her capacity for further change is arrested. But it is important to note that while Tess's actions and responses are at the central core of the novel, she is made to function in another way, a way which allows us to see the central core in another dimension and from another perspective.

As we have already seen, it is possible to see Tess as both active and passive, as both agent and victim of change. In the first half of the novel, she is more active, and, though victimized by Alec and exploited by her parents, capable of "rallying" and, indeed, moving beyond them. In the second half of the novel, she becomes more passive and consequently becomes more and more a victim. But like Eustacia Vye, who also occupies a point midway between past and present: as Tess loses her own capacity for change, she becomes an agent of change in others. Her effect is either to bring others closer to her own point of development or to stimulate them to transcend it. Thus, for example, she dispels the "natural" jealousy of the dairymaids and, temporarily at least, exerts such a powerful influence over them that they transcend their normal level. The influence she exercises over Izz, for example, is "of a warmth and strength quite unusual, curiously overpowering the less worthy feminine feelings of spite and rivalry" (p. 314). It is this "fascination over her rougher nature by Tess's character" that "impels" Izz "to grace" — that is, she admits to Angel that her love for him could never exceed Tess's, and thus sacrifices her chances of going with him to Brazil (p. 288).

Similarly, Tess has a positive effect on Alec D'Urberville. Although

TESS AS AGENT OF CHANGE

much has been made of Alec's effect on Tess, little attention has been paid to Tess's reciprocal effect on Alec. Through Tess, Alec undergoes an evolution of sorts, minor to be sure, but nonetheless positive. And because Alec's evolution serves as both echo and contrast to Tess's, it deserves some analysis.

Alec's change begins when Tess leaves him to return to Marlott. Although still aware of the social superiority of his position, he is struck by Tess's moral superiority and volunteers help if she needs it. Later, when he attempts to transcend his earlier values through religion, Tess "cures" him of his religious fanaticism by showing its hypocrisy:

"You and those like you take your fill of pleasure on earth by making the life of such as me bitter and black with sorrow; and then it is a fine thing, when you have had enough of that, to think of securing your pleasure in Heaven by becoming converted. Out upon such — I don't believe in you — I hate it!" (p. 328)

She makes Alec realize that what he has considered progress is no advance at all but merely a repetition of his former beliefs and attitudes in a more sophisticated form. (What Tess does *not* see is that her faith in Angel and her own hopes for absolute freedom in the future, either on earth or in Heaven, are equally self-delusive.) Tess tries to explain to Alec the superiority of her own values over his. Tess's values are closer to Hardy's but without the perspective that accompanies them: "Why you can have the religion of loving-kindness and purity, at least, if you can't have — what do you call it — dogma" (p. 349).

Alec's response to this assertion raises the typical question that the Victorian agnostics were forced to answer: "Hang it, I am not going to feel responsible for my deeds and passions if there's nobody to feel responsible [blame] to!" The answer that an enlightened ethical evolutionist such as Comte, Mill, or Hardy would give is, of course, that accountability to God is to be replaced by accountability to others, and the sense of the interdependence of the parts to the whole is superior to dependence upon a transcendent authority figure. But Tess cannot provide this explanation because her vision does not extend that far. Both in feelings and perspective she is midway between the "theological" and the "sociological" stage. She cannot "get on," for she has merely transferred her dependence on Providence to dependence on an idealized Angel, and, as Alec recognizes, her mind is "enslaved" to his.

However, despite Tess's inability to convince Alec by a full exposition of the tenets of ethical evolution, she does succeed in "chilling" his religious enthusiasm "to stagnation." And while she cannot convince Alec

123

abstractly that it is possible to be responsible without a Divine Taskmaster, her very situation makes him aware of his more limited responsibilities to her. Alec's second proposal is quite different in attitude and tone from his earlier one in the woods of The Chase. Since the difference has been overlooked by readers who see Alec as the unregenerate stage villain, it deserves quotation:

"If I cannot legitimize our former relations at least I can assist you. And I will do it with much more regard for your feelings than I formerly showed. My religious mania, or whatever it was, is over. But I retain a little good nature; I hope I do. Now, Tess, by all that's tender and strong between man and woman, trust me! I have enough and more than enough to put you out of anxiety, both for yourself and your parents and sisters. I can make them all comfortable if you will only show confidence in me." (p. 355)

He persists in his offers both at Kingsbere and at Marlott. And while we see that he can offer no more than material security, we can also see that there is some justice to his argument that he is more altruistic at this point than Angel: "I, at any rate, try to help you out of trouble, but he does not, bless his invisible face" (p. 350). The last section of the novel gives evidence that he has, indeed, kept his promise. When Angel returns he finds Joan Durbeyfield comfortably housed and Tess well clothed and cared for at the fashionable resort at Sandbourne. Within the limits of his capacity (which are, admittedly, narrow) and as a result of his experience with Tess, Alec comes to the point where "duty and desire run hand in hand" (p. 334).

Alec's evolution is interesting in that it serves as a minor echo of Tess's. Having begun further back along the ethical spectrum, Alec has advanced from egotism of the most primitive sort: he had been almost entirely self-indulgent. Like Tess, he is attracted to a being on a higher level of development. Again like Tess, he first attempts to escape from the past and undergoes, like her, a kind of religious conversion (though it is more obviously false) and is finally led to a greater sense of responsibility. He is not, however, capable of moving to the "metaphysical" stage of development, either emotionally or intellectually. He is incapable of envisioning the kind of transcendence both Angel and Tess yearn for. And it is for this reason that he, like Tess, is doomed to extinction by the very being who had brought him to this point.

Tess's positive effect on Alec is important for two reasons: in terms of the plot it makes their reunion psychologically more valid; and in terms of the structure, it allows us to see Alec's evolution and stasis as a prefiguration of Tess's. The narrowness of Alec's perspective emphasizes the scope of Tess's. At the same time its point of arrest underscores Tess's inability to move forward. Alec's fixation on Tess makes us more aware of the destructive aspects of Tess's fixation on Angel. Thus, we are made to see Alec as complementary rather than contradictory to Tess. Although the characters see each other as antagonists, we, as readers, see them as interrelated and complementary parts of a hierarchical continuum; that is, we see them from what Hardy would call the "altruist" perspective.

The briefly sketched scene at Sandbourne after Angel's return brings the two into closer conflict but also reveals their complementarity. The scene reverses their first encounter: Alec is now the victim and Tess the aggressor. It also recapitulates the central episode — the scene between Tess and Angel on their marriage night. This time, Tess takes the role of the avenging Angel, and Alec takes Tess's former place as victim. Just as Angel had earlier turned against her, now Tess turns against Alec, accusing him of having used deliberate deception to win her. She blames Alec for having betrayed her by deliberately lying about Angel's return, just as Angel had accused Tess of deliberately lying by witholding from him the story of her relationship with Alec. And just as Tess had not been as guilty as Angel had accused her of being, so Alec is not as much to blame as Tess claims. For Alec's judgment of Angel is based on his own limited perspective: he simply cannot believe in the ideal creature Tess remembers; and since Tess's Angel *is* an illusion, Alec is not as wrong as Tess makes him out to be. Tess knows this, for she has already been disillusioned by Angel. What she cannot bear is to see her own disillusionment mirrored and caricatured in another. And so, like Angel, she insists on her own righteousness and shifts the guilt to Alec. She destroys Alec for the same reason Angel had wished to destroy her: he is the embodiment of a disillusionment she prefers to reject, an obstacle in the way of her approach to the Ideal. Thus Alec, who has been brought close to Tess by her positive effect on him, becomes the victim of her illusions, just as she had been the victim of Angel's.

Her murder of Alec is both the immediate cause and a psychological foreshadowing of Tess's own death, and for the same reasons. For while both had moved forward, neither moves far enough. Tess can no more move out of the "metaphysical" stage than Alec can move into it. Alec's inability to conceive of the old Angel is matched by Tess's inability to conceive of the new one. And just as Alec was unable to see Tess as an objective being with a future beyond his own limited perspective, so Tess cannot see Angel as anything more than what she had known him to be earlier. In killing Alec, Tess attempts to obliterate her past; in going to Angel, she believes herself freed from it. She is not aware, however, that her view of Angel is also a part of the past; he is neither the Angel of Talbothays nor the absent Angel whom both she and Alec had judged so severely. For while her progress, like Alec's, had been arrested during his absence, Angel's has continued, and he is as far in advance of her as she had been of Alec. Her influence, while it has brought Alec closer to her, has increased the psychological distance between herself and Angel.

Fourteen

ANGEL CLARE

Most readers see Angel Clare as being placed as far ahead of Tess as Alec is behind her, for Angel Clare is presented as the "intellectual" who holds "modern views." And since we believe that the intellectual stage is the highest level of achievement, we cannot understand why Hardy makes his hero so unattractive. For Angel has neither the color nor vigor of Alec nor the stature or appeal of Tess. We ask ourselves, then, if Angel is more advanced than Tess, why isn't he also superior? Generally, we answer this question by saying that Angel, as a character, is an artistic failure because of Hardy's own lack of conviction, his skepticism about intellectual progress, and his preference for simpler ways of seeing and feeling. There is, however, another answer to this question, one which allows us to better understand our reaction as readers. Rather than projecting the conflicts we feel onto the novelist, we can examine the difference between our own assumptions and those of the novelist. If we do so, we will find that it is the conflict between these two value systems that has created our problem.

While we assume that the intellectual stage comes at the end of human development, we must remember that for Hardy, as for the other ethical evolutionists, the intellectual stage was a median one. It was preceded by the theological or mythic stage and followed by the sociological one. It was this last stage where the egotism of the earlier stages was finally overcome and the latent altruistic potential fully developed. This is the hierarchy that Hardy endorses when he says that the "higher passions" must be "ranked above the inferior," the "intellectual above the animal," and that above the intellectual were the "moral tendencies."

As we have already seen, these "moral tendencies" involve both seeing and feeling, for "altruism," in Hardy's sense, is more than a synonym for self-sacrifice or charity. It is a totally different kind of emotional and intellectual response from the earlier egotistic modes of seeing and feeling. It is a way of viewing life from a perspective outside the self, a way of standing back and seeing life as if one were at the end of it rather than standing in the center. From the end of the spectrum, all positions are relative, including one's own. From this perspective, the sense of self is diminished, the sense of pattern and interrelatedness strengthened. The fact that most readers recognize this distancing, pattern, and broad sympathy as characteristic of Hardy is not accidental, for it is this attitude that he valued most highly, and not simply as a way of resolving his own inner conflicts or even of achieving aesthetic effects. To Hardy, this way of seeing and feeling was the ethical one, characteristic of the highest stage of human consciousness. And it was toward this view that he sought to lead the reader.

An awareness of Hardy's perspective allows us to better understand his characterization of Angel Clare. If we read the text carefully, we can see what great pains Hardy took to portray him, to indicate the limitations of the "intellectual," and to trace his development.

The pattern Hardy established in *Tess* is similar to that which he had created in *Return of the Native*. The earlier novel had begun by focusing on Eustacia Vye and then, gradually, as Eustacia Vye's progress slows, by shifting the focus to Clym. Indeed, Eustacia Vye's decline serves as the stimulus for Clym's development. The same pattern is evident in *Tess*. In the first half of the novel, Tess's growth is the central focus. Gradually, however, as Tess becomes increasingly passive, she becomes the agent of change in others. Her effect on the dairymaids and on Alec has already been noted. But her effect on Angel is more profound, for while she brings Alec closer to her own level, she stimulates Angel to transcend it.

Before dealing with this effect, however, it is necessary to note the way Hardy characterizes Angel, for it is the very reverse of his characterization of Tess. Tess is created by positive strokes; her development is one of accretion. Angel, on the other hand, is developed by negative effects; his development is marked by losses rather than gains. Similarly, while Angel thinks of himself as clearly superior to those "less advanced" than he, Hardy takes great pains to show the similarity between him and others, especially his brothers and his parents. This negative shading is important to note, for it prevents us from being taken in either by Angel's view of himself or by Tess's idealized view of him. Furthermore, it accounts, in part, for our negative reactions to him.

What Hardy makes clear is that, at the time they meet, both Angel and Tess are at the same level of development, although they have arrived at it by different routes. They both believe themselves more free of the past than they actually are; they both try to escape from their sense of drift by fixing on the abstract and the idealized. When the two meet, they have arrived at the same median, or metaphysical, stage, although coming from different directions. When they separate, they go in different directions. While we have seen how Tess's direction is charted by her devotion to Angel, we have yet to see how Angel's direction is affected by Tess. Before seeing this, however, it is necessary to see how Angel is first defined by negatives.

Like Clym Yeobright, Angel is presented as the rational counterpart to the female "vessel of emotions." His history is described not as the heroines' are, by his sexual experiences, but by his intellectual development. As he had done with Tess, Hardy defines Angel by reference to his parents. The elder Clare is clearly a religious and traditionally ethical type: "he was the most earnest man in all Wessex—the last of the old Low Church sort" (p. 124). Although the son, who is almost two generations in advance of his father, does not share his views, he shares the temperament which has adopted them. The elder Clare had been a kind of religious radical: he was "a spiritual descendent in the direct line from Wycliff, Huss, Luther and Calvin; an Evangelical of the Evangelicals, a Conversionist, a man of apostolic simplicity in life and thought." Having in his "raw youth made up his mind once for all on the deeper questions of existence, [he] admitted no further reasoning thenceforward" (pp. 173-174). Angel is as radical for his day as his father had been in his. He has also the same kind of tenaciousness in maintaining his opinions and the same severely rigid morality. Although he consciously rejects his father's "negative" and "deterministic" beliefs, he shares the impulses which adopted them. Thus, for example, when his parents put away Mrs. Crick's mead for medicinal use and give away her black pudding to the poor, Angel feels that "they are right in their practice if wrong in their want of sentiment."

Although he is vaguely conscious of the similarities between himself and his father, he prides himself on the differences which make his father "the last of the old Low Church sort" and himself a "sample product of the last five-and-twenty years." He considers himself more liberated and therefore more advanced than his father. Like Leslie Stephen, he refuses to accept ordination, for, he asserts, "although [he] loves the Church as one loves a parent" he cannot be her minister "while she refuses to liberate her mind from an untenable redemptive theolatry" (p. 131). His father believes that a university education should be used for "the honour and glory of God"; Angel insists that "it may be used for the honour and glory of man." His "whole instinct in matters of religion is towards reconstruction." Angel considers his own attitudes more socially oriented and more positive than his father's. In quoting from his father's favorite Epistle to the Hebrews to define his position, he betrays, however, its negative side: "the removing of those things that are shaken as of things that are made, that those things which cannot be shaken may remain" (p. 132). Although he is critical of the negative aspect of his father's Paulinism, he is unaware of the negative aspect of his own more liberated and advanced views.

The relationship between Angel and his brothers is defined in the same way. The "lathe of systematic tuition" has turned Felix and Cuthbert into "unimpeachable models" of conventionality. And because of their conventional education, both are less authentic than the father: "Felix, though an offshoot of a far more recent point in the evolution of theology than his father, was less self-sacrificing and disinterested.... Cuthbert was upon the whole, the more liberal-minded, though, with greater subtlety, he had not so much heart" (pp. 175-176). Angel, having been deprived of the university education, is freer from stereotype, closer to the authenticity of his father and capable of change. Angel is conscious of the differences between himself and his brothers and feels superior to their narrow views and conventionality.

Having rejected both town and gown, Angel has selected farming precisely because he believes it will allow him to see and "set forth life as it is really lived." He believes that it will "afford him an independence without the sacrifice of what he valued more than a competency — intellectual liberty" (p. 133). He also selects this kind of living because it allows for greater freedom from moral and social conventions. But for all the apparent humility which his choice of farming implies, it is based upon a kind of moral arrogance which Angel finds so distasteful in his brothers. When his brother concedes, for example, that "high thinking may go with plain living," Angel reminds him that this was "proved nineteen hundred years ago" (p. 176). Having spent "years and years in desultory studies, undertakings, and meditations, he [had begun] to evince considerable indifference to social forms and observances. The material distinctions of rank and wealth he increasingly despised" (pp. 132-133). His experience with Tess, however, shows that he is not as entirely liberated from conventions as he imagines himself to be, and that, "with all his attempted independence of judgement this advanced and well-meaning young man . . . was yet the slave to custom and conventionality when surprised back into his early teachings" (p. 283).

Similarly, Angel prides himself on his lack of concern with his material future. In his "unworldliness" he sees himself "nearer to his father than was either of his brethren" (p. 184). What he cannot see is that this "unworldliness" has its negative, as well as its positive side. He is aware that his father's unworldliness "had necessitated Angel's getting a living as a farmer, and would probably keep his brothers in the position of poor parsons for the term of their activities" (p. 184). But he can see nothing wrong with his father's abiding by his principles, even when it means the sacrifice of their future. He himself will repeat his father's actions with even more dire consequences. By insisting on his own principles, he will place Tess in even more straitened circumstances than those in which his father's unworldliness had placed himself and his brothers.

The one positive feature that distinguishes Angel from both his father and his brothers is his openness to the future. When he first appears as a traveler in the company of his brothers, the difference between them is marked. The very amorphousness of his appearance implies that, unlike his brothers, Angel has not yet achieved the stage of development that will eventually characterize him. Like Clym Yeobright, "something and everything might only have been predicted of him" (p. 27).

By the time Clare appears at Talbothays, this openness to the future is leading him toward the proper "sociological" stage of development. He is shifting his concern with abstractions to concern with the particular, moving from the study of ideas to the study of people: "He soon gave up reading and preferred to read human nature." And, as a result of this shift of attention, his habit of stereotyping people begins to disappear:

The typical and unvarying Hodge ceased to exist. He had been disintegrated into a number of varied fellow creatures — beings of many minds, beings of infinite difference. . . . He grew away from old associations and saw something new in life and humanity. (p. 134)

Besides being aware of the differences among human beings, Angel also becomes aware of the changes in the natural world:

Secondarily he made close acquaintance with phenomena which he had before known but darkly — the seasons in their moods, morning and evening, night and noon, winds in their different tempers, trees, water and mists, shades and silences, and the voices of inanimate things." (pp. 134-135)

The appearance of Tess, however, seems to cause a strange kind of intellectual relapse in Angel. For while he had begun to look at the people around him as individuals, he sees Tess as a type, indeed, almost as an archetype. He prefers to think of her as a goddess or as a symbol of Rustic Innocence. He prefers to see her at dawn, for then her features are changed from being "simply feminine" to "those of a divinity." He prefers to call her Artemis or Demeter rather than Tess, and although he is amazed at her "advanced views," he dismisses their significance, preferring to believe that

131

"such a daughter of the soil could only have caught up the sentiment by rote" (p. 143).

It would seem, then, that Tess's initial effect on Angel is to cause him to regress intellectually to the position of a romantic. But what seems like regression on the intellectual level can be seen as development on the emotional one. That is, Tess's presence evokes feelings in Angel that he had previously been unaware of. And these feelings are shown to develop in a way that corresponds to what Hardy saw as the necessary steps toward altruism. They are remarkable in that they also reveal some degree of psychological insight. And because Angel's feelings are essentially reactions to Tess, who is also the focus of our own attention, they tell us something about our own reactions as readers.

Angel's initial reaction to Tess is what modern psychologists might describe as "infantile regression." He sees her (or wishes to see her) as a "divinity who could confer bliss." That is, she fills the place of both lost mother and rejected church. Hardy makes us immediately aware that this vision is a projection of Angel's need by contrasting what Angel wishes to see with what is. Angel prefers to see Tess at dawn, when she seems to "exhibit a dignified largeness both of disposition and physique, an almost regnant power," to one whose features in daylight become "simply feminine." In full daylight she is changed from "a divinity who could confer bliss" to *"a being who craved it"* (italics mine). The contrast is essential: we are never allowed to forget that Angel's illusions about Tess are projections of his own needs. He deliberately screens out what he would prefer not to know. Nor are we allowed to forget that the objective view, that is, the ability to acknowledge the "being who craves bliss," is superior to the subjective one.

As Angel's desires become more clearly defined, his view of Tess shifts. He shifts from the "pagan" to the romantic view: He sees her as Rustic Innocence, as symbol of an idealized Nature he knows does not exist. From having been a fructifying mother figure she becomes the unattainable Beloved. And when she proves, after all, attainable, and destroys his illusions of her innocence, "the new-sprung child of nature" becomes the "belated seedling of an effete aristocracy" (p. 250). This negative reaction is as subjective, or, as we would say, as adolescent, as Angel's earlier idealization. It is as much a defense against his accepting her objective reality as his earlier attitudes had been.

Although it is easy for us as modern readers to discount Angel's reactions to Tess's confession as conventional Victorian prudishness based on a false and outmoded social standard, his reactions do, in fact, have a good deal of psychological validity. Angel's desire for purity, which had led him to reject the complexities of the church and the social world, now

ANGEL CLARE

lead him to reject the complex and impure Tess. And just as his earlier desire for purity had been shown in its negative aspect as a delusive attempt to escape from the past, so his rejection of Tess is also an attempt to escape from complexities that threaten to enmesh him. He finds in Tess the very things he had attempted to escape from.

The strange description of Tess as she tells the story that concludes their romance and ends "Phase The Fourth" both foreshadows and explains Angel's rejection of her. For there is something both sinister and threatening about her. In the light of a fire that, from the "torrid waste" of ashes, casts a "Last Day" luridness about her and projects her enlarged shadow upon the wall and ceiling, causing the diamonds on her neck to give off "sinister winks like toads," Tess presses her forehead against Angel's and tells her story. She expects Angel to see the similarity between her own story and his. Angel does see a similarity, but not in the way Tess has anticipated. Angel had, it will be recalled, "been carried off his head" and "nearly entrapped" by a "woman much older than himself" (p. 133). At a time when he had been "tossed about by doubts and difficulties in London, like a cork on the waves," he had "plunged into eight-and-forty hours dissipation with a stranger." "Awakening" to a "sense of folly," he had "no more to say to her" and came home, "never to repeat the offense." Tess's story plunges him back into the experience; his reaction is not one of sympathy but of horror, for, rather than identifying with Tess as the victim, he sees her as the embodiment of the threatening female who would entrap him. Tess's story arouses both his fears and his guilt, just as she had formerly aroused his half-conscious desires. He sees her as threatening and destructive, as, indeed, she is, for she has destroyed the embodiment of his ideal. She is, indeed, what he says she is, another person from the one he had loved. She forces him to face the self from which he had been endeavoring to escape. Angel has, indeed, been betrayed and trapped, but not, as he says, "in the conventional way that nine-tenths of the world would merely laugh at."

Tess, then, who had first called forth Angel's desires for bliss and upon whom he had projected his need for purity and escape, now forces him to confront himself. Having admired "spotlessness," "though he himself could lay no claim to it," and "hating impurity," though it is part of himself, in loving Tess, Angel had been able to have the best of both worlds. But if Tess is as impure as he himself, there is no other world and hence no escape from having to confront the aspect of imperfection in himself. Angel cannot place his faith and hope in God, as his parents do, nor project them onto another, as Tess does. There is nothing in objective reality different from what is in himself. And what is now within himself is only part of what had been there formerly, for his confrontation with Tess has effectively destroyed his belief and his hope that he can find something "out there" that will correspond to his needs and his desires. In a way not unlike Hardy's method in *The Hand of Ethelberta*, by telling her story, Tess has defictionalized Angel's world.

Although Angel rejects Tess, he begins to accept, almost immediately, the new knowledge she brings. His dream that the "pure" Tess had died and that he is burying her reflects his unconscious acceptance of this new knowledge. He acts more like one bereaved than one who is morally outraged, and indeed he is bereft; for in burying the "pure" Tess he is burying that part of himself which the real Tess had destroyed. And the world which he awakens to is bleak, for it is devoid of the projections of the ego.

After three weeks of somewhat aimless wandering after he leaves Tess, Angel returns to his father's house. His position is analogous to Tess's when she had returned to Marlott after being betrayed by Alec. And just as Tess's perspective on nature had changed as a result of that experience, so now the picture of humanity changes for Angel:

Before this time he had known [life] but speculatively; now he thought he knew it as a practical man, though perhaps he did not even yet. Nevertheless humanity stood before him no longer in the pensive sweetness of Italian art, but in the staring and ghastly attitudes of a Wiertz Museum and with the leer of a study by Van Beers. (p. 277)

Like Tess, who could not take comfort in her earlier religious beliefs, Angel can no longer take comfort in the abstract and general teachings of the "great moralists." And again like Tess, who, after the death of her child, sees her own position with regard to the indifferent social world more objectively, so now Angel sees his own position from another perspective entirely. He returns "like a ghost" to his father's house, "the sound of his own footsteps almost an encumbrance to be got rid of." Angel looks at life with "a dogged indifference until at length he fancied he was looking on his own existence with the passive interest of an outsider" (p. 277).

We generally regard this attitude as characteristic of those who have suffered bereavement or severe depression and view it as an unhealthy lapse, something to recover from as quickly as possible. Our view of this attitude may indeed be the correct one; the ego may indeed need, as Erik Erikson in *Insight and Responsibility* suggests, greater satisfaction for its survival than this perspective provides. But we should also be aware that for Hardy such an attitude was to be striven for rather than rejected, since while diminishing the sense of self it provides the perspective and objectivity necessary for future survival. And while it denies the possibility of finding any objective correspondence to one's deepest needs and desires, it frees one from a frustrated search and from ultimate imprisonment in a solipsistic world from which there is no escape. The desire for purity, passivity, union, and bliss, whether projected onto a God or a Beloved, derives, as we now know (and as Hardy suggests), from our earliest infantile experiences; and it leads, unless sublimated or redirected, in only one direction — the direction taken by Tess — to death. Hardy's alternative, the complete sublimation of the demands of the ego, may be extreme, and the reasons for his extreme view might be interesting to probe. But the fact that he held this view is undeniable, and that he placed it at the highest stage of historical-ethical consciousness cannot be disregarded.

For Hardy, then, Angel's new perspective, his ability to "look on his own existence as an outsider," is a step in the right direction. He returns to life "like a ghost" and looks back at the pattern of his life from another perspective. And memory, which usually abstracts and idealizes, now de-fictionalizes. With the ideal Tess dead and his own sense of self diminished, the real Tess comes to life in a way Angel had discounted when he had been with her: she returns in his memory as a very real physical being: "He almost talked to her in his anger, as if she had been in the room. And then her cooing voice, plaintive in expostulation, disturbed the darkness, the velvet touch of her lips passed over his brow, and he could distinguish in the air the warmth of her breath" (pp. 282-283).

Returning to the Wellbridge farmhouse where they had spent their honeymoon, Clare relives first the happiness and then the disillusionment of the experience. He reenacts on the conscious level what he had formerly done during his sleepwalking. Kneeling by her bedside, he mourns for what he has lost. This time, however, he mourns for the loss of the real Tess, the Tess who had lain on the bed and had smoothed it with her hands. But while he is moving toward full acceptance of reality, the process is not yet complete: the division between self and other is not yet clearly defined. Although he would like to forgive her, he cannot, for "had he not been cruelly blinded?" In other words, he is still placing the responsibility for his self-deception onto Tess, and since she is made to assume the guilt, it is she who must suffer.

Further distance in space as well as in time finally gives him a clearer perspective, however. In Brazil, Angel comes to a "more just" conclusion:

During this time of absence he had mentally aged a dozen years. What arrested him now as of value in life was less its beauty than its pathos. Having long discredited the old systems of mysticism, he now began to discredit the old appraisements of morality. He thought they wanted readjusting. Who was the moral man? Still more pertinently, who was the moral woman? The beauty or ugliness of a character lay not only in its achievements, but in its aims and impulses; its true history lay not among things done, but among things willed.

How, then, about Tess?

Viewing her in these lights, a regret for his hasty judgement began to oppress him. Did he reject her eternally, or did he not? He could no longer say he would always reject her, and not to say that was in spirit to accept her now. (pp. 359-360)

Having proceeded this far, he needs, as Tess had needed, another human being to carry him farther. Luckily, he encounters a stranger with the kind of "large-mindedness" Tess had expected from Angel. The large-mindedness of the stranger is, in turn, the result of "sojourn[ing] in many more lands and among many more peoples than Angel." He tries to give Angel the benefit of his experience. He espouses the kind of moral relativity held by the Positivists:

To his cosmopolitan mind such deviations from the social norm, so immense to domesticity, were no more than are the irregularities of vale and mountain chain to the whole terrestrial curve. He viewed the matter in quite a different light from Angel, thought that what Tess had been was of no importance beside what she would be, and plainly told Clare that he was wrong in coming away from her. (p. 360)

Significantly, the stranger's words do not take effect until after he dies. They are "sublimed by his death" and then "influence Clare more than all the reasoned ethics of the philosophers" (p. 361). Just as the memory of Tess had affected Angel more than her presence, so the memory of the dead traveler exerts a greater influence than his presence. At this stage, experience alone is not enough. For the kind of advance Angel is to make, reflection upon experience is also required.

By contrasting himself with one more advanced than he, Angel sees his own "parochialism" and is "ashamed." He also begins to see the inconsistency between his "objective" view of history and his subjective judgment of Tess. He had preferred the relative freedom of pagan Hellenism to the "inherited creed of mysticism" of Christianity. Yet he had chosen to judge Tess by the values of that very creed of mysticism. He had despised Mercy Chant for embodying "the curiously unnatural sacrifice of humanity to mysticism" (p. 284). Now that judgment must devolve upon himself.

Having reached this stage of what Hardy would term the "devolution" of his moral arrogance, Angel moves from consideration of historical parallels and contrasts to more personal memories. He remembers Izz Huett's selfless admission of Tess's love. He remembers how Tess had appeared on the day of the wedding, "how her eyes had lingered upon him;

how she had hung upon his words as if they were a god's!" This memory is followed by his recollection of her utter faith in him and reliance upon him "during the terrible evening over the hearth." As a result of a reconsideration of these experiences, "from being her critic he grew to be her advocate." He recognizes his "mistake" in "allowing himself to be influenced by general principles to the disregard of the particular instance" (p. 361). Later, he wonders why he had not judged her "constructively, by the will, rather than by the deed" (p. 390). This shift of emphasis from general principles to specific instances, and to reliance upon motive rather than act, is clear evidence that Angel is coming closer to what Comte would have called the "sociological" stage of development. His experience with Tess and his reconsideration of that experience has brought him to the point where he can, unlike Tess, move into the future.

Angel's moral ratiocinations are, however, not the final stage of his development. They are still, consistent with his character, abstract and intellectual, and our impression of their abstractness is reinforced by the contrast between Angel's moral crisis and Tess's very real one at Flintcomb-Ash. We are also aware of some degree of moral arrogance and egotism in Angel's new position: he is too paternalistic and condescending in his willingness to forgive. Although he does not see himself in this way, we see him as indulging in the luxury of moral ratiocinations at Tess's expense; he becomes more and more culpable as he comes closer to forgiving Tess. Thus, Hardy is still defining Angel's progress in terms of negatives. The author's attitude toward Angel's intellectualizing, like ours, is ambivalent. It is against the reality of Tess's presence that Angel's new views must ultimately be tested.

"Phase the Sixth" had concluded with Tess's return to Kingsbere, the burial place of her ancestors, with Tess wishing for death but likely to be reunited with Alec. "Phase the Seventh: The Fulfillment," begins with Angel's return from Brazil to Emminster, and it is at this point that the focus shifts from Tess to Angel. Until this point, Tess has been in the foreground, and Angel's evolution has been only briefly and sporadically sketched. At the point when Angel returns to "find" Tess, we see her through his perspective, and his perspective is tested against the reality he confronts.

Like Clym, Clare returns as if from the grave to confront the echoes of his former life. When his mother tries to console him in the same terms that he had formerly used, he rejects the reassurance, seeing new meanings in the old terms: "'Child of the soil'! Well, we are all children of the soil." Later, he accepts the justice of the charges that Tess makes against him in her angry letter. And the Tess Angel finds is a kind of mocking echo of his former judgment of her. She is neither the Tess he had first imagined nor the one he had later remembered and forgiven. She is now in fact what he had formerly accused her of being: she is Alec's mistress by choice. She is, besides, a shadow of her former self: "Tess had spiritually ceased to recognize the body before him as hers, allowing it to drift, like a corpse upon the current, in a direction disassociated from its living will" (p. 400). Angel accepts the change and assumes the responsibility for it: "Ah! I am at fault," is all that he says.

When Tess catches up to Clare and tells him that she has murdered Alec, his response is quite different from his earlier reaction of horror when he had first suspected her of destructiveness:

It was very terrible if true; if a temporary hallucination, sad. But, anyhow, here was this deserted wife of his, this passionately fond woman, clinging to him without suspicion that he would be anything to her but a protector. He saw that for him to be otherwise was not, in her mind, within the region of the possible. (p. 407)

Rather than responding with horror or imposing moral judgment, Angel sees through the act to the motive behind it, and through the motive to its essence: Tess's utter dependence on him. His initial judgment is twice qualified: "it was very terrible if true; if a hallucination, sad." But he shifts from *his* judgment to perception of *her* need with the words "but, anyhow," and goes on: "here was this deserted wife of his...." This perception of her utter reliance upon him arouses his own feelings, which are, at last, adequate to the situation: "Tenderness was absolutely dominant in him at last." His vow to protect Tess "whatever [she] may or may not have done" follows and is proved valid by his subsequent actions.

The scene is, of course, a reversal of the earlier one when he had rejected Tess for much less. And the congruity in this scene between Clare's perceptions, feelings, words, and actions are in direct contrast to the earlier discordance between his perceptions and his actions. For earlier, Angel had perceived that "Tess was no insignificant creature to be toyed with and dismissed, but a woman living her precious life – a life which possesses as great a dimension as the life of the mightiest" (p. 170). And later, on the morning of their marriage, he had promised himself "never to neglect her, or hurt her, or even to forget to consider her" (p. 236). This perception and vow, however, had been unrelated to his feelings and detached from the real Tess. Now the words are felt as well as thought, and acted upon after they are spoken. At last Angel's feelings have caught up to his perceptions; his original perception of Tess's needs and fears as being different from his own is validated by his experience, and he accepts her on her own terms. Recognizing his own part in bringing her to her present

ANGEL CLARE

position, he assumes full responsibility. His sympathetic response to Tess proves he has "passed the test" and reached the altruist position. He has become in fact what Tess had seen in him from the first. Just as Lady Constantine had seen her ideal at last fulfilled in St. Cleeve, so in Angel, Tess's wishes are at last realized.

But in fulfilling Tess's expectations, in responding to her needs and desires rather than to his own, in becoming the altruist Tess had assumed he was, Angel experiences no sense of satisfaction. For, in reaching the altruist level he has transcended Tess; he is at a greater distance from her than ever before. And while Tess is happy in their union, Angel is essentially alone, for while he now responds to her, Tess is incapable of responding to him — to his new attitudes, feelings, and perspectives. We see the distance between the two in Clare's relation to her all during the last episode.

During their "escape," Clare indulges Tess's fancies as one would those of a dying person. He agrees to linger at Bramshurst Court because he sees that, for her, "the outside was the inexorable." And while Tess can dismiss both past and future in the happiness of the moment, her very presence and situation prevents Angel from doing so. While she sleeps on the altar at Stonehenge, he watches as the men move in to make the arrest. Their conversations underscore their differences: Tess prefers death to life without happiness, while Angel has returned to life with an acceptance of its accompanying pain. (As the chapter on Jude will show, Hardy's last fictional character is in much the same position when Sue leaves him.)

The last episode is effective partly because of the contrasts between Tess's position and Angel's. While Tess is happy and fulfilled in her reunion with Angel, he is made more unhappy by the sense of the increased distance between them. Angel has transcended Tess in now being capable of responses that Tess cannot fully share. In contrast with Angel's perspective, Tess's attitude now seems the more limited and confined, for while Angel now sees Tess as a real being with particular needs and desires, Tess still sees in her Beloved a projection of her own needs to escape from reality, differentiation, and change. She looks upon him as her Protector and is incapable of further response.

The position that the reader is left in at the end of the novel coincides with Clare's perspective and his reactions. We know, as Tess does only partially, that the demands she makes both of the world and of Angel are incapable of full realization; and though we sympathize with her, we can no longer identify with her. We accept her death as both inevitable and painful — as a loss of something that is also within us, for she embodies those things we also cherish: the desire for happiness, the belief in absolute purity and goodness, and the need to project these desires onto something

139

outside of ourselves — a God, a Utopia, or a Beloved. The depth and strength of her commitment to these values give her the stature of a tragic heroine. We see, with Angel, "the full depth of her devotion, its single-mindedness, its meekness; what long suffering it guaranteed, what honesty, what good faith" (p. 231). But these very values, which make her a latter-day Saint Theresa, disqualify her for life. We see, with Angel, that her faith, hope, and charity are too simple and "single-minded" for the secular world. The world is not heaven, nor human beings gods. We know, as we have known from the beginning, that Tess's Angel does not exist. The real Angel is very much less than what Tess imagines him to be. He has been defined more by what he is *not* than by what he is, by what he rejects rather than by what he accepts. By contrast to Tess, he is diminished in stature. That diminution is, however, a matter of choice, and is compensated for by more subtle responses and broader perspectives. As the projections of the ego are withdrawn, more of objective reality is allowed to enter. As the self becomes invisible, the pattern is allowed to emerge. Thus, as Tess, with all that she embodies, is distanced from us and placed in the past, we are left, like Angel, with a sense of a diminished self confronting a diminished world.

This is, of course, the altruist response: unresolved, painful, unsatisfactory. But it is the kind of response that Hardy prized most highly and that, in this novel as well as others, he tried to evoke. Such a response may not answer as satisfactorily as Hardy thought it did the problems confronting us. It may be altogether too demanding and too threatening for the ego to confront. We may, if we choose, reject the idea as invalid, and we may choose, after we have read the novel, to identify with the values of Tess rather than with those of the reformed Angel. But if we do so, if we allow our sympathy for Tess to shift back to identification with her, we should be aware that it is we who have chosen to do so, and that in this choice we also screen out other perceptions and reactions. We must be aware that the novel we choose to recreate is a reaction to the responses Hardy has evoked. We must acknowledge that, if Hardy failed in his effects, his failure was not the result of the weakness of his convictions, but rather of their strength. In his belief in the processes of ethical evolution he may perhaps have overestimated man's capacity for change and underestimated the tenacity and strength of the demands of the ego for satisfaction. He may even have overestimated his own strength as a novelist. He cannot, perhaps, defictionalize our world as effectively as Tess defictionalizes Angel's. Perhaps we will always prefer the fictions Tess herself creates to the reality she forces Angel to confront. On the other hand, the fact that we can never quite recreate the novel to our entire satisfaction indicates the power of the alternative Hardy confronts us with.

Fifteen

THE WELL-BELOVED

Between Hardy's two great tragic novels, *Tess of the D'Urbervilles* (1888-90) and *Jude the Obscure* (1895), lies another strange, obscure, and little-regarded work, *The Well-Beloved* (1891-2). But like such other "minor" works as *The Hand of Ethelberta* and *Two on a Tower,* it is significant in terms of Hardy's artistic development, for it reveals a further working out of previously unresolved problems and, in so doing, allows for greater mastery of his fictional techniques in the subsequent works. Although the grotesque and contrived plot would suggest that Hardy's creative genius was lying fallow, a careful analysis of the novel reveals that there is a great deal of seriousness in Hardy's play, and that the artist is sometimes at his most wakeful when he most seems to nod.

The plot of *The Well-Beloved* is palpably absurd. An artist, Jocelyn Pierston, falls in love with three generations of women — three "Avices" of the same family — grandmother, mother, and daughter. But a careful analysis of Jocelyn's state of mind in each of these situations reveals that such a plot summary is somewhat inaccurate, for in each case, Jocelyn's experiences are somewhat different, being cumulative and progressive rather than merely repetitive. What Hardy is doing with this plot, is, in effect, tracing the psychological development of his character's affective responses in a clearer way than he had done with his earlier characters. His treatment of Jocelyn's development through his series of love relationships casts a great deal more light on what Hardy had been suggesting in his treatment of earlier love relationships and what he will do with more dramatic effect in his portrayal of the relationship between Jude and Sue in his last novel.

We have seen how, in the earlier novels, the romantic characters become trapped by their own idealism, remaining at the metaphysical stage of development because they are incapable of moving beyond their disillusionment to a new level of response and feeling. We have also seen, to some degree at least, the psychological causes of such stagnation. We have seen how Tess fuses father figure and lover, and how St. Cleeve and Angel Clare fuse mother and mistress. Angel shifts from viewing Tess as a goddess to seeing her as a destructive mistress. He is finally able to see and accept her briefly as she is. Her death, however, transforms her into a kind of "late-espousèd saint."

In *The Well-Beloved* Hardy grapples with the oedipal problem head-on and comes to a rather strange conclusion — one that coincides with, and in some sense justifies, his theory of ethical evolution. The kind of charity or "loving-kindness" that Hardy espouses and sees as the end product of man's evolutionary history is a kind of purification of the sexual instinct while at the same time being a reassertion of the individual's earliest needs and desires. The infant's need for unselfish devotion and care becomes the goal for which all men strive. Men must become, in other words, the very responses for which they yearn. They are to become the very mothers and fathers that they themselves have lost. Thus, for example, Lady Constantine almost consciously transforms herself from St. Cleeve's mistress to his mother, and Angel Clare becomes at last a father to the fleeing Tess and to her younger sister, Liza Lu.

But such psychological transformations are only suggested in the earlier novels; the ethical overlay and terminology tend to obscure the psychology. In *The Well-Beloved,* Hardy is more daring: he reverses the pattern, and the psychological development is brought clearly into the foreground with the ethical value system forming the substructure of the work.

The Well-Beloved is what the seventeenth century would call an "anatomie" of love. That is, it provides a careful analysis of the kinds and qualities, degrees and shadings of those feelings that we generally combine under the generic name "love." As Jocelyn moves through his experiences with each of the three Avices, his feelings and attitudes change. In ethical terms he can be said to change from the egotism of romantic love to the detachment and charity of altruistic love. In psychological terms, he moves from son to lover to father. The first two relationships consciously parody literary love conventions. The third relationship is uniquely Hardy's.

The novel opens with the young artist returning to his provincial birthplace for a brief visit. He is met by Avice Caro, a childhood companion and next-door neighbor, and is greeted with a sisterly kiss. An "understanding" based on long years of childhood familiarity develops, and the couple are informally betrothed. The shallowness of Jocelyn's feeling is soon revealed, however, when he meets and immediately falls in love with another woman quite unlike the sisterly Avice. Resembling Eustacia Vye in her Junoesque stature, independence, and rebelliousness, Marcia Bencomb strikes Jocelyn as markedly different from his compliant and familiar betrothed. Though no "kimberlin" or foreigner to the island, she is sufficiently "romantic" in that she is running away from the constraints of her father. Like that between Dido and Aeneas, the first interview between Jocelyn and Marcia Bencomb takes place in a shelter during a rainstorm. Their encounter, in contrast to that between Jocelyn and his betrothed, has clearly sexual overtones. On discovering that Marcia Bencomb's father has been his own father's enemy, Jocelyn is struck with the heightened romance of their relationship, seeing it as paralleling that of Romeo and Juliet. The romantic illusion soon fades into the mundane, however, and Marcia returns to the island in obedience to her father's wishes.

For the next twenty years Jocelyn prospers as an artist and cosmopolite, seemingly having escaped from filial and romantic ties. However, just as he is about to propose marriage to an eligible and attractive widow, he learns of Avice's death. His interest in the widow is immediately dissipated by the news, and the memory of the dead Avice inspires a kind of love he has never before experienced. In the best *stil novisti* tradition, "he loved the woman dead and inaccessible as he had never loved her in life." He becomes conscious of "the intrinsic, almost radiant, purity of this new sprung affection for a flown spirit. . . . The flesh was absent altogether; it was a love rarefied and refined to its highest attar. He had felt nothing like it before."[1]

The lightness of tone and the detached attitude toward the hero suggests that Hardy has, up to this point, been parodying romantic attitudes and love conventions — attitudes that he himself had dealt with seriously before in his fiction and would deal with seriously again in his later poetry after the death of his wife. Here, however, he reveals some psychological insight behind the surface lightness. Jocelyn's first romantic experience with Marcia Bencomb had been presented as an escape from a more serious commitment, and the death of Avice I forces him to vaguely recognize what he had been escaping from. Immediately following the description of Jocelyn's feelings of "pure love" for the dead Avice comes a new insight into his own needs and feelings: Jocelyn begins to recognize that he can only love that which is familiar rather than opposite from his own nature (pp. 115-116). This shift from the need for an opposite and strange to the need for the familiar and congenial is extremely significant, both in terms of the novel and in terms of Hardy's love ethic. (It prefigures a similar pattern in the development of Jude, who is first attracted to Sue by her portrait and his sense of kinship with her.) It also suggests the psychological base for a more intense kind of kinship along with a more conscious attempt to disguise or conceal that need. Jocelyn's pattern of behavior after the death of Avice I reveals this conflict most clearly.

The death of Avice I marks the turning point in Jocelyn's search for the "well-beloved." Now, rather than looking for it in the foreign and strange, he begins to look for it in the familiar; rather than looking for an opposite, he begins to look for something complementary. With a conscious sense of direction he returns to his native island and, out of the grave of Avice I, sees arising Avice II, the daughter of his dead beloved.

Avice II is a compound of the strange and the familiar, being both an embodiment of her mother and a generation apart from her. But despite the fact that Jocelyn is now impelled by his need for the familiar, like Jude he consciously insists on the difference between them. Like Clym Yeobright and Angel Clare, Jocelyn is intrigued by the differences between himself and his beloved. They are separated not only by age but by intellect, class, and quality of feeling. Jocelyn acknowledges that the differences between them are far greater than they had been between himself and her mother, for while Avice II resembles her mother physically, she is neither as sensitive nor as well educated. She is "colder in nature, commoner in character" (p. 157). The social difference between them is also heightened. He is now distinctly a "town man" while she is an "artless islander"; she is an "uneducated Laundress" and he is a sculptor and Royal Academician. And where he had been her mother's next-door neighbor, he is now, in effect, lord of the manor and she is his servant. The situation is thus in the tradition of the pastoral romance, and, like Angel Clare, Jocelyn is attracted by the very contrast between his beloved's "innocence" and his own "experience."

Like Angel Clare's, however, Jocelyn's infatuation is shown to be based on an illusion of his own making. For Jocelyn, like Angel, embroiders his own fantasies on the romance by casting a halo around the head of his beloved, preferring to see her "rather as a sylph than as a washerwoman" and "veiling in her all that did not harmonize with his sense of metempsychosis" (pp. 139, 141).

But Jocelyn's fancy cannot cheat him so well as he would like it to, and when reality breaks through, he acknowledges his beloved's limitations. Like Angel Clare, at first he takes comfort in condescension, and emphasizes her inferiority so that he may feel superior. "Her limitations were largely what he loved her for. Her rejuvenating power over him had an ineffable charm" (p. 146). But Jocelyn comes to recognize, more clearly than Angel Clare, that the illusions he has created for his beloved are defenses against what he fears to face in himself, and he comes to see in the limitations of his beloved a reflection of his own: "He looked at himself in the glass, and felt glad at those inner deficiencies in Avice which formerly would have impelled him to reject her" (p. 158).

THE WELL-BELOVED

What Hardy makes explicit in Jocelyn's romantic attachment to Avice II is that behind the longing for the ideal that we normally characterize as romantic love is the conflicting desire both to discover oneself and, at the same time, avoid such a discovery. What Hardy makes explicit in *The Well-Beloved* is what he has suggested elsewhere: romantic love is, in essence, narcissistic. In searching for the familiar in his beloved, Jocelyn finds a projection of something within himself. His final illusion that he has found his beloved is broken when Avice confesses to the same fault in temperament that characterizes Jocelyn. She has behaved toward him as he had formerly behaved toward her mother; she shows herself to be essentially cold and inconstant, pursuing in one man after another "an impossible ideal." Thus, in looking for the familiar in the beloved, Jocelyn has found a mirror of himself.

The way in which Hardy conveys the narcissistic nature of romantic love in *The Well-Beloved* is admittedly awkward, contrived, and unconvincing. But its clarity throws greater light on what Hardy had been doing earlier in his portrayals of Bathsheba Everdene's attraction to Sergeant Troy, in Eustacia Vye's attraction to Wildeve, and in Angel Clare's attraction to Tess. It also helps explain his later portrayal of the relationship between Jude and Sue, who, like Jocelyn and Avice II, are kindred spirits, each seeking and failing to find the ideal for which they are looking. It is their sense of common heritage and common tendency that first unites and later separates them, for, in looking for someone like themselves, they find that they are indeed too much alike, echoing rather than complementing each other's needs. Like Jocelyn and Avice II, in looking at the other, Jude and Sue find only a mirror of that which is in themselves.

What happens to Jocelyn in *The Well-Beloved* thus explains, to some extent at least, why it is, as J. Hillis Miller points out, that Hardy's lovers characteristically fail in their quest for union with a beloved.[2] For what Hardy suggests in all of his portrayals of romantic love, and makes clearly explicit in this novel, is that what we call romantic love is essentially narcissistic in nature. The quest for the ideal is successful only insofar as it leads to a recognition of the real: finding in another that which one has unconsciously sought to avoid in the self. In seeking for the ideal, one is confronted by a mirror of the imperfections in oneself. (Angel Clare's shock at hearing Tess's sexual history, which is, in effect, a reiteration of his own, exemplifies this process.) Thus, what we regard as a possible and desirable goal, union with the beloved, is presented by Hardy as neither possible nor desirable. Romantic love is not an end but rather the means by which further psychological development becomes possible.

Hardy makes his point even more clearly by showing the destructiveness as well as the narcissism of idealistic love. In being rejected by

Avice II, Jocelyn is made to feel as Tess feels when Angel rejects her: "The seeking of the Well-Beloved was, then, of the nature of a knife which could cut both ways. To be the seeker was one thing; to be one of the corpses from which the ideal inhabitant had departed was another" (p. 164). While artificial and contrived here, this situation is dramatically worked out in the next novel, where Jude is similarly abandoned by the fearful and idealizing Sue.

But if Hardy shows romantic love not as we see it but as essentially narcissistic and destructive, what does he put in its place? It is this question that most puzzles readers of his novels, who may see the decline of romantic love as both necessary and inevitable in terms of the plot but fail to find a satisfactory explanation of why Hardy makes the failure inevitable. It is here, perhaps, that *The Well-Beloved* is most valuable, for it makes explicit the alternative that the novelist only suggests in the other novels. What is merely hinted at in the conclusions of *Tess* and *Jude* is spelled out in Jocelyn's relationship with the third Avice. In terms of Hardy's ideas, the transformation of romantic love to another kind of love is the most interesting part of the novel and requires a separate explanation.

Jocelyn's romantic relationship with Avice II abruptly ends when he discovers that she is both married and pregnant. Restoring her to her wayward husband after overseeing the birth of her child, Jocelyn leaves the island once more. He is recalled again twenty years later, however, by the dying Avice II, who wants him to look after her daughter. But instead of becoming her guardian, Jocelyn becomes her suitor. Superficially, the relationship between Jocelyn and Avice III resembles the previous two relationships. This love is, however, paradoxically both more distant and more intense. On the one hand, Jocelyn sees the third Avice as "better" than either mother or grandmother in that she is more graceful, more intelligent, and more sensitive than her predecessors. Furthermore, as Avice II had combined the strange and the familiar, so Avice III is an amalgam of mother and grandmother: "she was somewhat like her mother whom he had loved in the flesh, but she had the soul of her grandmother whom he had loved in the spirit" (p. 278). In other words, Avice III is the object of two opposite and heretofore contradictory attitudes toward women. (Tess had embodied a similar combination: she had been perceived as "all flesh" by Alec and "all spirit" by Angel. Similarly, Arabella and Sue are reflections of the contradictory attitudes in Jude.)

For his part, Jocelyn is more conscious of the ludicrousness of his position as a lover. He is painfully aware of the distance that age puts between them and tries desperately to conceal his imperfections, both from himself and from Avice III. But his attempts at self-deception fail, and he sees his age in his own mirror before he sees it in the eyes of the beloved.

Avice III's rejection of him completes the "cure" begun by her mother. While superficially the pattern of Jocelyn's relationship with Avice III is so repetitive as to be comic, the differences underlying the three relationships are distinctive, revealing familial and sexual impulses of which Jocelyn is only partially aware. The incestuous suggestiveness of the subsurface is what makes the novel both so repellent to the reader and so useful in clarifying Hardy's ideas about love. So far, we have looked at the novel in terms of Jocelyn's conscious responses to a succession of what he regards as romantic experiences. If we look at the pattern of his actions and the roles he plays, however, we see a somewhat different pattern emerge. For over against the conscious romantic superstructure is a familial substructure, which is apparent to the reader but which does not emerge in Jocelyn's consciousness until the end of the novel. Since it is the familial substructure that forms the basis for Hardy's alternative to romantic love, its examination warrants our attention.

It will be recalled that Jocelyn, in his complacent and familiar relationship with his childhood companion, Avice I, had avoided the direct sexual encounter which, by island custom, marked formal betrothal. Instead, he chose a mistress who was the direct opposite of Avice I. This affair is short-lived, however, and Jocelyn lives in a state of emotional limbo until the death of Avice I. The news of her death arouses new feelings of "pure love" but also releases equally dormant sexual desires. Unlike the *stil novisti* lover, Jocelyn does not remain faithful to his dead mistress but finds a new mistress upon whom he can focus both his feelings of "pure love" and his sexual desires. Jocelyn loves Avice II because she resembles her mother and is, in a sense, his "familiar" rather than his opposite. On the other hand, she is different enough from her mother (and Jocelyn emphasizes this difference) to arouse his sexual feelings. Avice II is "all body" while her mother had been "all spirit." Thus, by seeing Avice II as both mother and mistress, Jocelyn can be son and lover simultaneously. (Avice II's maternity is emphasized when she reveals, at Jocelyn's proposal of marriage, that she is already married, and to a Pierston at that, and about to become a mother herself.) Thus Jocelyn, who would be son and lover, is forced into a role he had sought to avoid. He becomes, in effect, Avice II's "father," rescuing her from her "trouble" and restoring her straying husband to her and to her infant daughter. The sexual relationship which had been avoided with the first Avice is now consciously sublimated, and Jocelyn is forced into the very father-daughter relationship he had sought, by romantic illusion to conceal from himself.

Jocelyn's relationship with the third Avice is more obviously familial, and consequently his attempts to conceal its true nature by romantic illusion are even more grotesque. For Avice III is not only young enough to be Jocelyn's granddaughter, but she is even more closely related to his own family. A Pierston by birth, she lives in his father's former house and sleeps in his own former bedroom. His first act is to rescue her from a kind of physical entrapment parallel to that from which he had rescued her mother.

Although Jocelyn tries to conceal the real relationship by romantic illusion, the veil he sheds over it is more transparent. He proposes marriage as a kind of protectorship, promising that he will "indulge her every whim" and suggesting that such a marriage will guarantee her material security and freedom after his death. Acknowledging that such arguments are the conventional ones for May-December marriages, he denies that he himself is selfishly motivated. Rather, his proposal is a reflection of the "substratum of old pathetic memory," which has engendered "the tenderest, most anxious, most protective instinct he had ever known" (p. 260). While seeing that his motives will be regarded as "the selfish designs of an elderly man on a maid," he himself feels that his desire to marry Avice III as being based on the least selfish of motives: "a cordial loving-kindness" (p. 313).

What is clear is that Jocelyn's feelings are by this time primarily parental rather than sexual and that, having been forced to play the role of father to Avice II, he has come to experience real paternal feelings in his relationship with the third Avice. These parental feelings are brought to the foreground by Avice III's rejection of Jocelyn as a suitor. When Avice III runs off with her lover on the eve of her wedding (thereby recapitulating Jocelyn's own sexual avoidance of Avice I), Jocelyn accepts the act with a sense of understood kinship and detachment — the kind of attitude that a parent shows for its child. The sexual impulse is entirely sublimated; Jocelyn no longer sees Avice III as physically desirable, but rather sees in her only those "good qualities" which will make her a "good housewife" to someone else in time. When she returns to him after a quarrel with her new husband, who has accused her of congenital inconstancy, Jocelyn automatically reacts as a parent, insisting that she patch up the quarrel, while he himself goes off to a business meeting, "leaving the couple to adjust their differences in their own way" (p. 337).

Thus, while Jocelyn consciously looks for romantic union with the ideal, unconsciously he progresses through his relationships with the succession of Avices from son to lover to father. Having been forced to play the role of father to Avice II, he experiences real parental feelings toward Avice III. The conflicting feelings of "pure love" and sexual desire that had been directed toward Avice II have been transformed and sublimated into disinterested parental feeling for Avice III. Thus, though he fails to find that which he consciously desires, i.e., the embodiment of the romantic ideal, he discovers, through his pursuit of the well-beloved, "the tenderest, most anxious, most protective feeling" he has ever known. It is this parental feeling that Hardy calls, both here and elsewhere, "loving-kindness" or "charity," and which he himself explicitly considered the best kind of love. Nowhere else, except perhaps in *Two on a Tower*, where Lady Constantine's maternal feelings are similarly developed, has he shown the context out of which this feeling of altruistic detachment arises, or so clearly delineated its relationship to romantic feelings and to oedipal desires.[3]

Most readers and critics have acknowledged Hardy's remarkable powers of evoking feelings of sympathy and tenderness. What they may not see, however, is how such evocative effects are related to the romantic hopes and disillusionments of his characters. His characterization of the development of Jocelyn Pierston's romantic feelings into paternal and protective ones reveals what he sees as the connection between romantic love and the altruist response. In *The Well-Beloved* the contrast between what Jocelyn feels and what he ought to feel is obvious and explicit, and the conflict is finally resolved when Jocelyn becomes aware of the direction that he has been unconsciously resisting. In the tragic novels, however, the contrast is implicit and the conflict unresolved, for Hardy arrests his characters at the romantic stage of disillusionment. By showing the inadequacy of this response, however, he evokes in the reader the feelings of sympathy that the characters *ought* to have. As we become increasingly aware of the inadequacy of the romantic responses of Angel and Sue, for example, we experience increasingly strong feelings of sympathy for Tess and for Jude.

Once we are aware of Hardy's love ethic as it is expressed in *The Well-Beloved*, we can see that our feelings of sympathy have been evoked as a reaction to the romantic responses of the characters and that these feelings are neither independent of the action of the novel nor contradictory to it, but rather that they are the final part of the continuum of feeling whose various aspects Hardy here anatomizes. What Hardy somewhat unconvincingly sketches out as the final stage in Jocelyn's development he will create more successfully through the response of his readers in his last and greatest novel, *Jude the Obscure.*

NOTES

1. *The Well-Beloved* (London: 1927), p. 114. The 1892 title, *The Pursuit of the Well-Beloved*, more accurately reflects Hardy's method.
2. J. Hillis Miller, in *Thomas Hardy: Distance and Desire*, presents the clearest exposition of this characteristic in Hardy's novels.
3. The parallels between Hardy's ideas about emotional growth and those presented by Erik Erkison in *Insight and Responsibility* (New York: 1964) pose an interesting subject for further study. For autobiographical aspects of Hardy's portrayal of Jocelyn Pierston see Michael Millgate, *Thomas Hardy: His Career as a Novelist* (New York: 1971), pp. 299-307.

Sixteen

THE DISILLUSIONMENT OF JUDE

"We want for light; but behold obscurity" (Isaiah 59:9)

Jude's world, as most readers are immediately aware, is the most repellent of all Hardy's fictional places. It has a kind of bleakness about it that is peculiar, even for Hardy. What makes it bleak, however, is not only, as some critics have suggested, that this world is lacking a God but that it is also lacking in characters with any moral values — particularly the moral value Hardy most prized — loving-kindness or altruism. By contrast, the world of Tess is congenial; and it is congenial not only because it contains the natural richness of the Froom Valley and Talbothays Farm but because there are other characters besides Tess who have some degree of altruism. Although there are egotists, there is also Dairyman Crick and the dairymaids and, to some extent, Angel Clare's parents and Angel himself. Even the egotists have some redeeming features: Tess's parents and even Alec are "shaded" by some feelings of concern for Tess. The situation is different for Jude, however; for, with the possible exception of the Widow Edlin, who appears late in the novel, all of the minor characters in Jude's world are either indifferent or hostile. Each one is engaged in pursuing his own egotistic course, and Jude becomes the victim not only of his own egotism but that of others. Sue's exploitation of him, like Angel Clare's of Tess, is simply the last in a series of similar acts of a less serious kind. Hence, the sense of loneliness which Alvarez sees as "the essential subject of the novel" is of a peculiar Hardyean kind.[1] It derives from his depriving his characters of those social values he believed most essential for human survival. Hardy deliberately isolates Jude by providing him alone with the characteristics he most valued. By making the contrast between Jude and the rest of the characters so sharp, it is as if he is making a last, desperate attempt to make his point as dramatically and effectively as possible.

Hardy's method in his previous novels had been to contrast a major egotist with a major altruist and to align the minor characters on either side, in order to provide a kind of historic perspective to the dramatic confrontation between the two central characters. In *Jude*, he stacks the cards. Except for Phillotson, whose course, for a time, runs parallel to Jude's, no characters show any signs of altruism. Jude is made to stand in relief against the contrasting background of the other characters. In terms of novelistic technique, this method has the obvious advantage of allowing Hardy to focus on the full dramatic impact of Jude's story. In terms of his ethical theories, it places the full weight of Hardy's ethical values on Jude alone. Much more depends on the success or failure of Jude's progress than on that of any other character in his previous novels. For unlike Clym, Angel Clare or Tess, Jude has no forebears by which to gauge his progress, and no heirs like Liza Lu or Elizabeth Jane who can take up the struggle after him.

Structurally the novel differs from the previous ones in that, where earlier the decline of one character, such as Eustacia Vye or Tess, had been accompanied by the rise of another character, such as Clym Yeobright or Angel Clare, in this novel the process is reversed: the rise of Jude is accompanied by the decline of Sue. The effect of such a technique is to deprive the reader of a comfortable fiction, or, as Kermode puts it, "the sense of an ending." The reader is left with an uncomfortable feeling of open-endedness, a sense of disequilibrium that is disturbing. But if we recall that it is just this sense of disequilibrium that is symptomatic of change, we can infer that this structural effect is deliberate. By depriving the reader of the consolatory response of a fictional character, Hardy shifts the burden of the response onto the reader. But what of the subject of this response? Where does Jude fit into the ethical continuum? Clearly he is one of the most sympathetic of all of Hardy's characters, and it is tempting to identify with his attitudes and values. Yet, as some recent critics have observed, it is not quite possible to do so, for at each stage of his progress we are made to see his ideals as illusions: at each step we are made to see him objectively as well as subjectively. His sense of being "in a chaos of principles" clearly indicates that he is not as far in advance as he thinks he is. We are aware of his moving forward but we are no clearer than Jude himself about what he is moving forward to. On the other hand, the failure of Sue's response makes us more aware of what Jude is "groping blindly" for. The very failure of Sue's response makes us aware of the necessity of a different kind of response. By seeing what Sue does, we are made to feel what she *ought* to do.

Jude is not, then, the "advanced" or "modern" type, but rather one

THE DISILLUSIONMENT OF JUDE

that is struggling to emerge out of the past. In terms of the plot, because of Sue's failure of response Jude relapses into a past from which he had valiantly struggled to emerge. In terms of their evocative effect, however, Jude's experiences evoke the kind of response that Jude himself had been seeking. Thus, like Hardy's other great tragic characters — Michael Henchard, Eustacia Vye, and Tess — Jude is a catalyst for change. But rather than stimulating the advance of another character, he stimulates a response in the reader. Through sympathetic interaction with the major character, our own attitudes are changed. We are moved from subjectivity to objectivity, from identification with the aims and values of Jude to an objective response to them.

The technique that Hardy uses in tracing the course of Jude's progress is similar to that which he had used in *Tess* and *The Well-Beloved*. Like Tess, Jude yearns for some "unattained goodness" in a world where he finds very little. As a reaction to the rebuffs of the real world, he creates ideals which prove to be self-delusive. Jude goes farther than Tess, however, in accepting the defictionalizing process of experience, until, like Jocelyn Pierston, he comes to confront the self-delusiveness of his former idealism and to recognize the emotional need at its base. In terms of ethical evolution, Jude moves from the theological through the metaphysical toward the sociological stage of development. Having reached this point, however, he finds no response to his needs and, as a result, like Tess, marks time for awhile and ultimately sinks back into the unconscious processes from which he has emerged.

As readers, we follow the course of Jude's history, seeing how his experiences, like Tess's, are a kind of purifying process, a means by which he is cured of his illusions and is moved toward a more objective view of reality and a more conscious awareness of his own motives. At each step we see how something of value is lost and how something of greater value is gained. In dealing with Jude, Hardy, like Angel Clare, follows the methods of God as suggested by one of his favorite biblical passages: "the removing of those things that are shaken as of things that are made, that those things which cannot be shaken may remain" (Hebrews 12:27). What makes the ending so painful is that we see how such progress is wasted: how Jude's progress is lost as an example to the world of Christminster and to Sue. It is the sense of the waste of what has been dearly bought that creates the tragic effect. In other words, the value system implicit in the novel is what creates its tragic effect.

Although Hardy deprives both Jude and the reader of an explicit value system, and hence of a clear sense of direction, he does establish the reader's position in advance of Jude from the very beginning. He does this by making Jude both the subject and the object of the story. As readers, we identify with Jude's aims and desires; at the same time we are made to see more than Jude does himself, and to see it earlier. We are thus placed in a position in advance of Jude's, a position toward which Jude strives but which he can never quite reach.

From the beginning, the contrast between Jude's subjective responses and a more objective perspective is explicit. As a reaction to the alien natural and social world of Marygreen, Jude creates an ideal world in the distant city of Christminster. He sees it as "a city of light," "a castle manned by scholarship and religion," a "place that teachers of men spring from and go to."[2] What *we* are made to see, however, is that Jude's idealism is both a reaction to his earlier experience and a projection of the need for a particular kind of response from another human being. The orphan of an unhappy marriage, he is grudgingly cared for by his Aunt Drusilla. The very first scene of the book describes the departure of his schoolmaster, Phillotson, who is either unaware of or chooses to ignore Jude's attachment to him. He is dismissed by Farmer Troutham for feeding the birds he was hired to frighten away. He is disappoiinted by Physician Vilbert's failure to bring him the promised grammars. The most he learns to expect from citizens of Marygreen is a kindly indifference, as when the local policeman ignores Jude's allowing the horse to lead the cart while he reads. Even the countryside is ugly.

As a reaction to this kind of world, Jude attempts to escape by fixing his hopes on Christminster. It gradually acquires "a tangibility, a hold on his life." But the reason for its hold on him is important: it is because Phillotson, "the man for whose knowledge and purposes he had so much reverence, was actually living there." Phillotson is associated with "the more thoughtful and shining ones therein" (p. 26). Thus, at the base of Jude's idealism is his need for a parent figure, for the kind of response he cannot find at Marygreen. What Jude is looking for is a place where he can be more at home, a place where he will be among people of his own kind, a place where he can be both free and happy.

The passage that describes how Jude arrives at his decision to go to Christminster is significant in that it reveals both Jude's real psychological needs and the way he creates an increasingly fictional ideal world as a retreat from the real one.

It had been the yearning of his heart to find something to anchor on, to cling to — for some place which he could call admirable. Should he find that place in this city if he could get there? Would it be a spot in which, without fear of farmers, or hindrance, or ridicule, he could watch and wait, and set himself to some mighty undertaking like the men of old of whom he had heard? As the halo had been to his eyes when gazing at it a quarter of an hour earlier, so was the spot mentally to him as he pursued

THE DISILLUSIONMENT OF JUDE

his dark way.

"It is a city of light," he said to himself.

"The tree of knowledge grows there," he added a few steps further on.

"It is a place that teachers of men spring from and go to."

"It is what you may call a castle, manned by scholarship and religion."

Jude's conclusion is supremely ironic, since it reveals a truth he is not yet conscious of: "After this figure he was silent a long while, till he added: 'It would just suit me'" (p. 29). Since the ideal place is a projection of Jude's needs, he is right in seeing its suitability. But the very biblical and medieval figures that he uses to describe this unreal place reveal the falseness of this notion. The place is too old and he is too young for him to have much in common with it. Furthermore, in identifying with the great men of the past, Jude reveals the grand illusions he has about himself.

Jude's illusions about himself are broken, however, when he encounters a real person closer to his own age and to his own unconscious desires. As most readers recognize, Arabella is the egotist in its most natural and most vigorous form. Her concern is simply to satisfy her own sexual and social needs. At first she seems like the very opposite of Jude. Yet what we also see is that Arabella's desire for Jude is simply a cruder form of Jude's desire for Christminster. For Arabella sees Jude as a means of social advance and as an escape from the squalor of her life on her father's pig farm. In this desire both for escape and for advancement she is not very different from Jude himself.

Jude's experience with Arabella is self-revelatory, for it makes him aware, for the first time, of his own sexual desires. Since Jude sees these desires as drawing him away from the fulfillment of his dreams, he regards them at the time as retrogressive. But if we are aware of Hardy's ironic treatment of these very dreams both before as well as after this episode, and of Jude's later changed attitude toward sexual love, we cannot regard Jude's sexual encounter with Arabella as altogether a bad thing. Nor can we regard Jude's decision to marry Arabella as altogether bad either; for although Hardy treats this kind of marriage ironically, he also makes it clear that Jude's willingness to take the consequences of his action is admirable. (Once again, a later action becomes a commentary on a former one. Jude's marriage to Arabella is contrasted to Sue's later marriage to Phillotson. The latter's is motivated by self-interest and the desire to escape from the consequences of her unconventional actions and attitudes. Jude at least is concerned with the ideal of honor and concern for Arabella's situation.)

Although Jude sees his experience with Arabella as a deterrent to the fulfillment of his dreams, he emerges from the experience with a greater awareness of himself and with more limited and hence more practicable aims. Instead of depending on childish notions of heroism, he depends on the guidance of a more advanced philosopher: "Surely his plan should be to move onward through good and ill – to avoid morbid sorrow even though he did see ugliness in the world. *Bene agere et laeteri* – to do good cheerfully – which he had heard to be the philosophy of one Spinoza, might be his own even now" (pp. 81, 82). What Jude does not yet see, however, is that, in continuing to maintain his habit of idealizing, he ignores what his experience with Arabella had taught him. He ignores the possibility that like Arabella's dimple, her innocence, and her hair, the real Christminster and the real Sue might be far different from what he imagines them to be.

With the break-up of his marriage to Arabella, Jude's desire to go to Christminster returns. But like the first impulse, this aim is based more on emotional than intellectual needs. Just as he had earlier wanted to go to Christminster to be with and become a man like Phillotson, now he is stimulated to go to Christminster because it contains Sue. Although Jude is only partially conscious of his motives, they are made clear to the reader. It is Sue's picture that "ultimately formed a quickening ingredient in his latent interest of following his friend the schoolmaster hither" (p. 86). Although Jude thinks he is going to Christminster for intellectual reasons, the novelist indicates that his decision "was one more nearly related to the emotional side of him than the intellectual" (p. 76). This half-conscious shift of interest from Phillotson to Sue is the result of his experience with Arabella, who has made him aware both of his sexual desires and his need to escape from them. In Sue he hopes to find all that Arabella is not. As Angel did with Tess, he sees her as an ideal of purity, an escape from that which he fears to confront in himself. And like Jocelyn with Avice II, Jude's sense of kinship with Sue draws him to her in a way quite different from his attraction to Arabella. Where he had seen Arabella as his opposite, he sees Sue as a reflection of himself.

As a result of his marriage with Arabella, Jude changes his attitude toward Christminster. As a child he had associated the city with intellect, freedom, happiness, and the great men of the past. Now he sees it as containing the embodiment of these values in Sue.

Jude's conscious shift in attitude toward Christminster occurs during the first twenty-four hours after his arrival. Wandering around Christminster during his first evening there, Jude feels himself ghostlike, sharing identity with its great intellectual and religious leaders of the past. In the morning, however, he awakes to find "the spirits of the great men disappeared," and he sees "the more or less defective real." He sees that the

THE DISILLUSIONMENT OF JUDE

ancient buildings have been "wounded, broken, sloughing their outer shape in the deadly struggle against the years, weather, and man" and feels a kinship with them (p. 92). Momentarily, Jude experiences a true illumination: ". . . here in the stoneyard was a center of effort as worthy as that dignified by the name of scholarly study within the noblest colleges" (p. 93). For his own reasons, he quickly extinguishes this illumination. It is "lost under the stress of the old idea." Further, Hardy adds, "he did not see that medievalism was as dead as a fern leaf in a lump of coal" (p. 93). From this point on, Christminster becomes a consciously maintained illusion.

What Hardy makes clear is that the reason Jude holds onto his illusion about Christminster is that he wishes to remain close to Sue. (Later, when he returns to Christminster after Sue's marriage to Phillotson, he sees a reflection of a former truth: as her presence had been more important than the ghosts of the ancient worthies, so now "hers . . . was the city phantom, while those of the intellectual and devotional worthies who had once moved him to emotion were no longer able to assert their presence there" [p. 197].)

Jude's underlying motive for maintaining his illusions is made clear by the fact that as soon as Sue leaves Christminster to become the schoolmistress for Phillotson at Shaston, Jude becomes restless. It is only after Sue has left that he makes his "sudden discovery" that "it would have been better never to have embarked in the scheme at all than to do it without seeing clearly where I am going or what I am aiming at" (p. 123). After the departure of Sue, suddenly "the whole scheme had burst up, like an irridescent soap bubble, under the touch of reasoned inquiry" (p. 125).

Once Sue has left Christminster, Jude gives up his illusions about it. He begins to acknowledge a preference for the real over the ideal, for the present rather than the past, and to prefer a life of action to a life of contemplation; and he begins to limit his own ambitions accordingly. The earlier brief "illumination" that had been lost "under the stress of the old idea" returns. Even before he gets the one disappointing reply from the Master, he "awakens to a sense of his limitations" and gets some comfort from the awakening:

He saw that his destiny lay not with these [learned men] but among the manual toilers in the shabby purlieu which he himself occupied, unrecognized as part of the city at all by its visitors and panegyrists, yet without whose denizens the hard readers could not read nor the high thinkers live. (p. 126)

Like Angel Clare at Talbothays, Jude has begun to prefer the real to the abstract, the ethical to the intellectual. But like Clare's, such a shift of point of view still reveals a good deal of egocentricity, for, instead of being willing to remain in the humble and obscure position of stonemason at Christminster, Jude decides to follow the career of another example. He decides to become a minister "at the age of thirty — an age which attracted him as that of his exemplar when he first began to teach in Galilee" (p. 140). The pride and egocentricity of this attitude is revealed by his trying to prove himself superior by drunkenly reciting the Nicene Creed in Latin.

With the return of sobriety, Jude looks back on his past dream of greatness as "but a mundane ambition masquerading in a surplice" (p. 139). Rejecting the desires of social ambition, he decides that he should still like to do "some good thing." He decides that "the career of the humble curate wearing his life out in an obscure village or city slum ... might have a touch of goodness and greatness in it; that might be true religion, and a purgatorial course worthy to be followed by a remorseful man" (p. 139).

In deciding to leave Christminster for Melchester, Jude consciously rejects some of the former illusions he had had about himself. He chooses ethical values over intellectual ones and subordinates the desire to be great with the need to do good. He believes that such restricted aims will be recognized and appreciated in Melchester: here "the altruistic feeling that he did possess would be more clearly estimated than the brilliancy which he did not" (p. 140). He recognizes, however, that such a decision has "an ethical contradictoriness" about it; for this time he is partially conscious that his real motive for going to Melchester is to be near Sue.

By the time Jude follows Sue to Melchester he is aware that his attitudes toward her, like his attitudes toward Christminster, have changed. Before he had met her, she had been "more or less an ideal character about whose form he began to weave curious daydreams" (p. 98). Because of his memories of Arabella, he tries to regard Sue as Arabella's opposite: he sees her as "a kindly star, an elevating power, a companion in Anglican worship, a tender friend" (p. 99). As he watches her from a distance at church, he believes he has at last found "an anchorage for his thought which promised to supply both social and spiritual possibilities" (p. 101). Although he becomes aware of the sexual bases of his attraction to her, he attempts to sublimate these feelings, acknowledging only that his desire to be with her "is partly a wish for intellectual sympathy and a craving for loving-kindness in [his] solitude" (p. 107). Although this is partially true, his idealism persists along with his repression, and he continues to regard her as "almost a divinity" (p. 157).

Gradually, however, Jude becomes more "objective" in his attitude toward Sue. When she insists on rehearsing the marriage ceremony with him, he begins to wonder whether she was "so perverse that she willfully gave herself and him pain for the odd and mournful luxury of practising long-suffering in her own person, and of being touched by tender pity for him at having made him practise it" (p. 189). Later he becomes more outspoken in his criticism of her. He tells her that in marrying Phillotson she is "as enslaved to the social code as any woman I know" (p. 262). Nevertheless, his blind devotion to Sue persists, and he allows himself to be subject to her will and performs it as dutifully as any medieval lover for his lady.

Their first kiss frees him, however, from his former devotion to Christianity. It is "the turning point in his career" for it leads him to reject the idea of becoming a "soldier and servant of the religion in which sexual love was at its best a frailty and at its worst a damnation" (p. 236). For a time he substitutes the religion of love for the religion of Christianity.

With the return of Arabella, however, Jude finally rebels, asserting that while Sue's constraints may have been excellent exercises in self-discipline, they are more than the natural man can bear.

With this declaration Jude's progress comes to a halt. Having shifted from the need for an intellectual mentor to the need for a mate, from illusions of becoming great to a recognition of the need to do good, from illusions about an ideal intellectual and social milieu to illusions about an ideal woman, Jude reveals his real needs and projects these needs onto Sue. Since Sue is incapable of an adequate response, Jude can progress no further, the next stage of this development requiring a reciprocal relationship.

Jude's moral and intellectual advance up to this point is most evident by the contrast between his own and Sue's attitudes toward the child, Father Time. Jude accepts his paternity but is not particularly concerned about whether or not the child is his:

"The beggarly question of parentage — what is it, after all? What does it matter, when you come to think of it, whether a child is yours by blood or not? All the little ones of our time are collectively the children of us adults of the time, and entitled to our general care. That excessive regard of parents for their own children, and their dislike of other people's is, like class-feeling, patriotism, save-your-own-soul-ism, and other virtues, a mean exclusiveness at bottom." (p. 299)

Sue agrees with Jude in the abstract, but, as with her later "save-your-own-soul-ism," she reveals a "mean exclusiveness." She prefers that Father Time not be Jude's, for then they can both have him as an "adopted child" and she can forget Jude's past relationship with Arabella. Jude's main concern is not whether or not the child is his, but that it be given the kind of response that he himself had missed. He has reached the stage of general,

159

detached parental feeling characteristic of the altruist position.

But despite Jude's good intentions, his paternal and altruistic feelings toward the boy are never fully developed. We are told that the arrival of Father Time "brought into their lives a new and tender interest of an ennobling and unselfish kind" and that "it rather helped than injured their happiness" (p. 313). It would seem that Jude and Sue have been able to pass beyond the "personal" stage and into the "domestic" stage of their evolution. What we see, however, is that this is not true. At the Agricultural Show, for example, Jude and Sue behave as lovers, ignoring Father Time almost entirely. Their main concern seems to be whether or not they should marry.

As Michael Hassett has pointed out, their interminable discussions about marriage reveal that Jude and Sue are trapped by conventional attitudes toward marriage and are incapable of creating a new relationship within the old institution.[3] What their hesitation reveals is not so much an intellectual problem as an emotional one. Their criticism of the institution is a screen that conceals their own inability to move beyond the courtship stage. In this inability they are no different from Grace Melbury and Fitzpiers, Eustacia Vye and Clym Yeobright, or Tess and Angel. Their unwillingness or inability to move into a new relationship is based upon the fear of losing whatever happiness they have. They finally conclude their discussions with the observation that "if we are happy as we are, what does it matter to anybody?" With what we know of Hardy's attitude toward the desire for absolute freedom and personal happiness, the result of such a judgment is predictable. What follows becomes a commentary on this hedonistic philosophy.

Although "they postpone action and seem to live on in a dreamy paradise," events in life move forward, and their position becomes increasingly precarious (p. 297). Forced more and more upon themselves by their inability to move forward within the legal and conventional sanctions of marriage (accepting the past and moving into the future), they become social outcasts, and Jude becomes increasingly unable to care for the material needs of his ever-increasing family.

The kind of physical degeneration that the two experience — poverty, illness, a migratory life — is similar to that of Tess as she "marks time" waiting for Angel's return. It is related to a kind of degeneration that has taken place within the relationship. There is, as most readers sense, a kind of atrophy about it.[4] Despite the fact that Sue has already borne Jude two children and is bearing his third, she is still frightened by the presence of Arabella at the fair at Kennetbridge. And Jude is ill and restless. He wants to return to Christminster. What has caused him to want to return to the place of his former illusions? Clearly, it is in part motivated by the failure of his relationship with Sue. Despite the fact that they are parents, they have remained within the courtship stage of their development. Their desire for absolute freedom and happiness has led to neither. Rather, it has resulted in effectively isolating them from any outside emotional or physical resources.

Jude's desire to return to Christminster expresses a desire to move — without much concern whether it be forward or backward. Christminster, Jude hopes, "will soon wake up and be generous." This awakening is precisely what Jude had hoped would happen to Sue. He wants to return to Christminster — he thinks he "should like to go back there — perhaps to die there" because he hopes to find something he had failed to find with Sue. As the latter half of his remark indicates, however, he is conscious that his hope is without much basis. And without that responsiveness that he hopes to find at last at Christminster, he senses that he cannot go on much longer.

Hardy makes explicit Jude's progress up to this point. By the time they return to Christminster, Jude is freed of his religious beliefs and of most of his earlier illusions. He is "mentally approaching the position which Sue had occupied when he first met her" (p. 335). But, as the subsequent analysis of Sue will indicate, this remark is as much an indictment as it is a mark of approval. For Sue is shown to be "shaded by limitations," and, once at Christminster, Jude begins to reveal his own limitations more clearly. Although his desire to return to Christminster indicates a desire to move on, it also indicates a relapse into his former idealism. This time the objective commentary of Jude is made by both Arabella and Sue. Arabella sees Jude's desire as a "ruling passion," and Sue admits that it is "a fixed vision which he'll never be cured of believing in" (p. 338). Sue's comment indicates that the remains of egotism dictate Jude's motive to return to Christminster:

> She thought of the strange operation of a simple-minded man's ruling passion, that it should have led Jude, who loved her and the children so tenderly, to place them here in this depressing purlieu, because he was still haunted by his dream. Even now he did not distinctly hear the freezing negative that those scholared walls had echoed to his desire. (p. 359)

Sue's comment, characteristically, tells as much about herself as it does about Jude. It is ironically self-deceptive and self-pitying. She is unwilling to admit her part in the return of Jude's obsession and sees herself only as its victim. Nor does she see the parallel between the "freezing negative" of the "scholared walls" and her own similar unresponsiveness. But despite the self-deception of Sue's comments, Jude's own actions *do* indi-

161

cate that there is some truth to them. He insists that they stand in the rain to observe the proceedings of the Remembrance Day celebrations without first looking for lodgings, and his speech before the workingmen of Christminster, which is generally regarded as an adequate defense and justification of his position, is actually a blend of truth and self-deception. While it is not as self-deceptive or as proud as his former drunken denunciation of Christminster, it is still, like Sue's later explanation to Father Time, only a half-truth. Certainly what Jude says about his loss of "fixed opinions" is true. That he is "in a chaos of principles — groping in the dark — " is also true. And that he is acting "by instinct and not after example" is evidenced by Sue's decline: he has followed Sue as far as she had been capable of leading him; beyond Sue there are no other examples to follow. But his comment that he has followed inclinations which "do me and nobody else any harm and actually give pleasure to those I love best" is self-deceptive. As readers, we see that his very action belies his statement, for he is standing in the rain with his homeless family. His self-deprecatory remarks do nothing but embarrass Sue. His public confession is a mixture of pride and self-scourging. Father Time's suicide and Sue's later collapse reveal to Jude the falseness of his present position, and he later recognizes the egocentricity of his former action.

Unlike Sue, however, Jude does not retreat into self-scourging after the death of their children. Rather, he accepts his portion of responsibility for the tragedy and is ready to move on. Recognizing that their past relationship had been to some degree false, he is yet willing to redeem what is best in it and to move forward. In terms of ethical evolution, Jude has moved from subjective attitudes toward theology and love to more objective ones. Having emerged from the metaphysical stage, he is freed of his past illusions and hence ready to move into a new stage in life. What he wants now with Sue is a new kind of relationship which Hardy had earlier described as "a sympathetic interdependence in which mutual weaknesses are made the ground of a defensive alliance" (*The Woodlanders,* p. 244). Aware now of both his own limitations and Sue's, and rejecting the ideal for the "more or less defective real," he is ready to move into the future.

What makes the ending of the novel so painful is Jude's final awareness that, for all his progress, there is no future to move into, for there is no one who shares his attitudes and values. He has moved so far ahead of the others as to be finally and utterly alone. He is clearly beyond the monotonously repetitious cycle represented by Arabella's egocentric plottings, nor is he able to evoke in Sue the kind of response adequate to his needs. For while he has been progressing, Sue has moved backward: she cannot provide the "intellectual sympathy" or "loving-kindness" that he craves and which he now sees as the end toward which he had been moving.

THE DISILLUSIONMENT OF JUDE

The loss of his belief in God, in romantic love, in social ambitions and conventions is as nothing compared to the loss of this last and final hope. Having given up the hope of finding the kind of response he craves in God, in the natural world, or in the social and intellectual world at large, Jude had focused his hopes on the one individual who had seemed capable of returning the kind of intellectual sympathy and loving-kindness he had to offer. When this last hope also turns into an illusion, Jude gives up the struggle.

Thus, in contrast to Hardy's other tragic characters, Jude is not trapped by a past of his own making but rather by a present in which he finds himself alone. Having freed himself from his own illusions, he is overcome by the regressive attitudes of others over whom he has no control.

At this point Jude's perception of his own position is made to coincide with that of the reader. Where we had earlier been made to see his former perceptions about himself and his world as half-truths, we are made to acknowledge that his present perception of his position is an accurate one. If his previous expectations had been too great, his present ones are minimal. We are made to feel that certainly such minimal subjective needs should have some kind of response in the objective world.

The congruence between Jude's perception of himself and that of the reader makes for the dramatic impact of the closing scenes. For here, Jude's consciousness is juxtaposed to the semiconscious or unconscious actions and attitudes of those around him. Gradually these semiconscious and unconscious forces overcome him, and, less dramatically than Father Time, Jude eventually gives up the struggle "because there are too many." Eventually, Jude yields to the pressure of the more powerful external forces and looks for similar unconsciousness, first in drunkenness and then in death. Consciously, he finally yields to the forces against him by bringing the curses of Job down upon himself. But it is neither God nor Satan but the egotism of the world that destroys the modern hero.

The curses that Jude calls down upon himself are answered by the "hurrahs" of the crowd cheering the day's winners. The crowd is as unconscious of the great alumni of the past they are supposed to be remembering as they are of Jude. The juxtaposition of the crowd's cheers with Jude's curses makes it seem as though Jude's judgment of the worthlessness of his life and that of those outside finally coincide. But Jude's death is being approved of in the same manner as that with which his life has been regarded — without consciousness of its value or its significance. The death of Jude would seem to represent a victory for the self-assertive, unconscious forces that are, like Arabella, seemingly forever moving forward, but are, in reality, merely repeating the same cycle endlessly.

As with all tragedy, however, the effect upon the audience, or the reader, is precisely the reverse of the action. The triumph of the unconscious, self-assertive forces represented by the crowd is apparent only to those unaware of what is lost. To those aware of the loss, such a triumph becomes a defeat. The lack of consciousness on the part of the crowd serves to heighten the reader's awareness of Jude's values and his singularity. "Obscurity" is no longer descriptive of Jude's vision but rather a reflex of the obscurity of vision of the others. The last scene brings the contrast into focus. Against Widow Edlin's report that Sue has found peace in forgetting Jude, Arabella asserts that, despite her attempts, Sue will be pained by his memory and the sense of what his loss entails. The truth of this final comment is supported by the reactions of the reader. And these reactions are the last, most effective countervailing pressure in fiction that Hardy brings to bear upon the forces against which he believed himself to be struggling.

NOTES

1. "Introduction to *Jude the Obscure*," in *Hardy*, ed. Guerrard, p. 120.
2. *Jude the Obscure* (New York: Doubleday, nd), p. 29.
3. "Compromised Romanticism in *Jude the Obscure*," *Nineteenth Century Fiction*, Vol. 25, March, 1971, pp. 432-444.
4. Irving Howe remarks that the relationship between Jude and Sue anticipates "that claustrophobic and self-destructive concentration on 'personal relationships' which is so pervasive a theme in the twentieth century novel" ("Literary Modernism in *Jude the Obscure*," *Jude the Obscure*, ed. Charles Child Walcutt [New York: Bantam Critical Edition 2nd], p. 517).

Seventeen

THE RELAPSE OF SUE BRIDEHEAD

Sue Bridehead puzzles Hardy readers almost, perhaps, as much as she puzzles Jude. Part of the reason for the difficulty is that Hardy, contrary to his former practice, provides no authorial comments to shape our attitudes or opinions about her: all that we have to go on are her own comments about herself and those of the other characters, primarily Jude. And from what we have seen of how Hardy limits the perceptions of Jude, we cannot be altogether sure of the reliability of his reactions. Nor can we find out much about Sue from her actions, for these are remarkable for their inconsistency. And if we attempt to resolve these inconsistencies psychologically, we find the psychological motivation too thin to allow for anything more than surmise.

But if some of the difficulties arise from Hardy's treatment of Sue, others arise from the imposition of our own values. For example, we generally assume that idealism, unconventionality, and rational skepticism are good in themselves and diametrically opposed to egotism, conventionality, and emotional immaturity. And when we see both groups of characteristics presented in one character, as we do in Sue, we tend to see the character as hopelessly contradictory. What Hardy does, however, is show them not as contradictory but as corollaries of each other. This point will become clearer during the course of our analysis.

Despite the difficulties in Hardy's presentation, Sue manifests some characteristics that all readers can perceive. One of the most outstanding is her unresponsiveness. She is consistently evasive, unwilling to commit herself physically, verbally, or emotionally. A second characteristic, apparently related to the first, is her inability to move in any direction for any

165

length of time: she vacillates between unconventionality and conventionality, courage and fear, honesty and self-deception. Although these characteristics are apparent to all readers, we do not know what to make of them, for underlying Sue's unresponsiveness and her seeming superficiality and fickleness there is a genuine striving after something worthy and admirable.

Although Hardy's characterization of Sue, like his characterizations of his other major tragic figures, eludes the categorizing attempts of critics, it can be at least partially understood in terms of the novelist's ethical values. What characterizes Sue, in terms of ethical evolution, is her singular lack of "loving-kindness" or charity. Although she continually makes demands upon the charity of Phillotson and Jude (and indeed acts as a catalyst to arouse and develop their altruistic impulses), she has none of her own to offer. And although her unresponsiveness is first presented in sexual terms, it is later shown to have ethical dimensions. When she rejects Jude for the last time with the knowledge that he is ill and, indeed, dying, her lack of responsiveness is shown in its most extreme form. She herself confesses that she had begun with the need to be loved, and although she later professes to love Jude, her rejection of him at the end clearly indicates the limitations of such love. Although her love for Jude at the time she rejects him might at last be considered passionate, it is clearly lacking in compassion. It is perhaps for this reason that she feels sexual love to be sinful and wishes to be rid of it. And although she talks to Jude of "the charity that seeketh not her own," she herself is singularly lacking in that trait. As Norman Holland notes, the lines that immediately precede Sue's biblical quotation form an ironic commentary on her actions: "Though I give my body to be burned and have not charity, it profiteth me nothing" (I Corinthians 13:3).[1]

It is Sue's very lack of fellow-feeling, her need for charity, which attracts her to the two men who are capable of giving it. The ideal, Platonic love that she demands is a projection of her need for the kind of love that requires no reciprocation. Sue's inability to respond also helps explain her vacillation, for she is driven by the need to conceal her absence of fellow-feeling even from herself.

But if Sue's unresponsiveness can be explained in terms of ethical evolution as a lack of altruism, how can she also be presented as an "advanced" character? It would seem that, in his presentation of Sue, Hardy is breaking his rule of presenting his "intellectual" characters as moving toward altruism. With Sue, he seems to be doing just the reverse. Certainly, in contrast to Jude, Sue regresses as Jude moves forward.

Actually, however, Hardy is not as contradictory as he seems, for he has always shown the advanced, intellectual type as being limited by residues of conventionality and egotism. What he is doing with Sue is revealing those residues more emphatically. As he had done with Clym and Angel Clare, and more obviously with Jocelyn Pierston and Jude, he reveals the underlying emotional immaturity behind the screen of Sue's "idealism."

If we examine the values that Sue maintains, we find that her "idealism" consists, essentially, in a belief in absolute freedom and happiness. She believes that "it is Nature's intention and Nature's law and *raison d'etre* that we should be joyful in what instincts she afforded us — instincts which civilization has taken upon itself to thwart." Whatever we may think of this notion, it is clear, by his manner of presentation, that Hardy does not approve of it. For example, he has Sue make the remark to Jude at a time when Jude himself has felt the full force of these very instincts and after he has found them to be not particularly joyful. At the time that Sue expresses this Rousseauistic notion, she is hardly aware of the power of such instincts in herself. Later, she quotes that portion of Mill that suits her needs to Phillotson. Although she argues for her own freedom and happiness, she is unaware that her demands severely restrict similar needs of Phillotson.

Sue's unconventionality and "rational skepticism" derive from her "idealism." She rejects social conventions because they thwart her freedom; she rejects Christianity because it denies man the possibility of achieving happiness in this life. And although she lives in a world dominated by social conventions and religious values, she believes she has freed herself from both.

From what we know of Hardy's own skepticism about the possibility of freedom and happiness, the idea that Sue has achieved an "advanced state" should be immediately suspect. And it is not long before he makes his position clear. What he shows is that the values Sue professes are, in themselves, negative ones: Sue's desire for freedom is shown to be escapist; her desire for happiness, egocentric and destructive; and her scorn for social conventions and for religion is based on ignorance rather than knowledge. Furthermore, although she *seems* intellectually advanced by the ideas she professes, it is soon made clear that these ideas have been acquired second-hand from the undergraduate she had known earlier. They are derived, not earned. Sue herself denies any claim to intellectuality. Although she appears to the naive Jude at first as "a product of civilization" because she quotes from authors he has never heard of, she herself confesses: "I like reading and all that, but I crave to get back to the life of my infancy and its freedom" (p. 149).

This confession is significant, and although Jude temporarily disregards it and continues to believe in her intellectual superiority, Sue's later actions reveal the truth of her statement. Her "advanced notions" are shown to be exceedingly superficial, being forgotten at every crisis. She uses her "learning," which is highly selective, in the same way that she uses people: to give support to her emotional needs. What Jude comes to see, as his later terms of endearment indicate, is that, far from being intellectually advanced, Sue is, emotionally and morally, a child. Heilman's description of Sue's reactions is particularly apt because it uses the same terms an ethical evolutionist would use to describe a very early stage of development: "she moves variously toward self-protection, self-assertion, and self-indulgence."[2] Sue's reactions show a great deal more consistency once we see that her "advanced ideas," like Jude's idealism, are a screen for her unconscious needs.

Like a child, Sue tries to free herself from any restraint. And like a child, she is totally unaware of the consequences of her actions. She is indignant, for example, after her overnight stay with Jude, at the discipline of the Training School and escapes once again to Jude without recognizing the fact that even harsher penalties will ensue. She marries Phillotson without any awareness of what marriage might mean (despite her previous experience with the undergraduate); and, escaping again to Jude, she is surprised to find that his expectations are the same as Phillotson's. She seems to expect each man in turn to behave toward her not as a lover but as a father. (Her insistence that Jude play the role of the father in giving her away and that he later protect her from Phillotson is thus a true expression of the immature state of her emotional development.)

Sue is not only unconcerned about the consequences of her actions to herself but she is even less concerned about the effect of her actions on others. Thus, for example, she insists that Jude rehearse the wedding ceremony with her and is surprised to find that the experience pains him. She leaves Phillotson without a thought about how such an action will affect his career. Later, she tells Father Time a "half-truth" about her pregnancy, without any concern for his reaction to it.

Sue reveals another trait of the egotist as well. She is not only unaware of the consequences of her actions, but she makes no connection between her past actions and her present ones. She sees each relationship as a discrete entity, and hence unconsciously repeats the pattern of her past actions. She realizes, for example, after the death of the undergraduate, that her withholding herself from him had caused him great pain, and yet she repeats the pattern, first with Phillotson and later with Jude. When she finally recognizes the fact that her insensitivity to Father Time had caused not only his death but the death of her own children, she feels great remorse — the same kind of feeling she had had for the undergraduate, for Phillotson, and for Jude — but she does not see that this remorse is, as Jude argues, another kind of self-indulgence, an obsession with the past that blinds her to the needs of the present and that prevents her from responding to the one person she claims to love. (As Morrell notes, Hardy characteristically treats remorse as he treats idealism: as an escape from grappling with the present.)³ Sue returns to Phillotson not to right the wrongs done to him but as an exercise in self-discipline for its own sake.

Closely allied to Sue's moral blindness and egocentricity, and perhaps the motivating force behind it, is fear, particularly fear of a future which might not fulfill her hopes for freedom and happiness. With no real sense of the values of the past and no understanding of the effects of her own past actions, Sue lacks any sense of direction for the future. Unable to draw upon her own intellectual or emotional resources, she tries to avoid situations that make too great demands upon them. Hardy's comment that "courage has been idealized; why not Fear? — which is a higher consciousness and based on deeper insight" may very well have been the germ of his characterization of Sue (*The Life*, April 25, 1893).

That Sue's reactions are based primarily on fear, both of the past and of the future, becomes increasingly clear. For example, she admits to Phillotson that she married him when "her theoretic unconventionality broke down" (p. 241). Later, she admits to Jude that she hasn't "the courage of her views" (p. 262). Every action bears out the truth of her statement. She buys naked statues of pagan deities and then attempts to conceal them. She runs away from the Training School, courageously rebelling against restraint, and then marries Phillotson to escape from the social consequences of her unconventionality. She leaves Phillotson, again to escape from constraint, and yet regrets her decision as soon as she is with Jude. She is unable to agree to marriage with Jude, for she fears it will force her into a conventional relationship and she is unsure of her ability to engage in a new kind of relationship within the conventional forms. Like Tess, she would like to restrict her relationship to Jude to its courtship stage, "living always as lovers . . . and only meeting by day" (p. 281). When she does at last enter into a sexual relationship with Jude, she does it from fear of losing him to Arabella. When she recognizes that their unconventional way of living is forcing them into a nomadic type of existence, she contents herself with only a pretense of marriage which convinces no one. She cannot bring herself to tell Father Time the entire truth for fear that he will see the part both she and Jude have played in their present predicament and condemn them for it.

Her reaction to the children's death is also one of fear. For a moment she feels that "all the ancient wrath of the Power above us had been vented upon us, His poor creatures, and we must submit" (p. 369). Although she is quick to retract this idea as that of a "superstitious savage," the fear remains. She cannot become Jude's wife in any real sense because that relationship brings with it the kind of responsibility and sympathy she fears herself incapable of. Since she cannot spontaneously return the kind of feeling he has for her, she chooses to take the more conventional position as wife to Phillotson, where the sense of duty, rather than spontaneous sympathetic feeling, is paramount. Although she cannot love Phillotson, she can respect his authority and sacrifice herself to him in the same way that she respects the authority of the church and partakes in its sacrificial rituals. Her retreat to the father figure, Phillotson, and the mother church is thus a safe escape from her fear of entering into a new kind of relationship with Jude.

But if Sue's return to Phillotson is an escape from her fear of the future, it is also a necessary return to the kind of past she had previously attempted to avoid. For awhile, she had believed that she had successfully escaped from it by returning to an even earlier time. At the Agricultural Show she had congratulated herself and Jude for having "blinded" themselves to "sickness and sorrow" and for having "forgotten what twenty-five centuries have taught the race." She believed they had escaped from the Christian attitude toward sickness and sorrow by returning to "Greek joyousness." It is doubtful whether such a condition ever existed, and, as her ignorance of Aeschylus later reveals, Sue's view of Greek culture is somewhat distorted. With characteristic irony, Hardy has Sue condemn medieval architecture for the very fault she reveals in herself. Sue dislikes it, she says, for its "childishness" in attempting to "imitate vanished Roman forms remembered by dim tradition only" (p. 332). In striving after "Greek joyousness" Sue is also attempting to imitate poorly remembered and vanished forms.

When at last, with the death of her children, Sue is forced to confront the pain and suffering she had been attempting to avoid, she begins to feel the relationship between cause and effect, action and consequence. For the ethical evolutionist, this is the first step toward moral progress. It is not, of course, the last. Sue's position is now intermediate, between childishness and maturity. Hardy makes this intermediate stage clear. Her reaction to the death of her children is neither "pagan" nor "modern." Although she admires the line from *Agamemnon* that Jude recites — "Things are as they are and will be brought to their destined issue" — Sue is no stoic. Her reaction is extreme, if not hysterical. For the first time, she experiences a sense of sin. So extreme is her remorse for the consequences of her act that she feels she must do penance and renounce pleasure altogether.

Jude's more sober reaction places Sue's in perspective. As Jude reminds her, Sue's religious hysteria has no relationship to her advanced views; rather, it is expressive of the very medievalism she had always abhorred. She begins to feel, in a way that she had not felt before, the conflict between flesh and spirit. Her reaction to this conflict is more typically medieval than either pagan or modern. She sees her remarriage to Phillotson as a means of resolving the conflict. It will be a kind of penance, an exercise in self-discipline, a means of mortifying the flesh. It is the same kind of reaction, though in extreme form, that Jude had undergone after the break-up of his marriage with Arabella and in his early relationship with Sue. (It is caricatured in Arabella's brief religious conversion after Cartlett's death.) Jude, however, has outgrown his medievalism: Sue cannot. Their positions are now reversed, and Sue is now experiencing the "traditionalism" she had disdained when she saw it abstractly in Jude. What she does not see is that her need for personal salvation is a more extreme form of her earlier egotism in that, in order to save herself, she is willing to sacrifice Jude.

Although Jude sees Sue's medievalism as a sudden reversal or relapse from her formerly superior position, we see it as a more conscious form of the role Sue had been unconsciously playing with Jude. For when she could no longer think of him as either cousin or father, she had accepted him as lover in a very limited sense. Like Elfride Swancourt, she had played, and enjoyed playing, the role of La Belle Dame Sans Merci. Although she is far from the person he imagines when he first sees her engaged in "the sweet, saintly business" of engraving "Allelulia" in an ecclesiastical warehouse in Christminster, she sees herself on a higher intellectual level than Jude and enjoys his adulation of her. Later, she admits that "she did want to ennoble some man to high aims" and had hoped that Jude might be the man. Like the noble lady of the courtly love tradition, she had enjoyed being wooed and had encouraged the man to love her "while she [didn't] love him at all" (p. 262). When she is not being superior to him intellectually, she enjoys calling forth her lover's chivalric nature. Jude is to be her protector, defender, and savior. He is at all times to make sacrifices and suffer pain for her sake. Sue would make Jude into a kind of Giles Winterbourne and would say of him what she says of the dead undergraduate and what Grace Melbury says of Giles: "He died for me."

Although Jude undergoes his lady's discipline for awhile like a true knight, emerging more altruistic and ennobled, Sue remains the same, for the courtly love relationship is not reciprocal. Even after their relationship changes from Platonic to sexual, and later, when they become parents, Sue remains at the metaphysical stage of development, regarding Jude still as a lover rather than as a husband and father of their children.

The fact that Sue cannot pass into the domestic or "sociological" stage by becoming a wife and mother is indicated by her relationship to Father Time. Although he calls her "Mother," Sue retains her distance and sees him as "an immediate shadow" to the happiness that she and Jude have achieved. When Arabella sees them at the Agricultural Show she notes that, despite the presence of Father Time, the couple still behave as lovers. Despite the fact that she bears his children, Sue never does become Jude's wife, either in the conventional or in the psychological sense, for she is incapable of going beyond the romantic, or medieval relationship: she is incapable of giving spontaneously, either sexually or emotionally. Thus Sue's sense that she is not Jude's wife after the death of their children, is, in the psychological sense, true.

But if Sue's rejection of Jude is not so much a relapse as a clarification of what her tendencies have been all along, is it a step forward or a step backward? The answer corresponds to our own reactions as we read the novel: it is, in a way, both. Jude sees Sue's loveless remarriage to Phillotson as a mental and emotional relapse. And from his vantage point it is. His experience with her and his bereavement have "enlarged" his views about duty and self-sacrifice. He would now neither escape from pain and suffering as Sue and he had done in the past, nor would he deliberately inflict it on himself as she does by returning to Phillotson. He is ready to enter into a new phase of their relationship and can find no satisfaction in a retreat to Arabella. Furthermore, as his reactions make clear, Sue's "new" attitudes are not as much of an improvement over her earlier ones as she believes. They are, in some ways, even more cruel because more conscious. Her desire for personal salvation is essentially as egotistic as her desire for personal happiness had been; she is willing to sacrifice Jude to secure peace of mind for herself. Even her sense of remorse and her desire to do penance are, like Eustacia Vye's self-pity, exaggerated forms of egotism. Like Eustacia, if she cannot be a heroine, she will be a victim.

But what we are made aware of both by Jude's reactions and Sue's former behavior, is that Sue is not as important as she thinks herself to be. It is all very well to recognize the part one has played in a sequence of events and to assume some responsibility for them, but to believe that one has been, like God, the principal actor is to assume a greater importance than any individual has. Such an attitude is, in terms of ethical evolution, still subjective. Similarly, while it is indeed necessary to recognize that suffering is an aspect of life that cannot be ignored or avoided, to suffer for the sake of suffering accomplishes nothing. While Sue's religion may satisfy her own needs, it has nothing to do with satisfying the needs of others.

But while Sue's medievalism is "placed" by Jude's reactions to it, it cannot, in Sue's terms, be considered regressive. Although she still lacks the responsiveness that Hardy would call charity or loving-kindness, she is now aware of that lack and does not try to evade it. In terms of ethical evolution, it is better to suffer remorse and do penance than to have no sense of duty, no sense of suffering, no sense of restraint at all; it is better to exaggerate one's responsibility than to have no sense of the relationship between cause and effect whatever; and it is better to be aware of one's relationship to the natural world, even if it means doing battle with it. In leaving Jude, Sue rejects one relationship she has outgrown and another that she cannot yet come to terms with. She has come to a full recognition of her own limitations. She can no longer be the lady of the courtly love tradition, nor can she be the kind of wife their future relationship would demand. She cannot move into the future with Jude until she has a clear sense of the direction of the past. In terms of ethical evolution, she must experience the last stage of moral egotism before she can move toward a future stage of altruism. Thus, although seemingly conventional, Sue's return to Phillotson is, for her, an act of honesty and courage, a movement forward. Although she has lost her belief in freedom and happiness, she is still striving for something worthy and admirable.

The last episode reflects the suspended, transitional quality of Sue's final position. The memory of Jude's devotion and loyalty, which had failed to move her in his lifetime, remains to disturb the peace she seeks in her return to Phillotson. It prevents her from feeling any kind of self-satisfaction in her present position. It is a constant reminder of what she herself lacks and what, possibly, she is striving for. Although she looks for peace by praying to one martyr, she is all the time aware of the more immediate memory of another being whom she herself has martyred by her own lack of charity. It is the consciousness of the latter which is given priority by Arabella's incisive comment at the conclusion of the novel: "She may swear that [she has found peace] on her knees to the holy cross upon her necklace till she's hoarse, but it won't be true! She's never found peace since she left his arms, and never will again till she's as he is now!" (p. 438)

Hardy's treatment of Sue, his revelation of her childlike and immature reactions beneath her idealism, of her fearfulness and lack of responsiveness, of her ambivalent relapse and progress subtly defines and structures our own reactions to her. As with Jude, we are made to see the psychological needs behind her "advanced" ideas, the unconscious desires motivating her seemingly capricious and egotistic actions. As a result, we cannot blame Sue as she blames herself nor yet fully accept her decision to renounce Jude physically while still loving him in spirit. The reaction we have to Sue is like the reaction we have to Jude: it is neither one of condemnation nor of identification. Rather, it is one of sympathy. Such a reaction derives not from a confused and contradictory portrait of a "modern type," but rather from a carefully developed characterization derived from Hardy's clearly developed system of values. The sympathy that we are made to feel for Sue, like the pity that we feel for Jude, is precisely the kind of "morality" Hardy believed the novel "made for." Having begun the work with his mind "fixed on the ending," Hardy achieves in this final novel, the kind of response in the real world that he eliminates from his fictional one. With *Jude the Obscure,* Hardy completes the defictionalizing process he had begun earlier. As he had related his value system ever more closely to psychological truths and made his fictional characters come closer and closer to grips with internal and external reality, in this last novel he bridges the gap between his own ideal value system and the real world of the reader. For, whatever we may think of its objective validity, Hardy's abstract value system is given living reality in the attitudes and responses of his readers.

NOTES

1. "*Jude the Obscure:* Hardy's Symbolic Indictment of Christianity," *Nineteenth Century Fiction,* June, 1954, pp. 50-60. Holland provides a lengthy and perceptive analysis of Hardy's view of the Christian ideal of self-sacrifice.
2. "Hardy's Sue Bridehead," *Nineteenth Century Fiction,* Vol. 20, 1965-66, p. 312. While Heilman sees Sue's intellectuality as genuine, he also makes a remark that calls into question Sue's assessment of herself: "though they like to think of themselves as ahead of their times, . . . this is rather a device of self-reassurance in people who are less ahead of their times than not up to them" (p. 318). Heilman also notes that Sue's resistance to marriage "keeps us from crediting her statement that she and Jude found a pagan joy in sensual life" (p. 313).
3. *The Will and the Way,* p. 109.

BIBLIOGRAPHY

Annan, Noel. *Leslie Stephen.* London, 1951.
────── *The Curious Strength of Positivism in English Thought.* London, 1959.
Bailey, J.O. *The Poetry of Thomas Hardy: A Handbook and Commentary.* North Carolina, 1970.
Bate, W.J. *Criticism: The Major Texts.* New York, 1952.
Bridges, J.H. *A General View of Positivism.* London, 1865. This is an abridged version of Comte's *La Systéme de Politique Positive; Ou Traité de Sociologie Instituant La Religion de L'Humanité.* Paris, 1851-4.
Buckley, J.H. *The Victorian Temper.* Massachusetts, 1951.
Burrow, John Wyon. *Evolution and Society.* Cambridge, 1966.
Chew, Samuel. *Thomas Hardy.* New York, 1928.
Darwin, Charles. *The Origin of Species* and *The Descent of Man.* New York, n.d. Modern Library.
D'Exideuil, Pierre. *The Human Pair in the Works of Thomas Hardy.* New York, 1970.
Edel, Abraham. *Ethical Judgment.* Illinois, 1955.
Eggenschiller, David. "Eustacia Vye, Queen of the Night and Courtly Pretender." *Nineteenth Century Fiction,* 25 (March, 1971), 444-458.
Erikson, Erik. *Insight & Responsibility.* New York, 1964.
Evans, Robert. "The Other Eustacia," *Novel* (Spring, 1968).
Graham, Kenneth. *English Criticism of the Novel, 1865-1900.* Oxford, 1965.
Gregor, Ian and Nicholas, Brian. *The Moral and the Story.* London, 1954.
Guerard, Albert. *Thomas Hardy: The Novels and The Stories.* Cambridge, 1949.
────── ed. *Hardy.* New Jersey, 1963.
Halévy, Elie. *The Growth of Philosophical Radicalism.* trans. Mary Morris. Boston, 1955.
────── *Hardy,* ed. A.J. Guerard. New Jersey, 1963.

SELECTED BIBLIOGRAPHY

Hardy, Evelyn. *Thomas Hardy: A Critical Biography*. London, 1954.
Hardy, Florence. *The Life of Thomas Hardy*. New York, 1962.
Hardy, Thomas. *Collected Poems*. New York, 1926.
―――― *The Dynasts* (1904, 1906, 1908). London, 1948-9.
―――― *Selected Writings of Thomas Hardy*, ed. Irving Howe. New York, 1966.
―――― *Thomas Hardy's Personal Writings*, ed. Harold Orel. Kansas, 1966.
―――― *Desperate Remedies* (1871). London, 1951.
―――― *Under the Greenwood Tree* (1872). New York, n.d.
―――― *A Pair of Blue Eyes* (1873). New York, 1960.
―――― *Far From the Madding Crowd* (1874). London, 1949.
―――― *The Hand of Ethelberta* (1876). London, 1951.
―――― *The Return of the Native* (1878). New York, 1959.
―――― *Two on a Tower* (1882). London, 1952.
―――― *The Mayor of Casterbridge* (1886). New York, 1962.
―――― *The Woodlanders* (1887). London, 1949.
―――― *Tess of the D'Urbervilles* (1891). New York, 1964.
―――― *The Well-Beloved* (1892). New York, n.d.
―――― *Jude the Obscure* (1896). New York, n.d. Dolphin Books.
Hassett, Michael. "Compromised Romanticism in *Jude the Obscure*." *Nineteenth Century Fiction*, 23 (1971).
Heilman, Robert. "Hardy's Sue Bridehead." *Nineteenth Century Fiction*, 20 (1965-66).
Himmelfarb, Gertrude. *Darwin and the Darwinian Revolution*. New York, 1962.
―――― *Victorian Minds*. New York, 1968.
Hofstadter, Richard. *Social Darwinism in American Thought*. New York, 1959.
Holland, Norman. "*Jude the Obscure*, Hardy's Symbolic Indictment of Christianity." *Nineteenth Century Fiction*, 9 (1954-5).
Holloway, John. *The Victorian Sage*. London, 1962.
Howe, Irving. *Thomas Hardy*. New York, 1967.
Huxley, Thomas H. *A Touchstone for Ethics*, ed. Julian Huxley. New York, 1947.
―――― *Essays*, ed. Frederick Barry. New York, 1929.
Irvine, William. *Apes, Angels, and Victorians*. New York, 1959.
Kermode, Frank. *The Sense of An Ending*. New York, 1967.
Lerner, L. and Holmstrom, J. *Thomas Hardy and His Readers*. London, 1968.
Maitland, F. W. *The Life of Leslie Stephen*. London, 1906.
Marsden, Kenneth. *The Poems of Thomas Hardy*. New York, 1969.
Martineau, Harriet. *The Positive Philosophy*. 2 vols., London, 1853. This is a trans. of Comte's *Cours de Philosophie Positive*. Paris, 1830-42.
Mill, John Stuart. *Auguste Comte and Positivism* (1865). Michigan, 1961.
―――― *Essays on Politics and Culture*, ed. Gertrude Himmelfarb. New York, 1962.
―――― *Essential Works*, ed. Max Lerner. New York, 1966.
Miller, J. Hillis. *Thomas Hardy: Distance and Desire*. Massachusetts, 1970.
Millgate, Michael. *Thomas Hardy: His Career*. New York, 1971.
Moore, G. E. *Principia Ethica* (1903). Cambridge, 1962.

SELECTED BIBLIOGRAPHY

Morrell, Roy. *The Will and the Way.* Singapore, 1965.
Paris, Bernard J. *Experiments in Life.* Detroit, 1965.
Parsons, Talcott. *The Structure of Social Action.* Illinois, 1949.
Paterson, John. *The Making of The Return of the Native.* California, 1960.
Pinion, F.B. *A Hardy Companion.* New York, 1968.
Purdy, Richard L. *Thomas Hardy, A Bibliographical Study.* Oxford, 1968.
Rousseau, J. J. *Discourse on the Origin of Inequality* (1754), trans. G. D. H. Cole. New York, 1950.
Shaftesbury, A. A. C. 3rd Earl of. *Characteristics of Men, Manners, and Opinions* (1711). London, 1900.
Simon, W. M. *European Positivism in the Nineteenth Century.* New York, 1963.
Southerington, Frank. *Hardy's Vision of Man.* New York, 1971.
Spencer, Herbert. *Illustrations of Universal Progress.* New York, 1881.
―― *Principles of Ethics.* 2 vols., New York, 1892-3.
―― *Science, Philosophy and Morals.* New York, 1872.
―― *The Study of Sociology* (1872). Ann Arbor, 1961.
Stang, Richard. *The Theory of the Novel in England: 1850-1870.* New York, 1966.
Stephen, Leslie. *The English Utilitarians* (1900). London, 1950.
―― *Freethinking and Plainspeaking.* New York, 1908.
―― *George Eliot* (1902). London, 1950.
―― *Hours in a Library.* 4 vols. (1874-9). New York, 1904.
―― *Men, Books, and Mountains* (1872). Minneapolis, 1956.
―― *The Science of Ethics.* London, 1882.
―― *Social Rights and Duties.* New York, 1896.
Tess of the D'Urbervilles: Twentieth Century Interpretations, ed. A.J. La Valley. New Jersey, 1969.
Walcutt, Charles. *Man's Changing Mask.* Minnesota, 1966.
Watt, Ian. *The Rise of the Novel.* California, 1967.
Weber, Carl. *Hardy of Wessex.* New York, 1965.
Webster, Harvey. *On A Darkling Plain.* Chicago, 1964.
Willey, Basil. *Nineteenth Century Studies.* New York, 1949.

INDEX

Alvarez, A. 151
Archer, William, 9, 15n.
Burrow, J.W. 16n., 27n.
Comte, A. 10-11, 18-24, 27n., 30-33, 90, 123, 137
Conrad, J. 95
Darwin, C. 10, 12, 16n., 18
Eggenschiller, D. 64n.
Einstein, A. 10
Eliot, G. 12, 27n., 100, 121n.
Erikson, E. 134, 150n.
Evans, R. 64n.
Graham, K. 29
Guerard, A. 106
Hardy, F. 15n.
Hassett, M. 160
Heilman, R. 168, 174n.
Himmelfarb, G. 10, 16n.
Holland, N. 166, 174n.
Holloway, J. 29, 107, 121n.
Howe, I. 10, 16n., 164n.
Hume, D. 16n., 18
Huxley, J. 10, 16n., 18, 22, 27n.
James, H. 93

Lawrence, D.H. 97, 100
Maitland, F.W. 27n., 45n.
Marsden, K. 15n., 16n.
Mill, J.S. 10, 11, 15n., 16n., 18-24, 27n., 123, 167
Miller, J.H. 38n., 51n., 112, 145
Moore, G.E. 16n.
Morrell, R. 16n., 46, 107, 169
Orel, H. 15n.
Paris, B. 27n.
Schopenhauer, A. 9, 15n., 16n.
Southerington, F. 19
Spencer, H. 10, 16n., 18, 22, 23, 27n., 32
Stephen, L. 10, 11, 19, 20-24, 27n., 32, 33, 38n., 42, 55n., 65, 90, 129
Von Hartmann, 9
Walcutt, C. 16n.
Watt, I. 14
Weber, C. 45n.
Webster, H. 15n., 16n., 45n.
Wordsworth, W. 25
Yeats, W.B. 15n.

DATE DUE			
DEC 8 1979			
MAR 2 0 1980			
APR 0 3 1980			
MAY 2 1 1980			
NOV 2 7 1980			
MAY 1 9 1983			
MAY 9 1985			
MAY 1 9 1988			
MAY 2 5 1990			
DEC 1 0 2002			

WITHDRAWN from the Alma College Library

HIGHSMITH 45-220